SPORTS
IN AMERICA
OPPOSING VIEWPOINTS®

Other Books of Related Interest in the Opposing Viewpoints Series:

American Values
Chemical Dependency
Drug Abuse
Economics in America
Education in America
Homosexuality
Male/Female Roles
Racism in America
Social Justice
War on Drugs

SPORTS IN AMERICA

OPPOSING VIEWPOINTS®

David Bender & Bruno Leone, *Series Editors*

William Dudley, *Book Editor*

OPPOSING
VIEWPOINTS
SERIES®

Greenhaven Press, Inc.   PO Box 289009   San Diego, CA 92198-9009

Cover photo: Worldwide Photos

Library of Congress Cataloging-in-Publication Data

Sports in America : opposing viewpoints / William Dudley, book editor.
   p.   cm. — (Opposing viewpoints series)
  Includes bibliographical references (p.) and index.
  ISBN 1-56510-105-7 (alk. paper) — ISBN 1-56510-104-9 (pbk. : alk. paper)
  1. Sports—United States—Moral and ethical aspects. 2. Sports—United States—Corrupt practices. I. Dudley, William, 1964– . II. Series: Opposing viewpoints series (Unnumbered)
GV706.3.S67 1994
796'.0973—dc20
                                    93-30961
                                           CIP

Every effort has been made to trace the owners of copyrighted material.

"Congress shall make no law . . .
abridging the freedom of speech,
or of the press."

First Amendment to the U.S. Constitution

The basic foundation of our democracy is the first amendment guarantee of freedom of expression. The Opposing Viewpoints Series is dedicated to the concept of this basic freedom and the idea that it is more important to practice it than to enshrine it.

Contents

Why Consider Opposing Viewpoints?

"The only way in which a human being can make some approach to knowing the whole of a subject is by hearing what can be said about it by persons of every variety of opinion and studying all modes in which it can be looked at by every character of mind. No wise man ever acquired his wisdom in any mode but this."

John Stuart Mill

In our media-intensive culture it is not difficult to find differing opinions. Thousands of newspapers and magazines and dozens of radio and television talk shows resound with differing points of view. The difficulty lies in deciding which opinion to agree with and which "experts" seem the most credible. The more inundated we become with differing opinions and claims, the more essential it is to hone critical reading and thinking skills to evaluate these ideas. Opposing Viewpoints books address this problem directly by presenting stimulating debates that can be used to enhance and teach these skills. The varied opinions contained in each book examine many different aspects of a single issue. While examining these conveniently edited opposing views, readers can develop critical thinking skills such as the ability to compare and contrast authors' credibility, facts, argumentation styles, use of persuasive techniques, and other stylistic tools. In short, the Opposing Viewpoints Series is an ideal way to attain the higher-level thinking and reading skills so essential in a culture of diverse and contradictory opinions.

In addition to providing a tool for critical thinking, Opposing Viewpoints books challenge readers to question their own strongly held opinions and assumptions. Most people form their opinions on the basis of upbringing, peer pressure, and personal, cultural, or professional bias. By reading carefully balanced opposing views, readers must directly confront new ideas as well as the opinions of those with whom they disagree. This is not to simplistically argue that everyone who reads opposing views will—or should—change his or her opinion. Instead, the series enhances readers' depth of understanding of their own views by encouraging confrontation with opposing ideas. Careful examination of others' views can lead to the readers' understanding of the logical inconsistencies in their own opinions, perspective on why they hold an opinion, and the consideration of the possibility that their opinion requires further evaluation.

Evaluating Other Opinions

To ensure that this type of examination occurs, Opposing Viewpoints books present all types of opinions. Prominent spokespeople on different sides of each issue as well as well-known professionals from many disciplines challenge the reader. An additional goal of the series is to provide a forum for other, less known, or even unpopular viewpoints. The opinion of an ordinary person who has had to make the decision to cut off life support from a terminally ill relative, for example, may be just as valuable and provide just as much insight as a medical ethicist's professional opinion. The editors have two additional purposes in including these less known views. One, the editors encourage readers to respect others' opinions—even when not enhanced by professional credibility. It is only by reading or listening to and objectively evaluating others' ideas that one can determine whether they are worthy of consideration. Two, the inclusion of such viewpoints encourages the important critical thinking skill of objectively evaluating an author's credentials and bias. This evaluation will illuminate an author's reasons for taking a particular stance on an issue and will aid in readers' evaluation of the author's ideas.

As series editors of the Opposing Viewpoints Series, it is our hope that these books will give readers a deeper understanding of the issues debated and an appreciation of the complexity of even seemingly simple issues when good and honest people disagree. This awareness is particularly important in a democratic society such as ours in which people enter into public debate to determine the common good. Those with whom one disagrees should not be regarded as enemies but rather as people whose views deserve careful examination and may shed light on one's own.

Thomas Jefferson once said that "difference of opinion leads to inquiry, and inquiry to truth." Jefferson, a broadly educated man, argued that "if a nation expects to be ignorant and free . . . it expects what never was and never will be." As individuals and as a nation, it is imperative that we consider the opinions of others and examine them with skill and discernment. The Opposing Viewpoints Series is intended to help readers achieve this goal.

David L. Bender & Bruno Leone,
Series Editors

Introduction

> *"Sport accurately reflects American society, its frustrations, its fantasies, its cultural values. The arena is at once apart from and a part of everyday life."*
>
> Larry Gerlach, *Vital Speeches of the Day*, March 15, 1984.

Sports play an undeniably important role in American life. An estimated 100 million people in this country participate in sports ranging from bowling to running to softball. Millions more watch live and televised sports events. Sociology professor Jay Coakley writes in the *World & I*:

> The popularity and visibility of sports events and sports participation in this country have grown dramatically over the past century. . . . Surveys indicate that nearly 75 percent of Americans participate in, watch, read about, or talk about sport with others on a daily basis. Sport makes up a significant part of our news coverage, and it is often an important part of our family lives, our educational experiences, our economy and our political system, and even our religious life.

Why is sport so fascinating for so many? University of Utah history professor Larry Gerlach identifies several attributes of sport that he believes account for its allure.

Sport, Gerlach argues, is simple enough to be appreciated by people of all backgrounds, abilities, and interests. People with differing economic situations and personal values can unite by competing in sports games or watching and cheering on favorite teams. Sports can be discussed freely among intimate friends or relative strangers in place of other topics—such as art, politics, and religion—that may be considered too personal, esoteric, or divisive. Sport lends itself to such a function, Gerlach declares, because it

> is the cultural activity in our society that is wholly intelligible to the lowest common denominators in society. My thirteen-year-old son can discuss basketball on an equal basis with me. It is the ideal cultural activity in a democracy, rather like the public school system. It is intelligible . . . and embraceable by all elements in the culture.

13

One important aspect of sport's simplicity and appeal, Gerlach argues, is that it is pure, with none of the interwoven values and assumptions found in literature, art, or other cultural diversions. One doesn't need deep knowledge or particular moral values to appreciate sporting events. Gerlach states:

> Sport is the only non-ideological cultural activity in our society, or any society. . . . Sport is only a kinetic enterprise. There is no value represented as two athletes line up to run 100 meters.

Gerlach also asserts that the basic, elemental idea of winning vs. losing is one of the main attractions of sporting events. They offer a forum in which the rules are clearly set, accomplishments are immediately recognized, and winners and losers are easily determined. Sport, Gerlach argues,

> involves confrontation between obvious good guys—my team—and obvious bad guys—your team. That conflict is cleanly, finely, and clearly resolved through the use of physical force. The more physical the game, the more popular the game.

Finally, Gerlach contends, the element of fantasy is an important part of the appeal of sports. One can watch a baseball game, for instance, and imagine making the plays oneself. Sociologist Gary Alan Fine notes that researchers have found that a large percentage of daydreams, especially in men, revolve around sports. Gerlach states:

> Sport turns on illusion, on fantasy, on dreams—whether dreams of future glory or nostalgic remembrances of glories that once were or might have been. . . . Sport represents in large part the maintenance of childlike innocence and values in a harsh, cynical adult world.

The broad and multilevel appeal of sport makes it a fascinating lens through which to study American society. *Sports in America: Opposing Viewpoints* does so by examining several areas of controversy surrounding sport. Topics debated include How Do Sports Affect America's Youth? How Should College Athletics Be Reformed? How Should Professional Sports Be Reformed? Is Discrimination Against Minorities a Serious Problem in Sports? Is Sexism a Serious Problem in Sports? Should Steroids Be Banned from Sports? Throughout the book the underlying question remains the same: Given Americans' love affair with sport, what do these issues reveal about American sport and American society?

How Do Sports Affect America's Youth?

SPORTS
IN AMERICA

Chapter Preface

Sports are highly popular with American children. Vern Seefeldt of Michigan State University's Institute for the Study of Youth Sports estimates that about 25 million American girls and boys participate in at least one organized sport each year. Popular youth sports leagues include Little League, with about 40,000 baseball teams worldwide, and Pop Warner League football, with about 190,000 boys and some girls participating.

Many educators and observers have extolled the benefits of organized sports. These benefits include exercise, lessons in sportsmanship, and the increase in self-esteem that comes with learning new skills. Sports physician Lyle J. Micheli writes:

> I see the products of well-organized sports programs every day: happy, confident youngsters with a glint in their eyes that tells me they're hooked on sports for life. . . . I'm sometimes in awe of the positive impact sports can have, especially on children with chronic illness or handicaps.

Organized sports are not without critics, however. Some people contend that many organized sports are marred by a win-at-all-cost attitude among coaches and parents. It is this domination by adults that can weaken organized sports' benefits. Joe Paterno, the noted football coach at Pennsylvania State University, echoed many of the concerns about sports and youth:

> We dress up our kids in uniforms, give them professional equipment, tell them where to play, when to play, organize their games for them, give them officials, and put them in the hands of a coach who doesn't know the first thing about the sport or what's good for an 8-year-old.

While some critics deplore what they see as overregimentation and the imposition of adult values on children's play, defenders of organized sports argue that such problems can be solved through better training of coaches and other reforms. They maintain that sport remains a valuable activity for children. The viewpoints in this chapter examine several issues relating to youth and sport.

16

> *"What we need to be teaching our daughters and sons is that it's possible to have a good time . . . without turning the playing field into a battlefield."*

Sports Create Unhealthy Competition

Alfie Kohn

Some people have criticized youth sports for placing an undue emphasis on winning. In the following viewpoint, Alfie Kohn argues that such a focus on competition is not necessarily the fault of zealous coaches or parents. The structure of many sports games themselves, Kohn asserts, creates winners and loser and thus fosters competition, which he believes can be psychologically unhealthy. He advocates activities in which people can band together as teammates toward a common goal rather than as competitive opponents. Kohn is the author of *No Contest: The Case Against Competition* and is a contributing editor to *Psychology Today*.

As you read, consider the following questions:

1. How does changing sport opponents into partners change the dynamics of sports, according to Kohn?
2. How do competitive sports harm both winners and losers, according to the author?
3. What does Kohn say about cheating and sportsmanship?

"No-Win Situations" by Alfie Kohn. Reprinted by permission of the author from the July/August 1990 *Women's Sports & Fitness* magazine. Copyright © 1990 by Alfie Kohn.

I learned my first game at a birthday party. You remember it: X players scramble for X-minus-one chairs each time the music stops. In every round a child is eliminated until at the end only one is left triumphantly seated while everyone else is standing on the sidelines, excluded from play, unhappy . . . losers.

This is how we learn to have a good time in America.

Competition

Several years ago I wrote a book called *No Contest*, which, based on the findings of several hundred studies, argued that competition undermines self-esteem, poisons relationships and holds us back from doing our best. I was mostly interested in the win/lose arrangement that defines our workplaces and classrooms, but I found myself nagged by the following question: If competition is so destructive and counterproductive during the week, why do we take for granted that it suddenly becomes benign and even desirable on the weekend?

This is a particularly unsettling line of inquiry for athletes or parents. Most of us, after all, assume that competitive sports teach all sorts of useful lessons and, indeed, that games by definition must produce a winner and a loser. But I've come to believe that recreation at its best does not require people to try to triumph over others. Quite to the contrary.

Terry Orlick, a sports psychologist at the University of Ottawa, took a look at musical chairs and proposed that we keep the basic format of removing chairs but change the goal, the point becomes to fit everyone on a diminishing number of seats. At the end, a group of giggling children tries to figure out how to squish onto a single chair. Everybody plays to the end; everybody has a good time.

Orlick and others have devised or collected hundreds of such games for children and adults alike. The underlying theory is simple: All games involve achieving a goal despite the presence of an obstacle, but nowhere is it written that the obstacle has to be someone else. The idea can be for each person on the field to make a specified contribution to the goal, or for all the players to reach a certain score, or for everyone to work with her partners against a time limit.

Note the significance of an "opponent" becoming a "partner." The entire dynamic of the game shifts, and one's attitude toward the other players changes with it. Even the friendliest game of tennis can't help but be affected by the game's inherent structure, which demands that each person try to hit the ball where the other can't get to it. You may not be a malicious person, but to play tennis means that you try to make the other person fail.

I've become convinced that not a single one of the advantages attributed to sports actually requires competition. Running, climbing, biking, swimming, aerobics—all offer a fine workout without any need to try to outdo someone else. Some people point to the camaraderie that results from teamwork, but that's precisely the benefit of cooperative activity, whose very essence is that *everyone* on the field is working together for a common goal. By contrast, the distinguishing feature of team competition is that a given player works with and is encouraged to feel warmly toward only half of those present. Worse, a we-versus-they dynamic is set up, which George Orwell once called "war minus the shooting."

The dependence on sports to provide a sense of accomplishment or to test one's wits is similarly misplaced. One can aim instead at an objective standard (How far did I throw? How many miles did we cover?) or attempt to do better than last week. Such individual and group striving—like cooperative games—provides satisfaction and challenge without competition.

The Lessons of Sports Competition

We can no longer assume that highly competitive, adult-supervised sports for kids automatically build character or teach them the right lessons. Adults—whether parents, coaches, or parent-coaches—bring a whole complex of frustrations and expectations to the Little League parks. What lessons does a child learn from a win-at-all-costs coach who orders his pitcher to "brush back" the best hitter on the opposing team? What feelings does an ex-pitcher take away from the game when he belatedly realizes that he "threw out" his arm by throwing curves on the orders of his untrained coach? What emotions are churning inside the less skilled players who are buried on the bench or run off the team? . . .

How many kids are afraid to leave the locker room after a bad game to face their parents? How many quit a sport permanently or are chased away? How many suffer career-ending injuries or use a real or imagined injury to escape from an overstressful activity? With kids being thrown into competitive leagues at the age of eight or sometimes even earlier, how many burn out before high school? Before junior high?

Tom McMillen with Paul Coggins, *Out of Bounds*, 1992.

If large numbers of people insist that we can't do without win/lose activities, the first question to ask is whether they've ever tasted the alternative. When Orlick taught a group of children noncompetitive games, two-thirds of the boys and all of the girls preferred them to the kind that require opponents. If our culture's idea of fun requires beating someone else, it may just be because we don't know any other way.

It may also be because we overlook the psychological costs of competition. Most people lose in most competitive encounters, and it's obvious why that causes self-doubt. But even winning doesn't build character. It just lets us gloat temporarily. Studies have shown that feelings of self-worth become dependent on external sources of evaluation as a result of competition. Your value is defined by what you've done and who you've beaten. The whole affair soon becomes a vicious circle: The more you compete, the more you *need* to compete to feel good about yourself. It's like drinking salt water when you're thirsty. This process is bad enough for us; it's a disaster for our children.

While this is going on, competition is having an equally toxic effect on our relationships. By definition, not everyone can win a contest. That means that each child inevitably comes to regard others as obstacles to his or her own success. Competition leads children to envy winners, to dismiss losers (there's no nastier epithet in our language than "loser!"), and to be suspicious of just about everyone. Competition makes it difficult to regard others as potential friends or collaborators; even if you're not my rival today, you could be tomorrow.

This is not to say that competitors will always detest one another. But trying to outdo someone is not conducive to trust—indeed it would be irrational to trust a person who gains from your failure. At best, competition leads one to look at others through narrowed eyes; at worst, it invites outright aggression.

Changing the Structure of Sports

But no matter how many bad feelings erupt during competition, we have a marvelous talent for blaming the individuals rather than focusing on the structure of the game itself, a structure that makes my success depend on your failure. Cheating may just represent the logical conclusion of this arrangement rather than an aberration. And sportsmanship is nothing more than an artificial way to try to limit the damage of competition. If we weren't set against each other on the court or the track, we wouldn't need to keep urging people to be good sports; they might well be working *with* each other in the first place.

As radical or surprising as it may sound, the problem isn't just that we compete the wrong way or that we push winning on our children too early. The problem is competition itself. What we need to be teaching our daughters and sons is that it's possible to have a good time—a better time—without turning the playing field into a battlefield.

"Through sports, children learn how to handle defeat as well as victory—no sulking, gloating or rubbing it in."

Competitive Sports Are Beneficial

John Leo

John Leo is a contributing editor for *U.S. News & World Report*, a weekly newsmagazine. In the following viewpoint he describes a recent trend of schools' deemphasizing competitive sports in their physical education (P.E.) classes. Leo questions the reasoning behind this trend, arguing that competitive team sports do teach valuable lessons to children.

As you read, consider the following questions:

1. What goals of noncompetitive physical education activities does Leo mention? What is his attitude about these goals? How can you tell?
2. What are the two main rationales behind the attacks on competitive team sports, according to the author?
3. What lessons do children learn from competitive sports, according to Leo?

"Phys Ed, or Self-Esteem?" by John Leo, *U.S. News & World Report*, May 31, 1993. Copyright 1993, *U.S. News & World Report*. Reprinted by permission.

If you read the *New York Times*, always look first at the bottom of Page 1. That's where the editors sometimes insert a warm and fuzzy article to get your mind off the real front-page news about Bosnia, famine, Sen. Bob Dole and other unsolvable problems.

One day the fuzziness and warmth radiated smartly out of an article headlined "New Gym Class: No More Choosing Up Sides." The story was that basketball and other games are disappearing from gym classes across America, mostly because gym teachers think the games damage the feelings of children who aren't outstanding.

Even games like dodgeball "have fallen into disrepute," wrote reporter Melinda Henneberger, who perhaps had a harrowing time in traditional gym class. She described PE past with "all but the best athletes hoping the bell would rescue them from some fresh humiliation," and said that "now competition is out and cooperation is in."

Sure enough, right above the article was a photo of six children in a gym, each up on one leg doing an interpretive dance. Nearby a grim phys-ed teacher looks on, perhaps to make sure that none of the kids makes a break for it and tries to start an illicit basketball game.

Kids can still shoot some hoops on their own, the *Times* said, but "even then, the goal is not so much to learn to score a basket as to develop body awareness, hand and motion skills and the confidence to try new activities."

A New Age Approach

This is a New Age approach to sports, drained of fun and skill. "Body awareness," "space awareness" and various feelings are excruciatingly important to this form of basketball. Actually putting the ball in the basket is not.

The *Times* article carries the implicit message that win-lose games are dangerous. Losing inevitably means humiliation. Kids have such fragile egos that it's better to avoid any challenge or competition that might send them into a tailspin. (Chalk up much of this attitude to the self-esteem movement.) There's also the hint that these games are vaguely undemocratic because the kids who play them are suddenly separated into winners and losers.

A lot of the anticompetition theory made the rounds in the late '60s, when giant balls were pushed around by whole classes so everybody could be on the same team.

Later, books of noncompetitive games started to appear, with titles like *Everybody Wins*, the first sign that losing at kickball was about to be defined as traumatic.

In fairness, the game theorists who stressed group fun and de-

22

emphasized competition had a point. This is a competitive, hyperindividualistic culture that undervalues cooperation. Sports shouldn't be used to turn out little predators or tomorrow's screaming Little League parents.

Losing Can Benefit Children

While many six- and seven-year-olds don't really care whether they win or lose, older kids often react with tears and disappointment. Telling a child, "It doesn't matter. It's only a game," is not the best approach to take, believes Dr. Judith Meyers-Walls. She says, "It's important to recognize that children's bad feelings are just as important as their good feelings."

Learning to deal with loss is one of the most valuable lessons kids can take with them from sports. Losing can become a positive experience when a child learns persistence and determination to come back and be successful next time. But a child will only learn those lessons if he has supportive adults to fall back on.

Richard Chevat, *Good Housekeeping*, June 1992.

The trouble is that the anticompetition people couldn't seem to hold up the ideal of cooperation without going berserk over team games. Alfie Kohn, author of the 1986 book *No Contest*, argues that competition in the classroom and in the gym inevitably has destructive effects. Even a choose-up game of hoops? Yes, he told me. "There are still destructive effects—anxiety, a sense of failure and lack of interest in exercise. Fun doesn't require adversarial activities. The way we feel about people is affected by the structure of the game."

But kids in a pick-up volleyball game are not learning the dangerous lesson that "other people are obstacles to my success" (Alfie Kohn's phrase). They are simply playing, and perhaps learning something about cooperation, discipline and excellence along the way.

Two Arguments

The attack on competitive sports in schools comes in two new forms these days. One has to do with gender. Since boys tend to grow up throwing a ball against a wall or a stoop, and most girls may not, there's a feeling that girls reach school age with an athletic disadvantage. The schools are addressing this problem, but some people want to avoid the whole issue by downgrading or eliminating team games. Rita Kramer, author of *Ed School Follies*, a book on theories at schools of education, thinks a feminist argument against competitive sports is emerging. "This is one of those hidden-agenda items for feminists," she says. "Some of them don't want masculine skills to be valued too highly in the schools."

The other, more serious argument comes from the cooperative learning movement and other school movements that promote "equity issues" and are less concerned with excellence than with equality. The basic teaching, that nobody is better than anybody else, leads believers to oppose any activity that produces winning individuals. From an "equity" point of view, it's better to have everybody hopping up and down on one leg than to risk the inequality of having winners.

There are many obvious things to say here. The anti-achievement ethic buried in the "equity" argument is a deadly one. People can lose without humiliation and win without feeling superior. Through sports, children learn how to handle defeat as well as victory—no sulking, gloating or rubbing it in. Aerobics and interpretive dancing have their place, but so do team sports. And it's always best to keep ideologues out of the gym.

Come on. Let's play ball.

"There's no question in my mind that well-organized athletic programs can provide a safe, wholesome environment where our children can enjoy their spare time."

Participating in Organized Sports Can Benefit Children

Lyle J. Micheli with Mark D. Jenkins

Lyle J. Micheli cofounded the world's first children's sports medicine clinic at Children's Hospital in Boston, Massachusetts. He is an associate professor at Harvard Medical School and served as president of the American College of Sports Medicine. In the following viewpoint, taken from his book *Sportswise* (written with sports and fitness writer Mark D. Jenkins), Micheli defends organized sports as a potentially valuable activity for today's youth. He describes several benefits of sports for children and calls for better coaching and greater parental involvement in order to ensure that sports provide these positive rewards.

As you read, consider the following questions:

1. What does Micheli think about the debate between proponents of organized sports and free play?
2. What are some of the rewards of sports, according to the author?
3. What qualifications should sports coaches have, according to Micheli?

While driving through the suburbs on a sunny spring afternoon, you chance upon an emerald-green patch of manicured grass upon which thirty youngsters in pristine white uniforms are learning the mysteries of that most American of pastimes, baseball. A timeless portrait of American youth, right?

Think again. Organized sports are such a prominent feature of American folk culture that we are inclined to imagine that Little League baseball and Pop Warner football arrived on these shores with the *Mayflower*. But in fact, organized sports for children became a part of the fabric of American society only after World War II. Only in the past quarter century have they become a ubiquitous part of the American scene. Before that time, free play and sandlot sports dominated the leisure time of American children. The change in the character of children's play from unstructured to organized doesn't please everyone. When I attend conferences I hear many of my colleagues waxing nostalgic about the bygone days of free play and decrying the rise of organized sports. "Those were the days" is their theme.

Frankly, I find the debate over the relative merits of free play versus organized sports irrelevant. Like those who miss the horse and carriage, many people mourn the passing of the old ways of play. But we must realize that several profound changes in our society have contributed to the organization of children's sports, among them the limited number of recreational facilities, the progressive loss of open space and vacant lots in cities and suburbs, and the decrease in spontaneous neighborhood activities. The American family structure has changed; separation and divorce are common, and in many families both parents work outside the home. These changes have made organized sports an attractive option for many parents who simply can't keep an eye on what the kids are up to. Our lives have become so busy and structured that organized programs fit well into our compartmentalized existence.

The Rewards of Sports

There's no question in my mind that well-organized athletic programs can provide a safe, wholesome environment where our children can enjoy their spare time. Goodness knows there are too many negative temptations available to our children. I'm not talking only about illegal temptations like drugs, alcohol, and unsafe, unwise sexual experiences. There are also television, video games, junk food, and fancy toys, which are perfectly legal as well as perfectly terrible for this nation's youngsters. You can extol the virtues of educational television, interactive video games, and brain-building toys as much as you want, but I've seen too many casualties of such modern technology to be impressed. I'm talking about fat children with a list of

26

heart-disease risk factors as long as their arms; I'm talking about children so weak they can barely do one sit-up; I'm talking about children whose muscles are so "tight" they can't touch their knees. These are kids who have been denied the chance to participate in fitness-building activities. Far too many of our youngsters are missing out on the physical activity their bodies need to reach their full potential, not to mention the rewarding experiences sports provide that help them develop into fully formed adults.

The Popularity of Youth Sports

Today's kids are participating in organized sports in a big way. According to Dr. Vern Seefeldt, director of the Institute for the Study of Youth Sports at Michigan State University, about 25 million American boys and girls—more than half of those between ages six and 18—regularly take part in at least one organized sport. And while the structure of play for children may have changed over the years, parents, pediatricians and psychologists generally agree that games and athletics continue to have real value for kids. At their best, sports help socialize children, promote mental and physical development, build self-esteem and strengthen family bonds.

Kevin Cobb, *American Health*, September 1992.

Health Fitness   "Health fitness" is the healthy state achieved through regular exercise. Its three components are heart-lung endurance (cardiovascular fitness), strength and flexibility (musculoskeletal fitness), and a good ratio of body fat to muscle (nutritional fitness). All three components are essential for children's short- and long-term good health. Kids who exercise regularly have bigger hearts, more muscle mass, less fatty tissue, stronger bones, and more flexible joints. Being fit in childhood helps people fight off a host of diseases in later life, including heart disease, back pain, and osteoporosis. Fit children are far less likely to be injured in sports than youngsters who aren't in shape. Recent evidence also suggests that regular exercise helps youngsters' academic performance; this is the "healthy mind in a healthy body" concept that has been with us since the time of the ancient Greeks. Health fitness is vital for us all—children, adults, and the elderly. I'm strongly in favor of youngsters balancing sports like football and baseball, which don't really promote fitness, with health fitness builders like swimming, running, soccer, cycling, and strength training with weights. These activities keep kids in shape and provide opportunities for lifetime participation. . . .

Good Health Fitness Habits   Those who play sports in childhood are very likely to continue to do so as adults. We get used to feeling good and strive to keep feeling that way. For that reason it's very important that children learn good health fitness habits early in life. In addition to encouraging kids to exercise, sports can teach why exercise is so important. For example, young swimmers can learn to read their pulses—they get a huge kick out of this—and from a very early age they can understand that maintaining a high pulse rate for at least twenty minutes three times a week is a good way to guarantee the long-term health of their hearts. By the same token, children must learn the life-threatening—this is no exaggeration—consequences of a sedentary lifestyle. Once again, it is very important that we promote the health fitness-building sports that can be played through life. That way, when baseball, football, basketball, and ice hockey are no longer available or appealing to them in adulthood, our kids will have a background in activities like cycling, jogging, and swimming to help them keep in shape.

Sports Skills   Children love learning new skills. It's a natural part of growing up to want to absorb as much knowledge as possible and use it in different situations. Having new knowledge makes kids feel more confident and self-assured. Sports skills are especially important because they are tools for staying fit and healthy throughout life as well as for effective participation in childhood activities. As far as I'm concerned, the more skills a child can learn, the better. The youngster who learns to play baseball, squash, soccer, and basketball and is taught to swim, cycle, and jog properly has a packed toolbox of sports skills that can be used throughout life. I'm much more interested in having children learn five different sports than getting them to specialize in just one. The rise of the young specialist athlete explains in large part the increasing incidence of overuse injuries. At the same time, it's extremely important that children be properly coached. Incorrectly learning a skill such as baseball pitching can lead to serious injury.

Sports and Competition

Healthy Competition   Children love to compete. Despite what some critics say, competition between kids didn't start with organized sports. It's been around since our ancestors were living in caves. What sports can do is teach children to compete fairly, to try their hardest, to congratulate the winners if they lose, and to accept victory gracefully if they win. This is the old-fashioned notion of sportsmanship, which I feel has been overlooked in recent times. Children exposed to healthy competition will soon learn that the reason they play sports isn't to win at all costs, but to strive to win by playing as hard as they can within the boundaries of a set of rules. I truly believe that when left to their own devices, children are much more interested in competing than in winning. These are not the same thing. Just watch kids playing a fierce game of soccer among themselves, and then ask them what the score is. Most of the time they won't know! Most important, children who learn to play hard and fairly will take this approach with them into other areas of their adult lives.

Self-Esteem One of the most important things sports can do is build self-esteem. Children have to grow emotionally as well as physically, and sports can help them develop a positive self-image and become much more confident. It isn't necessary to be the star of the team to be successful in sports. Any child who feels as if she is contributing to the team effort will learn self-esteem. The goals set for each child should be realistic; as they achieve these goals they understand that they are developing as athletes. If a child is having difficulty in a team sport like baseball or football, encourage him to take up an activity that allows greater scope for competing against himself—jogging, cycling, strength training, or swimming, for example.

Social Benefits

Friendship One of the great rewards of sports is socializing. Sports give kids the chance to be with a large group of peers in a stimulating environment. The more sports a child plays, the more friends she has the chance to make. It is a testament to the power of sports that these friendships often last through life. Children should be encouraged to make friends on opposing teams as well as their own. When a barbecue is held after a Little League game, the kids have an opportunity to get to know one another personally. That's where the true spirit of youth sports can be found. Children learn to leave rivalries on the field and discover that their opponents are kids like themselves who just want to have fun in sports.

Pleasure Ah, fun! For kids, this is the number-one reason to play sports. I suspect that many adults have forgotten how much fun we had in sports when we were kids. And many have forgotten *how* we had that fun. We impose adult measurements of success—trophies, uniforms, leagues, and so on. The rationale is that if we don't give kids these things, they'll quit sports. But that's simply not true. Children were playing among themselves long before anybody invented trophies or leagues. These criteria are merely icing on the cake. Kids in sports just want to have a good time, be with their pals, compete, learn how to play the sport, and get as hot, sweaty, and filthy as possible.

Along the same lines, adults far too often confuse winning

with having fun because winning is the measure of success in adult lives. For kids, success in sports mostly means having fun. In fact, winning at all costs usually gets in the way of having fun; the game becomes too serious. A good coach will know how to motivate his athletes to do their best while giving them the chance to enjoy themselves as much as possible. At the Sports Medicine Clinic at Children's Hospital I see the products of well-organized sports programs every day: happy, healthy, confident youngsters with a glint in their eye that tells me they're hooked on sports for life. If there's one memory that adults should have when looking back on their childhood sports, it's an overwhelming sense of fun. That virtually guarantees a lifetime interest in sports and fitness.

Sports and Self-Image

It may be a strong statement to make, but in my opinion, a parent who says that he or she is not interested in sports and doesn't value athletics for their child is acting irresponsibly. This is not to say that intellectual stimulation is unimportant, only that physical stimulation is equally important. This means that the same father who starts reading books to his one-year-old should also roll the ball back and forth across the floor to his child, and that the mother who plays classical music for her baby should also tumble around on the floor with her baby. . . .

Psychologists are not prone to agree on many things, but one thing we do agree on is the importance of a positive self-image to a healthy and active life. And the fact is, there is no more effective way of developing a child's self-image than by the early and frequent exposure of that child to athletic movement and eventually to sports.

Given the evidence, then, the question is not whether sports are good or whether they should be part of a child's life, but how to find the best way to make athletics a part of a child's everyday life and how soon to start.

Eric Margenau, *Sports Without Pressure*, 1990.

Organized sports have the potential to give children all the rewards described above. I'm sometimes in awe of the positive impact sports can have, especially on children with chronic illness or handicaps. . . . Sports and fitness activities are emerging as an important rehabilitative tool for conditions ranging from asthma to multiple sclerosis.

Unfortunately, our sports programs turn out so many well-adjusted child athletes *in spite of* the way they are run, not because of it. The organization of children's sports programs in this country is astoundingly haphazard. America simply hasn't responded adequately to the enormous changes involved in moving from unstructured activity to planned programs. You might argue that our "nonsystem" is working quite well—"If it ain't broke, don't fix it." But much of the evidence suggests that if our system ain't completely broke, it could certainly use some fixing. Otherwise, how do you explain the shocking fact that over 70 percent of our kids drop out of organized sports before the age of fifteen? How do you explain children's plunging fitness levels? How do you explain the new phenomenon of debilitating overuse injuries? How do you explain that organized sports have a 20 percent reinjury rate attributable to inadequate rehabilitation? These facts tell me that while there is great potential in our children's sports programs, the present situation is far from perfect.

Improving the Coaches

I'm especially concerned about the quality of adult leadership, especially in coaching. Think about it: we allow coaches to make our children run laps, lift weights, perform strenuous athletic tasks, and engage in many other potentially injurious activities. Yet in most cases we don't require volunteer coaches to have any training in injury prevention, techniques for safe training and playing, or basic first aid. This highly unsatisfactory situation exists partly because the demand for youth sports coaches far exceeds the supply, and most programs are reluctant to impose even minimum standards. As one sports organizer said, "Beggars can't be choosers." Although the vast majority of volunteer coaches are well meaning and committed, most simply do not have the training they should have, even though such training is available from numerous organizations.

Although I sometimes tire of comparisons between the health care system in the United States and that in Canada—a nation with a much smaller and more homogeneous population—I'm afraid our neighbors to the north are ahead of us when it comes to youth sports. All Canadian youth sports coaches must be certified by examination. Australia and New Zealand are following suit. . . .

I am convinced that certification of coaches will eventually come to this country, probably by the year 2000. When it does, it will be a win, win, win situation. Our coaches will win: they'll be better trained and therefore more knowledgeable in sports technique, health fitness principles, and injury prevention. Parents will win: they'll know that their children are being instructed by qualified personnel. And of course, the biggest winners will be our kids: they'll be better trained, less likely to be injured, and more qualified to participate in sports and health fitness activities throughout life.

Without training, most volunteer coaches wind up running their programs as they think a professional coach would. Too often, their criterion for success is the team's win-loss record, not whether the kids are having fun. These coaches subscribe to Vince Lombardi's credo: "Winning isn't everything; it's the only thing." I prefer the motto of the American Coaching Effectiveness Program: "Athletes first, winning second."

Pros and Cons

Therefore, while I sing the praises of organized sports for children, it troubles me greatly that too many American children are denied the very rewards these programs should provide. I'm also very concerned about the enormous numbers of kids who leave sports programs because they're cut from the team, injured, or just fed up with the overcompetitiveness. Indeed, for every potential reward sports offers, there's also the potential for a negative experience.

Here's what two people arguing the pros and cons of organized sports might sound like:

Pro: Organized sports are good for kids' health because they get systematic exercise in a psychologically sound environment.

Con: Kids stand around in organized sports too much to get fit, and competition increases the risk of psychological harm.

Pro: Organized sports are safer than free play and sandlot sports.

Con: There's no proof that organized sports are safer. In fact, kids never suffered overuse injuries until organized sports came along.

Pro: Difficult sports skills and playing techniques can be learned only in a supervised sports environment, with proper coaching and officiating.

Con: Team play spawns conformity rather than individuality, and acceptance rather than innovation.

Pro: Leagues, team rankings, and tournaments make it more fun for the kids.

Con: There's no evidence that organized competition is any more enjoyable.

The simple fact is that organized sports can be either good or bad. Whether a youngster has a safe and successful experience depends almost entirely on the quality of the program he is enrolled in. If the quality of adult supervision is high, our kids can achieve all the rewards that sports have to offer.

"One of the gravest concerns that psychologists have about organized youth leagues is that . . . they tend to overlook the spontaneous needs and desires of young children."

Participating in Organized Sports Can Harm Children

Rick Wolff

An estimated 25 million children in America participate in some form of organized sports. Sports activities range from Little League baseball and Pop Warner League football to such sports as tennis, running, and soccer. Some people have questioned whether sports—particularly highly organized sports supervised by adults—are an altogether healthy activity for children. In the following viewpoint, Rick Wolff argues that incompetent coaches, overbearing parents, and an emphasis on winning over having fun can make youth sports a harmful psychological experience for many participants. Wolff, a former professional baseball player and college coach, has written numerous books and articles on sports psychology.

As you read, consider the following questions:

1. Why do many professional athletes refuse to let their children play organized sports, according to Wolff?
2. What kinds of sports-related stress does the author discuss? What results does he predict from such stress?
3. What recommendations does Wolff make concerning youth sports?

According to Dr. Rainer Martens, one of the nation's leading psychologists and experts on youth sports, the worries about children and sports seem to run in cycles. "The first wave of concern started in the early 1950s, and then again, there was great controversy about Little League and the like in the early 1970s. Judging from those precedents, I can understand why it is happening again in the early 1990s."

Parents' concerns about youth sports have been with us for some time now. But what's curious is that while many well-meaning moms and dads have expressed all sorts of worries about the impact that organized youth sports have on their sons and daughters, precious little has been written about what the experts—the psychologists, psychiatrists, pediatricians, and educators—have to say about these youth leagues. But over the last decade, the experts have started to quietly observe children's behavior in these quasistructured play environments, and they've been conducting psychological experiments to see just how children react to sport, play, winning, and losing.

The Best and the Brightest?

Let's start with the athletes themselves. Most parents totally accept the premise that organized youth sports, such as Little League or Pop Warner football, are the launching pad for future major league players.

But what struck me as ironic, when I started to ask current and former major leaguers about their experiences in Little League baseball, was that one after the other told me that he wouldn't let his own children ever play in such organized leagues. Ron Leflore, a major league star for many seasons with the Tigers, White Sox, and Expos, and who now lives in Florida, was adamant that his son not play Little League ball. "Too many parents just don't know what they're doing when they're coaching, and I've seen too many kids hurt by the experience," says Leflore. . . .

Robin Roberts, a star pitcher for many seasons for the Philadelphia Phillies, is another who has stepped forward about the hazards of youth sports, and in particular about Little League baseball. Writing in an article for *Newsweek*, Roberts says:

> I still don't know what those . . . gentlemen in Williamsport had in mind when they organized Little League baseball. I'm sure they didn't want parents arguing with their children about kids' games. I'm sure they didn't want to have family meals disrupted for three months every year. I'm sure they didn't want young athletes hurting their arms pitching under pressure at such a young age. I'm sure they didn't want young boys who don't have much athletic ability made to feel that something is wrong with them because they can't play baseball. I'm sure they didn't want a group of coaches drafting the

34

players each year for different teams. I'm sure they didn't want unqualified men working with younger players. I'm sure they didn't realize how normal it is for an eight-year-old boy to be scared of a thrown or batted baseball. For the life of me I can't figure out what they had in mind. . . .

Let's not put the entire rap on Little League baseball; when it comes to ultracompetitive parents and uninformed coaches, psychological horrors abound in all youth sports leagues.

Youth Football

George Welsh, the highly successful football coach at the University of Virginia, has long been a critic of youth league football. Welsh has gone on the record as saying that organized football for eight- and nine-year-olds is just too demanding, both physically and emotionally. Even worse, he doesn't like the fact that young ballplayers become stereotyped at an early age. "A kid becomes a tackle at eight and he stays a tackle the rest of his life," observes Welsh. "How could that be much fun? At his age he should be learning all the skills. He should learn to throw and catch and run with the ball."

Welsh's comments are echoed by another Hall of Fame football name, Larry Csonka, a star running back at Syracuse and, for many years, in the National Football League. Some football fans, aware of Csonka's rough-tough image, might be surprised to find that he didn't allow his two sons to play in midget football leagues.

Observed Csonka about the youth football leagues in his neighborhood: "The coaches didn't know much about what they were doing. They just yelled a lot. They acted like they imagined Lombardi and Shula would act. Why, they had those eight-year-olds running gassers [long windsprints], for crying out loud."

Csonka continues: "The whole country loves football, and so do I. But parents don't stop to consider all the things that can go wrong for a young fellow pushed into that kind of pressure. For one thing, he can come home with a handful of teeth. Worse, he can come home soured on athletics for life."

Perhaps it shouldn't be surprising that it's the former professional athletes who so often step in and warn parents about letting their children play in organized youth leagues in which the coaching or supervising is out of sync with reality. After all, it's the professional athletes who have climbed that difficult pyramid of athletic success—and who knows better just what it takes to make it to the top of their profession?

But along with that competitive experience also comes lots of insight into the sport they "play." Galen Fiss used to play linebacker for the Cleveland Browns. One day in Kansas City, Fiss was coaching a youth football league when one of his linemen came out of the huddle, hopping and skipping up to the line of scrimmage.

"For an instant our coaches were horrified," said Fiss. "That's not the way you're supposed to approach the line. But then we realized he's a ten-year-old kid! That's his way of having fun."

© Peter Steiner/*The Washington Times*. Reprinted with permission.

The point is, rather than scream and yell at the little lineman to "get with it" and "look tough out there," Fiss and his coaching colleagues had the presence of mind to realize that the first priority in sports—as far as the kids are concerned—is having fun.

Winning and losing are secondary. . . .

While there are lots of really terrific youth sports coaches out there, there are also plenty of terrible ones—coaches who can inflict emotional damage on [a] child without even being aware of it.

Literally dozens of psychological studies have confirmed that kids are in a very vulnerable situation when they play youth sports. Among the key findings:

• There is strong evidence that children tend to form lifelong attitudes toward sports before they reach the age of ten.

• Kids need the constant approval of coaches, and they are much more sensitive to criticism than adults are.

• An adult declaration of success or failure, of worthiness or unworthiness, is a major determinant of a child's self-esteem.

• And perhaps most importantly, there are countless studies that indicate just how stressful the competition of youth sports can be for children—and just how detrimental that can be to their self-esteem. And who's providing most of the stress for the kids? That's right—the coaches and parents!

What Happens to Kids Who Are Stressed Out?

They give up. Or they turn away. Or they find some other nonathletic avocation to take up their time. Or they become depressed. You've heard of "burnout" among professional people, such as doctors, social workers, and other individuals in high-pressure jobs. The same kind of thing often happens to children.

How does burnout occur? Too often the parents mistakenly assume that the child really wants to continue the sport in which he's shown promise and wants to continue that activity to the exclusion of other youth activities. A common example is the young boy or girl who shows tremendous promise in the swimming pool or as a tennis player or gymnast. Such promise can be exhibited as early as six or seven years of age.

But this athletic promise often confronts the adoring parents with a difficult decision: to let the child devote her full leisure time to that one particular sport (swimming, tennis, gymnastics, and so on) or to allow her to sample all kinds of sports that little people tend to enjoy?

For many parents this can be a real quandary. After all, tennis stars seem to get younger all the time; the same goes for Olympic swimmers and gymnasts. But more and more psychologists point out the dangers of having a child devote all of his or her spare time to just one athletic pursuit at an early age. Imagine what must go through an eight-year-old's mind when he is told by Mom and Dad that "if he wants to become the best in his chosen sport, then he'll have to swim dozens of laps in a pool, day after day." That's kind of a tough sentence for a youngster who just wants to have fun. But the tragedy is that it happens every day, all over the country.

Whenever you find yourself worrying about a child's dedication to just one sport, keep in mind a classic book on athletics entitled *The Pursuit of Sporting Excellence*. David Hemery, an Olympic hurdler, interviewed sixty-three of the world's greatest athletes about their development in sports. In his results he found that only five of these great athletes ever specialized in just one sport before the age of twelve, and that the average age of one-sport specialization for these athletes was sixteen.

One of those athletes who didn't specialize in a particular sport until he was sixteen was Carl Lewis, the world-class sprinter and jumper. O. J. Simpson, the great football star, didn't fully decide on a career in football until he was nineteen years old.

What happens to children who do specialize at a very young age? At the very least many of them end up experiencing burnout. And at the other end of the spectrum many simply miss out on the normal developmental patterns of childhood, such as making friends, enjoying creative games, and trying out other sporting activities.

You've seen all the magazine and television reports about the next young tennis star or Olympic hopeful. And chances are you've asked yourself, "I wonder why the parent pushes that child so hard?" The answers are numerous, but more often than not there is usually an underlying adult drive that's pushing that little person's need to achieve and to win.

According to a widely quoted study, one psychologist has concluded: "Adult egos too often turn the game into a victory drive or a training ground for future stars, with their children as pawns."

Children's Experience

The point is, parents must come to grips with the simple reality that a child's perspective on sports and games is much, much different from that of an adult. As George F. Will, the well-known columnist and author of the best-selling book *Men at Work*, points out, "Children are an enlarging if sobering experience, and often amusing. But childhood is frequently a solemn business for those inside it."

To Will, and to many other parents, it is clear that children take their play very seriously, and they ought to be wary that in the context of youth league play, their children don't take it too seriously. Whereas the adult can usually put winning and losing into proper perspective in the scope of life, a child is still grappling with those abstract concepts. And unless those concepts are placed into a proper philosophical framework, the realities of winning and losing can be skewed way out of proportion for the youngster.

38

The famous developmental psychologist Erik Erikson pointed out that from the ages of seven through twelve, children are constantly learning about their worldly environment. During this time they are driven to master certain skills and roles in their daily world. They are constantly overcoming feelings of inferiority (ever notice how a child will keep practicing a skill over and over again, until he or she perfects it?). And when kids do master a certain skill, they feel proud of their own personal accomplishment.

Of course, a major driving force in this pursuit of mastery comes from a desire to please one's parents. Parental approval is very significant in this period of a child's existence.

But what parents look upon as "simple child's play" is, to the child, a very serious matter, and too often parents forget that—a particularly common failing when a parent pushes a youngster into one sport at too early an age. . . .

The "Has-Been" Syndrome

There are other common syndromes for young athletes as well. Perhaps the opposite of the burnout syndrome—the case of a kid who plays one sport too much—is the child who doesn't get to play enough—the so-called "has-been" who never "was."

In some ways this is an even more dangerous and tragic situation than that of the burnout victim.

• According to a recent study as many as 80 percent of all children who play youth sports drop out of competitive sports by the time they reach the ripe old age of twelve.

• In Canada, where ice hockey is practically a religion, you might be surprised to learn that according to a Canadian Amateur Hockey Association poll of a few years ago, there were 600,000 players registered with the CAHA, of whom 53 percent were under the age of twelve; 35 percent were between twelve and fifteen; and only 11 percent were over the age of fifteen. In other words, by age fifteen, only about one out of every ten kids in Canada is actually playing youth ice hockey. And there is every indication that similar percentages apply to kids in the United States in such sports as baseball, football, and soccer.

Why do these trends exist? Because somewhere along the line early in their sporting careers, too many of these kids had the misfortune to have fallen into the hands of coaches who decided that they weren't good enough to play or who simply didn't want them to play.

Even worse, too many coaches just flat out decide that they want to "show kids that sports can be a positive experience—but that it can only be positive if they play on a winning team." Hence, the coach plays the more advanced players most of the time while the less talented kids play limited amounts. From the coach's point of view the "lesser" kids share in their teammates' on-the-field successes.

You can imagine how much fun it must be for an eight-year-old to be always in the position of having to congratulate his teammates for playing well, while he's relegated to the role of bench reserve. And it doesn't take a Ph.D. in psychology to figure out that if a child doesn't get to play much, then after a while he won't show much enthusiasm for signing up the next year. . . .

Spontaneous Play

One of the gravest concerns that psychologists have about organized youth leagues is that because they are set up by adults, run by adults, and maintained by adults, they tend to overlook the spontaneous needs and desires of young children. Experts in child development, dating back to Jean Piaget, have long noted that kids like to fantasize and fabricate the "rules" of their games as they play them. You have seen your own child engage in a playful fantasy land, in which he or she is "lost" in conversation with playthings or imaginary playmates. This kind of spontaneous play is the stuff of creativity and tends to fuel the child's enjoyment of her own games.

Indeed, because these spontaneous games are played on a plane of fantasy, the so-called "realistic consequences" of winning or losing are never even considered a risk. That's a vital consideration for the child, because for her, the act of playing is supposed to be fun and of no risk at all.

But as soon as the concept of "rules" and the idea of "victory or defeat" is injected into the child's mind, then much of the simplistic, refreshing spontaneity vanishes. After all, there's no time to fantasize about one's play when one is being judged according to "the rules of the game," a game usually set up by— you guessed it—parents.

Does this mean that, without the interference or leadership of parents, kids would never learn the rules of a sport? Not at all. Piaget pointed out that from his observations, kids, when left to their own devices, will ultimately develop their own rules of fair play, and of competitive right and wrong. Piaget pointed out that if several children are left to play with marbles, eventually they will figure out on their own how to develop a sense of equitable play. In effect, learning the rules of fair play is critical not only to the child's sense of creative spontaneity but also to her moral growth and the development of social cooperation. . . .

What does all this mean in terms of the young athlete? Concludes Edward C. Devereux, a psychologist at Cornell University:

> In Little League ball the spontaneity is largely killed by sched-
> ules, rules, and adult supervision—a fixed time and place for

each game, a set number of innings, a commitment to a whole season's schedule at the expense of alternative activities. Self-pacing? Obviously not. Fun? Yes, in a hard sort of way; but, please, no fooling around or goofing off out there in right field; keep your eyes on the ball! Instant feedback? Yes, loud and clear from all sides, if you make a mistake; but mostly from adults, in terms of their criteria of proper baseball performance.

The major problem with Little League baseball, as I see it, is that the whole structure of the game is rigidly fixed once and for all. It's all there in the rule books and in the organization of the League and the game itself. . . . Almost all the opportunities for incidental learning which occur in spontaneous self-organized and self-governed children's games have somehow been sacrificed on the altar of safety (physical only) and competence (in baseball only). . . .

A few years ago a couple of psychologists recommended the following guidelines for youth sports. Even though they may sound a bit unorthodox to you, they're worth bearing in mind:

1. All score books should be eliminated.

2. Let the players select their coaches and let them umpire or referee their own games.

3. Let each player play the same amount of time.

4. Don't be afraid *not* to enforce a rule if it gets in the way of the kids' playing.

In other words, if you let your top priority be the children's amusement and the sheer fun of playing the sport, you'll ensure that they're keeping their priorities straight as well. Surely you have heard the old sports maxim, "It's not whether you win or lose, but how you play the game."

Playing for Fun

As far as kids are concerned, that particular phrase carries more truth than most parents imagine. One telltale study proves exactly that point. Back in 1974 a landmark study on children in sports asked these questions:

1. Would you rather play simply for fun, or would you prefer to win?

2. Would you rather be on a winning team but sit on the bench, or would you rather play a lot on a team that loses a lot?

The results shouldn't surprise you. Over 95 percent of the kids replied that they would rather simply have fun than worry about winning, and over 90 percent said they would prefer to be on a losing team if they were able actually to play in the games rather than be bench warmers on a winning team.

The results are clear: On the whole kids would rather simply play and have fun. Too often, sadly, it's us—the adults—who get in the way of their fun and enjoyment.

> *"I don't think we can accept all the glory and the money that comes with being a famous athlete and not accept the responsibility of being a role model."*

Athletes Should Be Role Models

Karl Malone

Fans have traditionally viewed star athletes as heroes and role models. But increasing media coverage of athletes' off-field lives, which in some cases have included incidents of drug abuse, gambling, and other questionable activities, has caused many people to question whether athletes should be seen as proper role models for America's youth. In 1993 Charles Barkley, a star NBA (National Basketball Association) basketball player and member of the 1992 U.S. Olympic team, declared in a controversial television commercial that "I am not a role model." In the following viewpoint, Karl Malone, Barkley's teammate on the Olympic team and an NBA star for the Utah Jazz, takes issue with Barkley. Malone argues that by virtue of their public prominence, athletes are role models whether they desire to be or not, and therefore they should strive to be good role models.

As you read, consider the following questions:

1. What does it mean to be a good role model, according to Malone?
2. What statement of Charles Barkley's does Malone agree with?
3. What are some of the advantages and disadvantages of being a famous athlete and role model, according to the author?

I love Charles Barkley like a brother, and except for the times when we're banging and pushing each other under the boards in games between my team, the Utah Jazz, and his, the Phoenix Suns, we're great friends. We don't necessarily like the same things: Charles loves golf so much he would play at halftime if he could, but I think a golf course is a waste of good pasture-land. One of the reasons we get along so well, though, is that we both say what's on our minds without worrying about what other people are going to think—which means we disagree from time to time. Here's an example of what I mean: I disagree with what Charles says in his Nike commercial, the one in which he insists, "I am not a role model." Charles, you can deny being a role model all you want, but I don't think it's your decision to make. We don't *choose* to be role models, we are *chosen*. Our only choice is whether to be a good role model or a bad one.

I don't think we can accept all the glory and the money that comes with being a famous athlete and not accept the responsibility of being a role model, of knowing that kids and even some adults are watching us and looking for us to set an example. I mean, why do we get endorsements in the first place? Because there are people who will follow our lead and buy a certain sneaker or cereal because we use it.

I love being a role model, and I try to be a positive one. That doesn't mean I always succeed. I'm no saint. I make mistakes, and sometimes I do childish things. And I don't always wake up in a great, role-model mood. There are days when I don't want to pose for a picture with every fan I run into, when I don't feel like picking up babies and giving them hugs and kisses (no matter how cute they are). Those are the days I just try to steer clear of the public.

A Positive Role Model

But you don't have to be perfect to be a good role model, and people shouldn't expect perfection. If I were deciding whether a basketball player was a positive role model, I would want to know: Does he influence people's lives in a positive way away from the court? How much has he given of himself, in time or in money, to help people who look up to him? Does he display the values—like honesty and determination—that are part of being a good person? I wouldn't ask whether he lives his life exactly the way I would live it or whether he handles every situation just the way I would handle it.

I do agree with Charles on one thing he says in his commercial: "Just because I can dunk a basketball doesn't mean I should raise your kids." But sometimes parents need a little assist. There are times when it helps for a mother and father to be able to say to their kids, "Do you think Karl Malone or Scottie

Pippen or Charles Barkley or David Robinson would do that?"
To me, if someone uses my name in that way, it's an honor.
Sure, parents should be role models to their children. But let's
face it, kids have lots of other role models—teachers, movie
stars, athletes, even other kids. As athletes, we can't take the
place of parents, but we can help reinforce what they try to
teach their kids.

Athletes Have Influence

Celebrities like Charles Barkley may decline the honor, but their
high visibility obliges them to behave with at least an awareness
that they are being watched by millions. Like it or not, they have
a power of influence on worshipful young fans multiplied by the
huge factor of television—perhaps even more so among the minority poor, who have few other avatars of success to excite their
hopes. It may be well and good to point out, as most child psychologists do, that parents are the main role models in a child's
life. But that smugly assumes an intact and caring set of parents to
do the job. "What does it say to the kid who doesn't really have
anybody?" asks Dr. Robert Burton, a Northwestern University
psychiatrist who specializes in treating athletes. "Kids need to
have someone they can idealize in order to aspire to become better themselves. Without that, there's not much hope for them."

David Gelman et al., *Newsweek*, June 28, 1993.

Parents just have to make sure they don't take it too far.
Sometimes they put us on a pedestal that feels more like a
tightrope—so narrow that we're bound to fall off eventually.
This is not something I'm especially proud of, but I've had parents in Utah say things to me like, "You know, Karl, in our family we worship the ground you walk on. In our house your picture is right up there on the wall beside Jesus Christ." Now,
that's going too far. Is it any wonder some athletes don't want to
be role models? Who wants to be held up to that kind of impos-
sibly high standard? Imagine someone putting a lifesized picture
of you on a wall and saying things to your picture before they go
to bed. That's scary.

Public Scrutiny

The scrutiny gets to be overwhelming at times. I feel for
Michael Jordan's having to deal with the negative publicity he
received about gambling. I don't think most people can imagine
what it's like to be watched that closely every minute of every
day. I was told once that it wouldn't be that bad for me because

no one would know me outside of Utah, but that's not true. Ever since I played on the Dream Team in the Olympics, I can't go anywhere without being the center of attention, and that's very confining at times. For instance, there have been occasions when I've felt like buying a big Harley-Davidson motorcycle and riding it down the street. First, the Jazz would have a fit and say it's too dangerous. Second, everyone would be watching to see if I wore a helmet, if I was obeying the speed limit, if I was taking turns safely—you name it. The first time I didn't measure up to expectations, I would hear, "What kind of example is that to set for other people who ride motorcycles?"

But the good things about being a role model outweigh the bad. It's a great feeling to think you're a small part of the reason that a kid decided to give school another try instead of dropping out or that a kid had the strength to walk away when someone offered him drugs. But one thing I would encourage parents to do is remind their kids that no matter which athletes they look up to, there are no perfect human beings. That way, if the kids' heroes should make mistakes, it won't seem like the end of the world to them.

I would never knock someone for saying what he thinks. If Charles doesn't consider himself a role model, that's certainly his right. But I think he is a role model—and a good one, too. And if he gets that NBA championship ring, I might just make him my role model.

"It's probably misguided for society to look to athletes for its heroes—any more than we look among the ranks of, say, actors or lawyers or pipefitters."

Athletes Should Not Be Role Models

Matthew Goodman

Many people have held up professional athletes as heroes or role models for America's youth. In the following viewpoint, Matthew Goodman questions the wisdom of doing so. He argues that the qualities that make for a successful athlete—competitiveness and a single-minded concentration on developing athletic skills—are not the attributes of heroes. Besides, he says, the way society pampers and treats its young star athletes hampers their social development and sense of ethics. Goodman has written about sports for several publications, including the *Village Voice, Washington Monthly* and *Z Magazine*.

As you read, consider the following questions:

1. Why do people wish for athletes to be heroes or role models, according to Goodman?
2. How does being an athlete change one's sense of self-worth, according to the author?
3. What does Goodman believe is the social function of athletes?

These days, it seems, the sports pages have come to resemble a police blotter. The fan seeking box scores and game recaps must first wade through news stories about drug abuse among athletes, arrests for drunk driving, betting and recruiting scandals, and, most disturbingly, reports of rape and other sex-related crimes. What's going on here? American sports fans ask over their morning toast and coffee. *What's happening to our heroes?*

It's not difficult to understand our desire for athletes to be heroes. On the surface, at least, athletes display many of the classical heroic attributes. They possess a vital and indomitable spirit; they are gloriously alive inside their bodies. And sports does allow us to witness acts that can legitimately be described as courageous, thrilling, beautiful, even noble. In an increasingly complicated and disorderly world, sports is still an arena in which we can regularly witness a certain kind of greatness.

Yet there's something of a paradox here, for the very qualities a society tends to seek in its heroes—selflessness, social consciousness, and the like—are precisely the *opposite* of those needed to transform a talented but otherwise unremarkable neighborhood kid into a Michael Jordan or a Joe Montana. Becoming a star athlete requires a profound and long-term kind of self-absorption, a single-minded attention to the development of a few rather odd physical skills, and an overarching competitive outlook. These qualities may well make a great athlete, but they don't necessarily make a great person. On top of this, our society reinforces these traits by the system it has created to produce athletes—a system characterized by limited responsibility and enormous privilege.

How Athletes Suffer

The athletes themselves suffer the costs of this system. Trained to measure themselves perpetually against the achievements of those around them, many young athletes develop a sense of what sociologist Walter Schafer has termed "conditional self-worth": They learn very quickly that they will be accepted by the important figures in their lives—parents, coaches, peers—to the extent they are perceived as "winners." Their egos come to rest, all too precariously, upon the narrow plank of athletic success.

Young athletes learn that success, rather than hard and honest play, is what brings rewards. And for those successful enough to rise to the level of big-time college sports, the "reward" is often an artificially controlled social environment, one that shields them from many of the responsibilities other students face. Coaches—whose own jobs, of course, depend on maintaining winning programs—hover over their athletes to ensure that nothing threatens their eligibility to compete. If an athlete gets into trouble with the law, for instance, a coach will very likely intervene—hiring an attorney, perhaps even managing to have the case quietly dismissed. In some schools, athletes don't even choose their own classes or buy their own books; the athletic department does all this for them. It's not unheard of for athletic department staff to wake up athletes in the morning and to take them to class.

TANK McNAMARA®   by Jeff Millar & Bill Hinds

Given this situation, it's not too surprising that many young American athletes seem to have been left with a stunted ethical sense. Professor Sharon Stoll of the University of Idaho has tested more than 10,000 student athletes from all over the country, ranging from junior high to college age; she reports that in the area of moral reasoning, athletes invariably score lower than non-athletes—and that they grow worse the longer they participate in athletics.

Spoiled by Society

Coddled by universities, lionized by local communities, accorded star status by the public, endowed with six- and seven-figure salaries, successful athletes inevitably develop a sense of themselves as privileged beings—as indeed they are. The danger arises when the realistic (and thus probably healthy) understanding of personal privilege mutates into a sense of personal entitlement.

Mike Tyson, of course, is the most blatant example of this phenomenon. Having been taught as a young man that he was special—his mentor, Cus D'Amato, reportedly had one set of rules for Tyson and another, more stringent, set for all his other boxing protégés—and having lived his entire adult life surrounded by a cortege of fawning attendants, Tyson eventually came to believe, like a medieval king, that all he saw rightfully belonged to him. Blessed with money and fame enough to last a lifetime, he spent his time outside the ring acquiring and discarding the objects of his desire: houses, automobiles, jewelry, clothes, and women. In the wake of the publicity surrounding his rape trial, countless women have come forward to relate stories of Tyson propositioning them and then, upon being rebuffed, exclaiming in what was apparently genuine surprise, "Don't you know who I am? *I'm the heavyweight champion of the world.*" Needless to say, not all athletes are Mike Tyson; there are plenty of athletes who recognize that they have been granted some extraordinary gifts in this life and want to give something back to the community.

Some remarkable individuals will always rise above the deforming athletic system we've created. After retiring from football, defensive tackle Alan Page of the Minnesota Vikings became a successful lawyer and established the Page Education Foundation, which helps minority and disadvantaged kids around the country pay for college. Frustrated by the old-boy network by which Minnesota judges had traditionally been appointed, Page challenged the system in court and finally won election to the state Supreme Court, becoming the first black ever elected to statewide office in Minnesota. Tennis star Martina Navratilova joined six other lesbians and gay men as a plaintiff in a lawsuit filed by the cities of Denver, Boulder, and Aspen challenging Colorado's anti-gay law as unconstitutional. Thankfully, there will always be some legitimate heroes (or, to use the more contemporary term, role models) to be found among professional athletes.

Still, it's probably misguided for society to look to athletes for its heroes—any more than we look among the ranks of, say, actors or lawyers or pipefitters. The social role played by athletes is indeed important (imagine a society without sports; I wouldn't want to live in it), but it's fundamentally different from that of heroes.

The Beauty of Sports

Thanks to the years of hard and uncompromising work that athletes have invested in themselves, sports is often able to provide us a glimpse of that "supreme beauty" that Bertrand Russell wrote of as characteristic of mathematics: "sublimely pure, and capable of a stern perfection such as only the greatest art can show."

Can't we just leave it at that?

Periodical Bibliography

The following articles have been selected to supplement the diverse views presented in this chapter.

Mark Anderson	"Playing with Pain Is Not Good for Kids," *USA Today*, April 1993.
Ira Berkow	"Should Sports Heroes Be Role Models at All?" *TV Guide*, March 21, 1992.
Julie Cart	"Sports Heroes, Social Villains," *Los Angeles Times*, February 2, 1992.
Richard Chevat	"Keeping the Fun in Team Play," *Good Housekeeping*, June 1992.
Kevin Cobb	"Child's Play: Organized Sports Should Be Fun and Games," *American Health*, September 1992.
David Gelman et al.	"I'm Not a Role Model," *Newsweek*, June 28, 1993.
Tom Junod	"Ordinary People," *Sports Illustrated*, March 29, 1993.
Charles Mahtesian	"Budget Chicken: The Newest High School Sport," *Governing*, August 1993.
Barry J. Maron	"Sudden Death in Young Athletes," *The New England Journal of Medicine*, July 1, 1993. Available from 10 Shattuck St., Boston, MA 02115-6094.
Lyle J. Micheli	"Children and Sports," *Newsweek*, October 29, 1990.
Mariah Burton Nelson	"Who Wins? Who Cares?" *Women's Sports & Fitness*, July/August 1990.
Rosemary Parker	"Learning by Intimidation?" *Newsweek*, November 8, 1993.
Aric Press	"Old Too Soon, Wise Too Late?" *Newsweek*, August 10, 1992.
Mike Royko	"Role Models of Past Worked for the Job," *Liberal Opinion Week*, July 19, 1993. Available from 108 E. Fifth St., Vinton, IA 52349.
Vern E. Smith and Aric Press	"Who You Calling Hero?" *Newsweek*, May 24, 1993.
E.M. Swift	"A Pro Vote for School Sports," *Sports Illustrated*, October 12, 1992.
Rick Telander	"The Wrong People for the Job," *Sports Illustrated*, December 23, 1991.

How Should College Athletics Be Reformed?

SPORTS IN AMERICA

Chapter Preface

People who run college sports programs, especially men's basketball and football, must try to foster and complement higher education while running a big-time entertainment business. Defenders of college sports argue that the two functions can be combined and that giving athletic scholarships to gifted athletes enables many poor students to attend college. But critics say that the goals of education and entertainment are fundamentally incompatible and that student-athletes are often deprived of a chance at a meaningful college education.

The gross revenues generated by successful football and basketball teams can run in the millions of dollars, part of which is often used to support other university athletic programs. But partly because of this, and because the expenses of running competitive programs can be considerable, college athletic directors and coaches are often under great financial pressure to win. Critics argue that in trying to attract the best athletes, many directors and coaches resort to practices that severely compromise the academic integrity of their institutions.

These practices include recruiting players who lack the educational background necessary to succeed academically in college, falsifying transcripts, and steering students toward easy classes that do more to keep their academic eligibility than to further their education. In one well-publicized case, Creighton University basketball player Kevin Ross received athletic scholarships and passed enough college classes to stay eligible to play for four years while remaining functionally illiterate. After failing both to graduate and to establish himself as a professional basketball player, Ross returned to elementary school.

Supporters of college athletes argue that, ultimately, student-athletes themselves must combine their academic and athletic pursuits and that many have succeeded. One example is former University of Virginia basketball star Ralph Sampson, who resisted entreaties to turn professional before completing college. Noted tennis player Arthur Ashe wrote that Sampson, far from being exploited, greatly benefited from his college experience:

> He is not being used. It would have been well worth it to him to borrow money to attend a school like the University of Virginia. If anyone is "using" someone, Sampson is using the University. . . . He decided to "use" Virginia to market his basketball skills while attending classes.

People disagree on whether Ralph Sampson's or Kevin Ross's experiences as a college athlete are more typical. Those disagreements are the focus of the viewpoints of this chapter.

"Those who come to college hoping to exchange their physical skills for a degree often discover the promise of an education is an illusion."

Sports and Academic Studies Are Incompatible

Shannon Brownlee and Nancy S. Linnon

Many people have criticized colleges' athletic programs as being incompatible with their academic mission. They argue that such programs exploit the amateur athletes who participate in them. Although student-athletes are often given scholarships and are supposed to combine their athletic endeavors with academic pursuits, they often have little opportunity to pursue an education or receive a degree. In the following viewpoint, Shannon Brownlee and Nancy S. Linnon examine college sports and conclude that the ideal of the student-athlete who combines athletics and schooling is a myth that has little bearing on past and present major college sports programs. Brownlee is a senior editor at *U.S. News & World Report*. Linnon was a reporter-researcher for the weekly newsmagazine.

As you read, consider the following questions:

1. Do many schools make profits on athletic programs, according to Brownlee and Linnon?
2. What are the lessons of history from early college football programs, according to the authors?
3. Who shares the blame for the current state of college sports, according to Brownlee and Linnon?

From "The Myth of the Student-Athlete" by Shannon Brownlee and Nancy S. Linnon, *U.S. News & World Report*, January 8, 1990. Copyright 1990, *U.S. News & World Report*. Reprinted with permission.

College sport is being undermined by its own mythology. The entire enterprise is founded on the whimsical notion of the amateur, the scholar-athlete who studies and trains hard and is rewarded for his efforts, not with money but with sporting values and, above all, an education. But this implicit bargain has today become a mockery, and the cause is an overriding need—both psychological and economic—to win.

Consider the economics: The teams competing in Pasadena's Rose Bowl will each walk away with $6 million. Bowl games alone were worth more than $55 million in 1989, and basketball powers will rake in a $1 billion bonanza over seven years starting in 1991 for granting CBS the privilege of broadcasting college games.

Big Business

That's big business—a business sustained by the dreams of athletes, a disproportionate number of whom are black. Few of those dreams come true. Fewer than 30 percent of football and basketball players graduate, a rate far lower than for all students, and only a tiny fraction make it to the pros. While a handful of exemplary programs can claim to graduate nearly 100 percent—Notre Dame, Duke and Penn State, for example—too many follow the lead of Memphis State, which graduated six out of 58 basketball players between 1973 and 1983.

These broken bargains can be traced to the peculiar economics of college sports. Despite the enormous sums of money involved, athletics are not a profitable enterprise for most colleges. Only about 45 athletic departments operate in the black each year. And only a few of those—notably Penn State, Notre Dame and Miami—do so consistently, because college sports as they're staged today, and football in particular, are very expensive businesses. Says John Slaughter, former chancellor of the University of Maryland, who is now president of Occidental College, "Winning is the thing that ensures the income. Football and basketball have to make money, and they have to win to make money, and that's how the cycle becomes so vicious."

The cycle has become vicious indeed. In 1989, 21 universities were penalized by the National Collegiate Athletic Association (NCAA) for infractions ranging from falsifying entrance exams to wooing recruits with cash to paying players, while an additional 28 were under NCAA investigation. Such ethical lapses belie the myth that college sports provide a moral education, and the effect is clear in the behavior of athletes. Since 1987, more than 250 college athletes have been arrested for violent crimes ranging from fistfights to attempted murder.

Why do universities tolerate a business that is exploitative and violent—and loses money on top of it all? First, and most obviously, a lot of people—from coaches to recruiters to concession-aires—make their living off it. And some make a very good living; college coaches earn as much as $1 million a year in salary and endorsement fees. But more to the point, big-time college sports satisfy a psychological need. As Robert Atwell, president of the American Council on Education, notes, "It's the nature of this highly competitive society of ours that loves winners and hates losers. College sports feed the insatiable appetite of the American male to be a couch potato and watch all this stuff."

Margulies/*Houston Post*. Reprinted with permission.

Corruption and violence are nothing new in college athletics, but the money has increased the pressure on recruiters to pay more attention to athletic prowess than to character. In January 1989, the University of Oklahoma's athletic dorm was the scene of a gang rape. The same month, one teammate shot another over a cassette tape, and quarterback Charles Thompson sold cocaine to an FBI agent. Four Sooners [went to] prison, and the NCAA put the team on three years' probationary exclusion from TV appearances and postseason play for "major violations" including drug use and payments to players.

Oklahoma has plenty of company in its misery. . . . While NCAA Executive Director Richard Schultz insists that "99 percent of everything that is going on in intercollegiate athletics today is exceptionally positive," the truth is that 10 to 20 percent of Division I athletic programs are in trouble with the NCAA's enforcement office at any given time.

There are signs that educators have reached their limit. A *U.S. News* poll conducted in 1989 revealed that nearly 86 percent of college presidents believe the pressures for success on the playing fields interfere with the primary educational mission of America's schools. Their frustration is evident in the words of Gordon Gee, president of the University of Colorado, who says, "We've got to deprofessionalize college athletics and return to the Greek notion of amateur competition."

A Mythical Past

But those days never existed, not in Olympia, and certainly not on the college gridiron, and it is the perpetuation of that myth that has college sports so conflicted. From its beginnings shortly after the Civil War, football has been soiled by violence and commercialism, as teams made use of older, tougher "tramp" players, students in name only. After numerous deaths on the gridiron, President Teddy Roosevelt ordered colleges in 1905 to take control of their student-run teams.

In doing so, administrators found that football was profitable. Yale's nationally ranked team, for example, had amassed a reserve of $100,000 (about $2 million today). Professional sport was considered degrading for institutions of higher learning, but money and football were so intimately entwined that the colleges could not possibly disentangle the two without killing the sport altogether. Instead, the universities created the illusion of amateurism by forming the NCAA to "retain a clear line of demarcation between college athletics and professional sports."

While college athletes are technically amateurs—their scholarships cover tuition, fees, books, room and board—their sweat is the fuel that runs an enormous machine. In 1988, Division I-A football generated $500 million in gate, TV and licensing revenues and untold amounts from corporate sponsors and boosters. Ironically, this income rarely shows up on university ledgers. At many big-time schools, athletic departments are run as separate corporations—financially shaky corporations. The University of Michigan, for example, one of the largest athletic departments in the country, operates 21 sports on a $21.3 million budget. In 1989, the Wolverines were $2.6 million in the hole. . . .

Boosters, athletic directors, presidents and coaches like to claim that a winning program translates into something they call "the intangibles," prestige and donations for a school. "How many people know we have a Nobel Prize winner this year?" asks Jon Burianek, Colorado's associate athletic director. "Not many compared with the number who know this football team's Cinderella story."

Maybe so, but the fact is a high-profile team benefits the athletic department, not the university. James Frey, a sociologist at the University of Nevada at Las Vegas, citing 12 different studies conducted over the past 50 years, concludes, "There's no relation between a winning record and donations that come into the university for academic programs."

Need for Reform

The reform of college sports is clearly an idea whose time has come. No one expects athletic programs to clean themselves up: they have become too independent, too unrestrained, too powerful. At some universities, coaches now earn salaries two or three times higher than the highest-paid professor, higher even than the president. Student athletes are (in the phrase of Wayne Duke, former commissioner of the Big Ten) "compartmentalized": they live apart in specially reserved dormitories, train and practice in specially reserved facilities, and have scant contact with other students. Through the booster club, people who know little and care less about the work of a university are invited to have a hand in its activities. And perhaps as a direct result, almost anything is tolerated—from illegal cash payments to counterfeit grade reports—as long as the team is winning. Between 1984 and 1989, the National Collegiate Athletic Association (NCAA) publicly reprimanded 83 programs for rules violations, but not even public opprobrium seemed to have much of an effect. . . . As a successful football coach at a Western university explained, "I'll be fired for losing before I'm fired for cheating."

D. G. Meyers, *Commentary*, December 1990.

As critics see it, the most hypocritical justification offered for football's excesses is that the game builds character. The values that truly can be gained from sports—an appreciation for hard work, sportsmanship, the joy of playing—have been distorted by the desperate need to win. Boosterism is the perfect example. As Rick Telander, author of *The Hundred Yard Lie*, points out, "The Bull Gators, the booster club of the University of Florida, is giving money to win—not to build character but to beat the living daylights out of Florida State. That's got nothing to do with education."

To be sure, not all athletes object to the system. Some view college as a mere formality standing between them and lucrative professional contracts. Colleges serve as farm teams for the National Football League and National Basketball Association, which have struck a cozy deal with the NCAA by agreeing not to take an athlete before his college eligibility is up. Deion "Neon" Sanders, a defensive back of electrifying physical talents who signed a $4.4-million four-year contract in April 1989, with the Atlanta Falcons, graced few classrooms with his presence during his senior year at Florida State. Asked whether he wanted to be in college, Sanders told Telander, "No, but I have to be."

But for every athlete who makes it to the big time there are hundreds more who neglect their studies in the mistaken belief that they too can cash in on their physical skills for a shot at a sweeter life. In reality, the road to the pros, where salaries in the NFL average $256,000 and in the NBA $650,000, is long and narrow. More than 17,600 young men play Division I-A basketball and football, and each year only 150 of them will reach the big leagues; even fewer will last more than a year or so. Yet according to a NCAA Presidents Commission study of athletes, more than 23 percent of college athletes (and 44 percent of the blacks) believe they are headed for the pros. "There's nothing wrong with having those dreams," says Thomas Tutko, a sports psychologist at San Jose State University. "It's when you sacrifice everything else that the problem occurs."

Shared Blame

The blame for the dismal state of college athletics must be shared—with the media for worshiping athletes and with the high schools for failing at basic education. "Colleges and universities are receiving products of an inferior educational system," says Richard Lapchick, director of the Center for the Study of Sport in Society at Northeastern University. "They didn't create the attitudes of the players, the high schools did." And increasingly, the sins of the colleges are being visited upon the lower schools. In many parts of the country, high-school coaches recruit elementary-school students. In 1989, high-school games began appearing on television.

Arthur Ashe, the only black male tennis player ever to win at Wimbledon, believes that black athletes suffer most acutely from the worship of sports. Only 4 percent of Division I college students are black, yet they represent 56 percent of basketball players and 37 percent of football players—in part, says Ashe, because "the screening of black athletes in black communities starts very early. It is cold-blooded; and by the time a young black boy is 13, we know if he's a good athlete or not, and junior-high coaches have already started recruiting him."

Even those who come to college hoping to exchange their physical skills for a degree often discover the promise of an education is an illusion. And no wonder. The NCAA Presidents Commission study found that football and basketball players devote, on average, 30 hours a week to their sport, 16 more hours than they spend in class. Detroit Lions running back Barry Sanders, 1989's Heisman Trophy winner, quit school early to turn pro, saying that college athletes spend so much time on sports they "might as well get paid for it.". . .

Some proponents of reform would go so far as to pay college players, thus ending the hypocrisy of the amateur student-athlete. Certainly, the NFL and NBA ought to be contributing to the training of their future recruits, if not by starting farm teams then by aiding college programs. But more than anything, coaches, athletic directors, college presidents and the NCAA must acknowledge—as polls reveal the general public already has—that college basketball and football are careering out of control. "[Football] has become a business, carried on too often by professionals, bringing in vast gate receipts, demoralizing student ethics and confusing the ideals of sport, manliness and decency." These words were delivered at the University of Wisconsin by historian Frederick Jackson Turner. The year was 1906.

"The concept of the student-athlete *is alive and doing quite well in the groves of academe."*

Sports and Academic Studies Are Compatible

Raymie E. McKerrow and Norinne Hilchey Daly

Raymie E. McKerrow is a professor of communication studies at the University of Maine at Orono. Norinne Hilchey Daly was a senior executive editor for the publisher Harcourt Brace Jovanovich. In the following viewpoint, they refute the notion that college athletics are a sham whose participants are not true students. They argue that many college athletes have had successful academic careers, and that sports may provide educational opportunities for athletes who otherwise may lack them. Conceding that some student-athletes have had troubled records, they point out that the same holds true for students who are not athletes.

As you read, consider the following questions:

1. What is the relation between sports and society, according to McKerrow and Daly?
2. How do the authors respond to the claim that commercialization has corrupted college sports?
3. What is characteristic of most student-athletes, according to McKerrow and Daly?

Trashing student-athletes has long been a favored occupation of academics with more time than talent on their hands. Generally, such diatribes can be ignored as the histrionics of individuals long since inured to the effects of reason or research as the ground for advancing an idea. One despairs of ever getting past the jaundiced view that the purity and dignity of pristine academic life has been sullied by the presence of athletic competition. Whether in coffee "cliques" at the university club or in faculty contributions to university athletic advisory boards, the assumption articulated (or left implicit) is that the "student-athlete" equation is an impossible dream and a search for a balanced perspective a chimera of "soft," sports-minded academics who lack the proper standards of judgment. . . .

Sports is neither a "cause" of nor a "solution" to society's ills; rather, sports are a reflection of the values and mores of the culture. If there is cheating in the society at large, one should not be surprised to find it in sports. Banning sports from academic life because of instances of cheating makes as much sense as banning mayors from running cities because of alleged or known isolated instances of corruption. This does not mean that cheating or corruption is to be condoned in either instance, but simply that one needs to put the respective issue in perspective.

A Balanced Perspective

Here we argue for a balanced perspective in viewing the achievements as well as the abuses surrounding sports in the academic environment. One impetus for writing this essay is to answer the argument that the student-athlete concept has died— that it is no longer possible to sustain the image. Another stimulus is the recognition that statistical data hide as much as they reveal. While such data are useful in identifying what is happening to student-athletes (e.g., graduation rates), statistics alone do not provide *reasons* for good or poor performance. In arguing for a balanced perspective, we hope one assumption will be clear: whatever the abuses or faults in sports, there is nothing *inherent* in the structure or attitude toward athletic competition that *decrees* such abuses must inevitably occur.

Is it possible to sustain the student-athlete image? *Yes*. The assertion that it had experienced "death at an early age" is an instance of overkill—the concept of the *student-athlete* is alive and doing quite well in the groves of academe. The image of students participating in athletic competition yet retaining integrity in the classroom is in danger in some quarters and on some campuses, but the wounds inflicted on the "image" are not fatal.

Finding patients in a critical condition among all students is a relatively easy task. . . . However, athletes are more likely to see their names in the sports pages for alleged criminal acts or even allegations of cheating; their academic ineligibility is likely to be paraded before the public on Sports Channel and in local and national newspapers (e.g., *USA Today*). In far too many such cases, what would otherwise be minor news confined to the "police beat" of a local paper (or ignored entirely as being un-newsworthy) ends up being reported as if it were major news.

Athletes Are No Worse Than Others

There is a societal fascination with the lives of "public fig-ures"—hence the reporting of their antics will be out of propor-tion to that of nonathletes at the same institution. What is im-portant to remember is that the behavior, whatever its cause, is not the result of some innate predisposition on the part of ath-letes to engage in improper actions. Decrying the involvement in sports on the basis of such reports damns all for the excesses of one person or at least one persona. For every Brian Bosworth on any campus, there are a dozen other athletes, young men and women, who reflect values and engage in behaviors that link them with other students. They all make mistakes, and even act immaturely at times, but on the whole they are young people of whom we can be justly proud. They do well in some courses, not as well in others. Their academic profile need not be that much different than that of nonathletes. At the University of Maine, for example, the combined SATs for 1988-89 (to the extent that scores on SATs are predictive of potential success—and that is an arguable proposition) reflect favorably in comparisons—the differences are not extreme. In fact, student-athletes at the university possess a higher-than-average score in comparison with Maine college-bound high school seniors and with all nationally college-bound high school seniors:

```
UM-bound HS Seniors...................966
UM-bound Student-Athletes.........923
National college-bound..................904
Maine college-bound.....................896
```

As one might expect from these comparisons, the academic performance of athletes is not that much different from the gen-eral student population. Students in twelve sports programs at UM earn grades above the institutional GPA. The six programs below the average are within .200 of the average. The average for all sports programs is above the minimum requirement of 2.00 for graduation. Dean's List representation also reflects well on the participating athletes: every athletic program has stu-dents who have made the list. The percentage of athletes on the list varies from 8% to 76%. In general, the representation from women's sports is greater than from men's sports. In citing these statistics, we are not trying to suggest that student-athletes are better, or that our institution is inherently superior to those in which this is not the case. The point is that such comparisons are *possible:* there is nothing inherent in the nature of sports or academics that prevents the successful combination of the two.

The same comparison would hold for athletes and nonathletes at the "bottom" of the academic scale. For every athlete allowed to remain in school with a 1.43 academic average and only 48 semester credits after four semesters (the minimum required by the NCAA), there is a nonathlete (often more than one) who is in a similar situation. The only just way to treat both, from an *academic* perspective, is to either dismiss both or allow both to remain for an additional semester, in accordance with the academic policies of the institution. To do otherwise is to sanction preferential treatment based on external and academically irrelevant criteria.

Sports Are Educational

Games and sports are educational in the best sense of that word because they teach the participant and the observer new truths about testing oneself and others, about the enduring values of challenge and response, about teamwork, discipline and perseverance. Above all, intercollegiate contests—at any level of skill—drive home a fundamental lesson: Goals worth achieving will be attained only through effort, hard work and sacrifice, and sometimes even these will not be enough to overcome the obstacles life places in our path.

The value and successes of college sport should not be overlooked. They are the foundation of our optimism for the future. At the 828 colleges and universities which comprise the National Collegiate Athletic Association (NCAA), over 254,000 young men and women participate in 21 different sports each year in about one quarter of a million contests. At the huge majority of these institutions, virtually all of these young athletes participate in these contests without any evidence of scandal or academic abuse.

The Knight Foundation Commission on Intercollegiate Athletics, *Keeping Faith with the Student-Athlete*, 1991.

While the national statistics on the graduation rates of student-athletes in the high-profile sports is alarming, there is a need for a balanced perspective. While in college, the majority of athletes advance toward a degree at about the same rate as other students. The University of Maine's graduation rates for athletes (51%) and nonathletes (48%) compare favorably with that reported nationally (athletes 52%; nonathletes 41.5%). To appreciate truly the image created by statistics on numbers of players

63

not graduating after four years in college, we must point out that not every nonathlete graduates in eight semesters. Illness, dropping out for a semester to work or travel or just to contemplate one's future choices, or taking fewer than 15 credits each semester—all contribute to a student's taking more time to finish a degree. . . .

In today's world, student-athletes with the possibility of professional contracts, and many without such prospects, are coming to summer school *during* their years of eligibility. Where the image used to be one of athletes making up eligibility deficiencies, this is no longer the primary reason. At the University of Maine, for example, approximately 75% of the student-athletes enrolled in summer courses do *not* have to be there to retain eligibility. Football players may take summer classes in order to reduce their course load in the fall and still remain "on track" toward graduation. Others may take courses simply to "get ahead" and to be sure that they will graduate on time.

The experience at Memphis State, where no Black basketball player graduated in a 10-year time span, is possible anywhere. The converse experience at Georgetown, where 90% of the basketball team graduated, also is possible. Neither experience is a *necessary* consequence of the coupling of sports with academics. Likewise, the experience at the University of Georgia, involving favoritism in the assignment of grades, is possible anywhere. So is "clustering" students in courses and academic majors in which they are likely to retain their eligibility. These abuses have and will continue to occur, they are not *necessary* by-products of the sports ethic in this country. Lax academic standards are not the universal result of the presence of athletic programs; nor are lax standards exclusive to courses and programs in which athletes enroll. Such standards are a reflection of the values of the institution and of the people hired to promote those values.

Is the past recoverable? *Hopefully not.* In his presentation to chapter delegates from the Eastern Region of Phi Kappa Phi in 1988, Marvin Eyler, head of the department of Physical Education and Recreation at the University of Maryland, lamented the passing of what he referred to as the "league of educated gentlemen" in academe and sport. If this "noble tradition" is what has passed from the scene, there is cause for celebration rather than mourning. For many, to mourn its passing is to call for the return of a sexist, macho image of an establishment-oriented, elitist club of "gentlemen." In spite of all of our efforts to eradicate it, sexism remains a feature of the sports world. . . .

The Commercialization of Sports

Seen in this context, the "league" is a reference to an outmoded and outdated public persona whose passing is to be lauded, not lamented. While eradicating sports is not the answer, neither is recovering a past which exacerbates the problem.

Is the student-athlete image irreparably compromised by the commercialization of sports? *No.* One cannot deny that commercialization and "big money" have had an enormous effect on sports in America. The temptation to win by any means becomes greater as the rewards to a campus reach "megabuck" proportions. The pressures to succeed result in illegal recruiting tactics, in "hiding" athletes in easy classes, and in other actions that detract from the sense of "fair play" that dominates our society's response to sports (and life in general). Not all of the pressures are equally deleterious. For example, Professor Eyler notes, in the context of decrying the influence of "big money," Kareem Abdul Jabbar's five-million-dollar salary. Is that excessive? Is 20 million dollars for approximately one and one-half minutes work in the ring too much money for Mike Tyson?

Comparing Salaries

Salaries paid to sports professionals need to be properly placed in a business context—they are entrepreneurs with a "life earning potential" that is markedly less than CEOs of major companies. . . . If one disparages an athlete who markets his or her skill at "top dollar," one should also disparage corporate America's penchant for paying the Lee Iacoccas of the country their salaries and bonuses. To deny a baseball player or any other athlete the opportunity to "cash in" on talent at marketplace values is to discriminate against them as business people. In fact, a five-million-dollar contract over two years is "small change" in the high-powered business circles in this country. As Dean A. Purdy notes in *The World & I:*

> . . . while the six-figure salaries paid to professional athletes may seem excessive, they pale in comparison to the "pots of gold" earned by individuals in other segments of the entertainment world, such as the recording and movie industries. For his employment, the professional athlete embarks on an extremely short and oftentimes perilous career. In professional team sports the [average] length of an athlete's career is less than four years.

There is only one Nolan Ryan. Few are the student-athletes who have the opportunity to place themselves in this highly restricted market: 1 in 10,000 youths will end up in pro football or basketball; of the 30,000,000 youths involved, less than 18,000 will make it to college level Division I play, and less than 200 of those will move on to the professional level. Should we discourage those who do have the chance? Many suggest that we should. The now-well-advanced trend toward using college sports as the "training ground" for the pros is decried by those who feel this view of college sports has no place in an academic setting.

Is the "training ground" image inherently negative—is it totally incompatible with the mission of an academic institution? As faculty members, and as advisors to students, we would prefer to have an athlete of college age *in school* rather than in the pros. The assumed disjunction between "preparation for adult life through college education" and "preparation for the pros" is a false one. We would rather take the chance that the prospect of getting a good education would actually rub off on the young athlete with visions of pro life dancing in his or her head (and we have witnessed such transformations on more than one occasion) than have the person miss that opportunity entirely by jumping from high school to the pro life.

Incentive for Academic Study

There is a built-in incentive to do well academically if one is "in training" for the pros while in college. If one flunks out, the ability to negotiate is far less than if one is doing well and has the option of returning to school for another year. Besides, the college experience plays a role in the maturing process and thereby enhances the student's ability to enter the pros with a more refined and stable sense of self—as a "responsible adult." For every Len Bias [a University of Maryland basketball star who died in 1986 of a drug overdose], there will be other students turning pro, quietly and without fanfare, who represent the qualities sought in a student-athlete. As further evidence of the importance of an academic background, some pro teams are willing to write contracts which enable an athlete to finish a college degree—either by providing a lump sum payment equivalent to the remaining costs for the degree or by paying tuition and books for summer school courses during the life of the pro contract. Obviously, the student whose own immaturity and lack of motivation results in flunking out diminishes the chances of such favorable negotiation.

In the midst of all of these pressures, or in spite of them, the *majority* of students participating in collegiate athletics, at both Division I and other levels, continue to balance their interest in a sport with the desire to obtain an education. For the majority, professional sports are not in their immediate future, and most athletes who are students are mature enough to realize what they have to do in order to benefit themselves once their playing days in college are finished. Certainly, there are athletes who come to school to play a sport and for whom the prospect of getting an education is the furthest thing from their minds. They are *not unique* when one compares their motivation to that of some nonathletes. For every athlete with an "illicit" motive, there are many nonathletes attending college because of parental pressure or because they do not know what else to do. More often than

66

not, representatives of both groups will be in the 8-10% of a freshman class who earn less than a 1.00 (a D average) in their first semester. In those cases where the athlete and the nonathlete survive the first few semesters, there will be a large number who change their minds about why they are attending college—they may not have entered with the "proper" motivation, but they mature and grow into the experience and profit from the opportunity nonetheless. Certainly there will be students who abuse the system, who do not profit from their time in academe. But they are students *first*, and *occasionally* are also athletes. To brand all athletes as uninterested in an education, as attending only in the hopes of entering a pro career, is to risk consigning the majority to oblivion for the excesses of the minority. . . .

Hand wringing and wailing need not characterize our response to the abuses in the system. Abuses are not an inherent result of the relationship between sports and academics. Thus, the image of the student-athlete on those campuses where excesses have occurred can be changed in a positive direction. There always will be students who do not perform to expectations, who will take advantage of the "system" as it is presented to them. To be sure, some of these will be athletes. The conclusion that the student-athlete is dead, however, is unfair to all those who do struggle and ultimately achieve both on the field and in the classroom. The premature burial is a disservice to these students, men and women alike, who will quietly pursue their interests on and off the field. . . . We need not prematurely bury the student-athlete just to protect ourselves from the excesses of those undeserving of the name.

"If we make graduating the priority of every student-athlete, . . . we'll be true to the values that our institutions are supposed to embody."

Student-Athletes Should Be Students First

Charles B. Reed

Charles B. Reed is chancellor of Florida's state university system. The following viewpoint is taken from a speech Reed made to college presidents and administrators involved with the National Collegiate Athletic Association (NCAA). In it, Reed argues that education should remain the primary focus of all college students, including athletes, and that colleges should make greater efforts to ensure that their student-athletes receive an adequate education and graduate. College athletic programs, combined with reforms such as Proposition 48 (a 1983 NCAA reform that bars freshmen from athletic scholarships and competition if they fail to meet minimum grade and test requirements), motivate athletes to take their own education more seriously, Reed argues.

As you read, consider the following questions:

1. What questions does Reed pose in his address?
2. What message needs to be sent to young athletes, according to the author?
3. What proposals for change does Reed recommend?

Charles B. Reed, "Education Is What It's All About," a speech given at the NCAA Presidents' Commission National Forum, San Francisco, April 1, 1989. Reprinted by permission of the author. This speech also appears in *Vital Speeches of the Day*, April 1, 1989.

To begin my comments, I want to borrow a line from Governor Mario Cuomo of New York. He told an audience in Washington that, back when he was considering running for president, late one night, the devil came to him and offered him a deal.

Governor Cuomo said, "He offered me the presidency in exchange for my soul. So I said: What's the catch?"

I think we need to . . . ask the question: If we are going to have big-time intercollegiate athletics in an environment of academic excellence, what's the catch?

That catch is, I think, not that we're trying to do two things that are totally incompatible, but that we've lost our sense of proportion and our sense of priority.

We often hear conversations within the NCAA that come to the conclusion that we "must not kill the golden goose"—meaning television contracts. Well, I think the golden goose really isn't broadcast revenues, but American higher education itself.

What Is More Important?

Our sense of proportion should tell us that. Anyone who has trouble deciding whether education or athletics is more important should recognize that we could easily have higher education without athletics.

Ask yourself: what would we do differently if tomorrow there were no such thing as intercollegiate athletics?

We'd still teach every course in the college catalogue. That wouldn't change one bit. We'd still conduct research at the same pace. We'd still perform public service.

What we wouldn't be doing in American higher education is bending or breaking the recruiting rules, stealing players and coaches from each other, struggling to keep our more rabid and fanatical boosters under control and trying to prevent the academic reputations of our institutions from being mocked or disgraced by our athletic programs.

Ask yourself another question: Is there another single reason why more university presidents have had to resign, or have been dismissed, than problems with athletics?

And finally, ask yourself this one:

What's more important in the life of a student-athlete—winning, or graduating?

I say, graduating is more important. And I think the real values of our universities are not merely what we say they are. Our real values are reflected not in words, but in the way we conduct ourselves. No institution is value-free. We either live up to high standards, or we don't.

Sometimes the recognition of our own imperfections prompts us to consider abandoning all pretense of amateurism and declaring the tradition of the scholar-athlete an unattainable myth. Some say we should openly pay our athletes, not require them to make progress toward a degree, and create a semi-professional feeder system for professional sports.

I disagree. I think the way to avoid hypocrisy is not to abandon our ideals, but to make a greater effort to live up to them.

Setting Priorities

And so we return to the issue of setting a priority. I think that priority ought to be graduating—on time—and at the same rate, if not at a higher rate, than students as a whole. Notre Dame, Penn State and Georgetown show us clearly that this is possible.

I know this can be done because I've seen it happen time after time. And frankly, I would not be here today as Chancellor of the State University System of Florida were it not for the athletic scholarship that made it possible for me to attend George Washington University, where I ultimately earned all three of my degrees.

I think we have to set graduation rates—not the score of the game or the won-lost record—as the priority, for three reasons.

First, it gives the student-athlete a chance at life after college.

Second, it sends the right message to younger students.

Third, it preserves the values of our society and of our universities.

The Purpose of Universities Is Education

We reject the argument that the only realistic solution to the problem is to drop the student-athlete concept, put athletes on the payroll, and reduce or even eliminate their responsibilities as students.

Such a scheme has nothing to do with education, the purpose for which colleges and universities exist. Scholarship athletes are already paid in the most meaningful way possible: with a free education. The idea of intercollegiate athletics is that the teams represent their institutions as true members of the student body, not as hired hands. Surely American higher education has the ability to devise a better solution to the problems of intercollegiate athletics than making professionals out of the players, which is no solution at all but rather an unacceptable surrender to despair.

The Knight Foundation Commission on Intercollegiate Athletics, *Keeping Faith with the Student-Athlete*, 1991.

Let's look at these three points one at a time.

The first point is the future of our student-athletes. Our system today throws up the photos of—to name two athletes from my own system—Deion Sanders and Sammy Smith, off to the

National Football League without degrees, to make millions of dollars.

Those two students will make enough money that, with some good advice, they'll be set for life even without degrees. But if they'd finished college, they'd be in a better position to evaluate the financial advice they'll get, and also have the basis for a second career after their knees give out. But they are two in a million.

Most of our student-athletes never get a shot at professional sports. Most who do don't last long enough to have what could reasonably be called "a career" as a professional athlete. What about those people who, having been exploited, now compete in the job market with former students who earned their diplomas?

Ask yourself this question: which applicant would you rather hire—someone whose academic focus was on remaining eligible for sports, or on graduating? Someone who barely passed a freshman algebra course, or someone who majored in computer science?

Second, we need to send a message to the younger students in the junior high schools and high schools of the nation that goes beyond the message of Proposition 48. We need to tell them that sports can be a meaningful part of life, but that hardly anybody makes a living in sports. Your odds of becoming a rock star or an astronaut are about the same as starting for the New York Knicks.

So we need to tell the next generation of student-athletes that, if they are unprepared academically to do college work, they can forget about playing college sports. In my experience, there are few better motivators for athletes than threatening to withhold participation in sports. Make it stick and you'll make it work.

A Focus on Education

Third, making academic success the true focus of intercollegiate athletics keeps us true to the purpose of our universities. Education is what it's all about—not touchdowns, skyhooks or home runs.

So let me make the following modest proposal:

1. Abolish spring training for football. . . . Athletes spend less time on the books than they do on sports. Let's cut back on some of the athletic distractions.

2. Reduce eligibility from four years to three. Let our freshmen find out where the library is and experience a degree of academic success first.

3. Report annually our graduation rates by institution, by sport, and by gender. We've started doing this in Florida, and we're beginning to see the results. Until now, only the coaching staff has been held accountable, because we don't keep score in the academic area.

71

Let's start keeping score—and compete with Notre Dame and Penn State and Georgetown not just on the field, but on Commencement Day.

4. Finally, let's extend the score-keeping to junior high and high schools, by making it clear that we do not recruit and will not accept as athletes students whose grades and test scores predict academic failure.

I realize not everyone is going to agree with everything I say here today. That's fine. But I think one thing we can all agree on is this:

Education is what it's all about. And if we make graduating the priority of every student-athlete, we'll be dealing honestly with our student-athletes, we'll set a positive example for younger students coming up, and we'll be true to the values that our institutions are supposed to embody.

Otherwise, when the devil offers us a bowl bid in exchange for our souls, we'll ask—what's the catch?

"It's time for schools to choose between real amateurism and real professionalism. They can't have a little of both."

Student-Athletes Should Be Athletes First

Louis Barbash

Louis Barbash is a writer and television producer based in Washington, D.C. In the following viewpoint, he argues that college sports such as football and basketball serve two different programs—education and generating money for the institutions. He argues that the latter goal has overshadowed the former in too many instances. Many student-athletes, he argues, are unprepared for college and have little interest in education. They are instead lured by the prospect of professional athletic careers. Barbash proposes that colleges acknowledge that their athletic programs are essentially minor leagues for professional sports and pay their athletes as such professionals. Barbash concludes that this may be the only way to end the hypocrisy of the present system.

As you read, consider the following questions:

1. What two main alternatives does Barbash propose to reform college sports?
2. Why does the author think the current system is hypocritical?
3. What does Barbash find shocking about the story of Dexter Manley?

From "Clean Up or Pay Up" by Louis Barbash. Reprinted with permission from *The Washington Monthly*, July/August 1990. Copyright by The Washington Monthly Company, 1611 Connecticut Ave. NW, Washington, DC 20009. (202) 462-0128.

Tom Scates is one of the lucky ones. He has a bachelor's degree from Georgetown University, where he played basketball under the fabled John Thompson, one of the best college basketball coaches in the country, and one of the few who insist that their players go to class. Ninety percent of Thompson's players at Georgetown receive degrees, about three times the national average.

More than a decade after Tom Scates received his diploma, he managed to parlay his Georgetown degree and education, his athletic skills, and the character he developed during his career in intercollegiate athletics into a job as a doorman at a downtown Washington hotel.

Still, Scates *is* one of the lucky ones. He played for a good team at a good school, under a moral coach, and under a president, Father Timothy Healy, who believed that Georgetown was a school with a basketball team, not a basketball team with a school. He was not implicated in drug deals, shoplifting, violence, grade altering, point shaving, or under-the-table money scandals. He didn't have his scholarship yanked. He didn't emerge from school functionally illiterate. He got a job.

Many of the men Scates played against when he was at Georgetown, and their basketball and football counterparts at major colleges and universities, have not been so fortunate. Less than half the football and basketball scholarship athletes will graduate from college. And what education athletes do get is often so poor that it may be irrelevant whether they graduate or not.

In addition to corrupting the university's basic academic mission, big-time sports have been a lightning rod for financial corruption. College athletes are cash-poor celebrities. Although their performance on the field or court produces millions in revenue for the university, they receive in return only their scholarships—tuition, room, and board—and no spending money. They are forbidden from working part-time during the season. Athletes have been caught trying to make money by getting loans from coaches and advisers, selling the shoes and other gear they get as team members, taking allowances from agents, and getting paid for no-show summer jobs provided by jock-sniffing alumni—all violations of National Collegiate Athletic Association (NCAA) rules.

The NCAA

Things might be different if the NCAA would show some real inclination to clean up the college sports mess. But that organization has a well-developed instinct for the capillaries: instead of attacking the large-scale academic, financial, and criminal corruption in college sports, too often the investigators from

Mission, Kansas, put their energies into busting athletes for selling their complimentary tickets and coaches for starting their practices a few weeks ahead of schedule. Meanwhile, the real problems of college athletics continue to fester. . . .

Is there any way out of this mess? Yes. Actually, there are *two* ways out. Because the NCAA has so utterly failed, because in the present system the big-money pressures to cheat are so enormous, and because, like it or not, sports have such a widespread impact on the country's moral climate, there should be a federal law that requires schools *either* to return to the Ivy League ideal in which players are legitimate members of the student body, judged by the same standards as everybody else, *or* to let players on their teams be non-student professionals. All the trouble comes from trying to mix these two alternatives— from trying to achieve big revenues while retaining the veneer of purity.

Paying Football Players

College football could follow the example of other profit-making entities in U.S. sports, including pro football, and reserve a percentage of the gross for the players.

The rationale:

• A college player's football-work schedule and conditioning program are about as time-consuming as an NFL player's.

• The probability of crippling injury is similar.

• On Saturdays and Sundays, students and pros provide similarly professional entertainment for thousands of Americans.

NBA and NFL players are now receiving well over half the gross revenues in their leagues. Universities, however, have many financial responsibilities, meaning, possibly, that their players should get less—perhaps only a third or a fourth of the gross.

Bob Oates, *Los Angeles Times*, October 3, 1993.

The pure alternative doesn't have to ignore athletic ability among prospective students—there were plenty of good football teams before today's double-standard disaster got firmly entrenched. You want to consider the athletic ability of college applicants for the same reason you want to consider musical or theatrical ability; a university should be a wonderfully diverse collection of talents that together stimulate people to develop in all sorts of positive ways. Athletic skill is one such talent—one that even academic purists ought to look at. But the key is that universities must consider athletic ability as only *part* of what they take into account when they accept a student. The fundamental mistake of today's college sports system is that it supposes a student could be at a university *solely* because of his athletic skill.

While the purely amateur option is probably the more desirable of the two, the professional one isn't nearly as horrible as it might seem at first. After all, coaches were originally volunteers, and now they're paid. (Army's first head coach, Dennis Michie, received no pay. Jess Hawley coached for free at Dartmouth from 1923-28. His 1925 team went undefeated and was the national champion.) So why not players?

How Much Should Players Make?

How much would a salaried college athlete make? If the example of minor league baseball is anything to go on—and such authorities as Roger Meiners, a Clemson University economist who specializes in the economics of college sports, and Ed Garvey, the former head of the NFL [National Football League] Players Association, think that it is—college salaries would be enough for a young athlete to live on, but not so much as to bust college budgets. Minor league baseball players start at around $11,000 for their first full professional season and range upward to the neighborhood of $26,000 for players on AAA teams under major league option. So it seems fair to estimate a salary of about $15,000 for an average player on an average team.

The professional option's chief virtue is honesty. The current student-athlete system requires both students and universities to pretend that the young athletes are not full-time professionals, but rather full-time students who play sports in their spare time. But does anyone suppose that high school athletes reading four and five years below grade level would be considered for college admission, much less recruited and given full scholarships, if they were not football or basketball stars? Can the abuses of NCAA rules that have been uncovered at almost half of its biggest schools have any other meaning than that giving these athletes a real education is not what universities are trying to do?

The hypocrisy begins with the fundamental relationship between the players and the university: 18- to 20-year-olds, many of them poorly educated, inner-city blacks, coerced and deceived into playing four years of football or basketball without pay so that the university can sell tickets and television rights.

The coercion comes from the colleges' control of access to professional football or basketball: It is virtually impossible to go to the pros without playing college ball first. Colleges open that opportunity only to athletes who will agree to perform for the college for four years without getting a salary or even holding an outside part-time job. The athlete does receive a four-year scholarship and room and board while he is enrolled, a package the NCAA values at about $40,000. The deception lies in the fact that the inducements held out to athletes by colleges—the chance to play pro ball and getting a college education—are essentially worthless, and the schools know it.

The athlete's first priority is to play pro ball. Forty-four percent of all black scholarship athletes, and 22 percent of white athletes, entertain hopes of playing in the pros. That's why they will play four years for nothing. But in fact, the lure of sports that keeps kids in school is a false hope and a cruel hoax. "The dream in the head of so many youngsters that they will achieve fame and riches in professional sports is touching, but it is also overwhelmingly unrealistic," says Robert Atwell, president of the American Council on Education. The would-be pro faces odds as high as 400-1: of the 20,000 "students" who play college basketball, for example, only 50 will make it to the NBA [National Basketball Association]. The other 19,950 won't. Many of them will wind up like Tom Scates, in minimum wage jobs, or like Reggie Ford, who lost his football scholarship to Northwest Oklahoma State after he injured his knee, and now collects unemployment compensation in South Carolina.

Worthless Scholarships

The scholarships and promises of education are also worthless currency. Of every 10 young men who accept scholarships to play football at major schools, according to NCAA statistics, just 4 will graduate. Only 3 of every 10 basketball players receive degrees.

Not only are these athletes being cheated out of a promised education, but they and their universities are forced to erect elaborate, meretricious curricula to satisfy the student-athlete requirement, so of those who *do* get degrees, many receive diplomas that are barely worth the parchment they're printed on. Running back Ronnie Harmon majored in computer science at the University of Iowa, but took only one computer course in his three years of college. Another Iowa football player also majored in computer science, but in his senior year took only courses in billiards, bowling, and football; he followed up by getting a D in a summer school watercolor class. Transcripts of the members of the basketball team at Ohio University list credit for something called "International Studies 69B"—a course composed of a 14-day/10-game trip to Europe. . . .

No case illustrates the cynicism that poisons big-time college sports better than that of former Washington Redskins star defensive end Dexter Manley. Manley spent four years as a "student-athlete" at Oklahoma State University only to emerge, as he admitted years later, functionally illiterate. But OSU President John

Campbell was not embarrassed: "There would be those who would argue that Dexter Manley got exactly what he wanted out of OSU. He was able to develop his athletic skills and ability, he was noticed by the pros, he got a pro contract. So maybe we did him a favor by letting him go through the program."

Plantation Slaves

Although top colleges see a winning athletic team as a jewel in their crown—and a huge money-maker—the reality is often quite different for the athletes themselves. Jan Kemp, a professor at the University of Georgia who has studied the treatment of athletes at her school, believes many college players are exploited for their talent, then tossed aside. "Athletes are just plantation slaves," she says. "They're given passing grades to earn money for the plantation. Then, when the athlete's service to the plantation is over, no one cares if he or she has made progress as a student."

In fact, only 1 in 5 college basketball players ever graduates, according to a recent federal study. The figures for football players were only a little better.

Myles Gordon, *Scholastic Update*, May 1, 1992.

One scarcely knows where to start in on a statement like that. It's appalling that an accredited state university would admit a functional illiterate, even recruit him, and leave him illiterate after four years as a student. It's shocking that it would do all this in order to make money from his unpaid performance as an athlete. And it is little short of grotesque that an educator, entrusted with the education of 20,000 young men and women, would argue that the cynical arrangement between an institution of higher learning and an uneducated high school boy was, after all, a fair bargain. . . .

Sports Without Strings

A system of sports without strings—releasing college athletes and their universities from the pretense that they are students, and instead paying them for their services—would cure the student-athlete system's chief vices: its duplicity and its exploitiveness.

Athletes who want to get started on careers in sports, including those whose only way out of the ghetto may be the slam dunk and the 4.4-40, would find paying jobs in their chosen field. Overnight, thousands of new jobs as professional football and basketball players would be created. Players with the ability to get to the NFL and NBA would get paid during their years of apprenticeship. For those of lesser abilities, playing for college teams would be a career in itself, a career they could start right out of high school and continue as long as skills and bodies allowed. And as they matured and their playing careers drew to a close, the prospect of a real college education might seem more inviting than it did at 17.

Releasing athletes from having to be students would, ironically, make it easier for those who want an education to get it. Even with the best intentions, today's college athletes have little hope of being serious students. Basketball practice, for instance, begins October 15, and the season does not end for the most successful teams until after the NCAA championships in early April; in other words the season starts one month after school begins and ends one month before school is out. During the season, athletes spend six or more hours a day, 30 to 40 hours a week, on practice, viewing game-films, at chalk talks, weight lifting, conditioning, and attending team meetings. The best-prepared students would have difficulty attending to their studies while working 34 hours a week—and these are not the best-prepared students.

But under no-strings sports, athletes who want educations will fare better than they do now, because the pace of their education need not be governed by their eligibility for athletic competition. A football player could play the fall semester and study in the spring. Basketball players, whose season spans the two semesters, might enroll at schools with quarter or trimester systems, or study summers and after their sports careers are over. Instead of being corralled into courses rigged to provide high grades like "Theory of Volleyball," "Recreation and Leisure," "Jogging," and "Leisure Alternatives," athletes would be in a position to take only the courses they want and need. This would be even more likely if, as part of the pro option, universities were still required to offer full scholarships to athletes, to be redeemed whenever the athletes wanted to use them.

Under these changes, those athletes who end up going to college would be doing so because they were pursuing their own educational goals. This reform would replace today's phony jock curriculum with the kind of mature academic choices that made the G.I. Bill such a success.

Such considerations make it clear that it's time for schools to choose between real amateurism and real professionalism. They can't have a little of both. From now on, in college sports, it's got to be either poetry or pros.

"What is needed from Congress is not short-term grandstanding, but a full-court press for systemic, fundamental reform."

Legislation Is Needed to Reform College Athletics

Tom McMillen with Paul Coggins

Tom McMillen was a high school and college basketball star who played on the 1972 U.S. Olympic team. Following an eleven-year career in the National Basketball Association (NBA), McMillen was elected to Congress, and represented Maryland's Fourth District from 1986 to 1992. He was a member of the Knight (Foundation) Commission on college athletics and signed their 1991 report recommending university reforms. However, in his 1992 book *Out of Bounds*, which he wrote with lawyer and novelist Paul Coggins and from which this viewpoint is taken, McMillen describes his differences with the commission on whether the college athletic establishment can be trusted to reform itself. McMillen argues that federal legislation is needed, and describes a reform bill he proposed while in Congress.

As you read, consider the following questions:

1. Why does McMillen fear that the National Collegiate Athletic Association (NCAA) is incapable of fully reforming itself?
2. What are the shortcoming of the 1991 Knight Commission report, according to McMillen?
3. What federal legislation does the author propose?

Excerpted from *Out of Bounds* by Tom McMillen with Paul Coggins. Copyright © 1992 by Tom McMillen and Paul Coggins. Reprinted by permission of Simon & Schuster, Inc.

There are many tragedies of "stars" who had no life after sports, and act one of the tragedy often begins in the schools. True reform of college sports will be a long, hard process with many false starts. The roots of the problem lie in skewed societal values that are widespread and deeply held. And reform will impinge upon powerful forces not only within our educational institutions but also outside the schools, such as TV executives, boosters, and agents.

As a result of our misplaced priorities, we have allowed vast entertainment complexes to reshape our schools and deflect them from their true educational missions. It is sheer folly to think that school officials have the time, energy, or resources to educate their charges and to run vast, multimillion-dollar entertainment empires at the same time.

Sports reformers often speak of restoring the balance between academics and athletics, but this does not mean that athletics and academics should be equally weighted. Athletics are not as important as academics for the individual, the school, or our society. Under the proper circumstances, sports can play an important role in the schools—the key is to ensure that athletics are serving educational aims and not subverting them.

Because of the vast sums of money washing through the sports system, it is more accurate to assume that there is a natural disequilibrium, rather than a balance, between academics and athletics, and that the system will require great energy and commitment to correct. Reform will be won not by a short flurry of corrective measures but by a constant battle against our national sports addiction.

There is a tendency to romanticize a distant age, when the sporting lion lay down with the academic lamb. Yet, as the Carnegie Report of 1929 makes clear, the "good old days" of college sports were not all that good, and most of the evils that bedevil college sports today were rampant then, long before the age of television. A key issue is whether the NCAA [National Collegiate Athletic Association] can reform itself. History is replete with examples of its inability to do so. And the NCAA will continue to be unable to reform unless it controls the money generated by college sports; but only Congress, through an antitrust exemption, can restore the power of the purse string to the NCAA, since the Supreme Court stripped the NCAA of control over the football broadcasting contracts in 1984. Even that would not, however, guarantee fundamental reform. . . .

A Trade Association

At its heart the NCAA operates chiefly as a trade association for athletic directors and coaches. . . .

We should not overlook the contributions of the many athletic directors and coaches who want reform, such as Dean Smith and Joe Paterno, but today they are like ants trying to move an elephant. . . .

Ironically, the organization is losing the clout to effect fundamental change. The NCAA has done little to check the "balkanization" of college sports, which faces a war for the broadcast pie not only among its divisions but also between the haves and have-nots within a division. Eventually the NCAA will lose its grip on the riches of college sports and, hence, its "stick" over the out-of-control programs. The NCAA will probably awaken to the need for real reform only after it is too feeble to curb its unruly members.

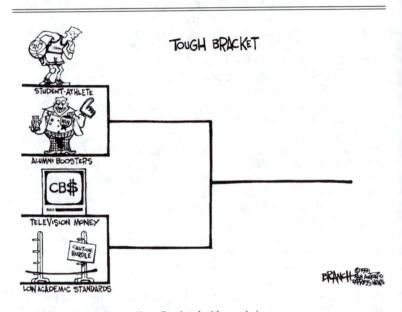

© Branch/*San Antonio Express News*. Reprinted with permission.

With the NCAA fiddling while Rome burns, scores of blue-ribbon panels have tackled the thorny issue of college sports in this century. The Knight Commission held hearings over eighteen months before issuing a forty-seven-page report in 1991 entitled "Keeping Faith with the Student-Athlete: A New Model for Intercollegiate Athletics." The crux of the report was its "one-plus-three" model—the "one" being [university] presidential control of college sports and the "three" being academic integrity, financial integrity, and certification.

My qualms about the Knight Report stem from its failure to

follow its recommendations to their logical conclusions. . . .

The fundamental flaw of the report was its failure, after insisting that college presidents assume control of their athletic departments and the NCAA, to explain how they could do so. Indeed, even if all the specific reforms in the report were adopted, many college presidents would still not be able to gain control of their athletic departments from powerful coaches and boosters.

I proposed in my first footnote to the report that the NCAA be restructured so as to ensure presidential control of the organization. This can be accomplished either by requiring that presidents make up a majority on the NCAA Council or by creating a higher body that is controlled by presidents and possesses power to establish broad policy for the conduct of intercollegiate sports.

Today college presidents theoretically control athletics through the selection of delegates to the NCAA conventions, but the reality is far different. Even absolute presidential control of the NCAA, however, is no panacea. To begin with, any model of governance that requires college presidents to devote the bulk of their time to athletics is fundamentally flawed. College presidents ought not be forced to choose between an out-of-control athletic department and inattention to the other facets of university life. Moreover, on some campuses college presidents have been part of the problem; and presidential interest in athletic reform, while hot now, will inevitably cool in the coming years. . . .

Money Is Key

True presidential control will have little long-term impact on college sports unless the incentives for winning (and cheating to win) are removed or greatly reduced. The NCAA has failed to accomplish this, and the Knight Commission was too timid in pursuing this necessary goal. The central difference between the majority on the Knight Commission and me was the focus of our reform effort. In the "one-plus-three" model of the Knight Report, the "one" was presidential control. In my view, however, the big "one" should be financial reform.

For example, in 1991 the NCAA distributed nearly $73 million from the basketball tournament to Division I schools under a formula that was weighted heavily toward the ACC [Atlantic Coast Conference], the Big Ten, and other traditional powers. "When 66 percent of the money still goes back to the traditional powers," charged Jeffrey Orleans, the executive director of the Ivy League, "some individuals will see this as solely a commercial enterprise.". . .

Convinced that here again the Knight Commission had not been bold enough, I inserted my second footnote into the final report:

I do not fully agree with this report's recommendation regarding the revenue distribution plan that presidents need only "review" the new formula. This is the most important reform necessary in intercollegiate athletics—without it, all other reforms will be difficult, if not impossible, to enact. While the NCAA and this Commission have focused primarily on basketball revenues, we have not begun to address conferences' and institutions' revenues from athletics, including bowl games. I recommend that an independent panel review this issue and propose a new model for revenue distribution that eliminates the "winner-take-all (or most)" mentality that results in violation of NCAA rules, exploitation of student-athletes, and the commercialization of college athletics.

As further evidence that the Knight Commission was too "soft" on the NCAA, the final report failed to address the fairness of its enforcement procedures. In 1991 the NCAA belatedly established a commission to study the enforcement process and make suggestions to change it. This effort, however, may be too little, too late. My third and final footnote in the report urged outside entities, including the government, to devise fairer rules of enforcement and not to count on the NCAA to clean its own house. . . .

Caring Only About Money

Members of the National Collegiate Athletic Association feign deep despair over the crisis in education, but their only real concern is how to cart home the booty. The NCAA hierarchy and college presidents say it's time to clean up sports. They promise to support academic integrity by passing Proposition 48, which sets tight scholastic standards for incoming freshmen on sports scholarships, and then undo their good deed by pushing through a watered-down version that loosens those standards so better athletes—but lesser students—ultimately can join the varsity. They promise that no Division I football schedule will begin before September, yet allow the Kickoff and Disneyland Pigskin Classics—which reward participating teams with approximately $500,000 apiece—to be played in August, ensuring that a university's sports "students" will be banging heads in football pads well before they ever set foot in a classroom. They promise that student-athletes will attend class, yet slate basketball games for week-nights halfway across the country in order to maximize television revenue.

Wayne M. Barrett, *USA Today*, November 1990.

Each year the United States invests $160 billion in higher education, more per student than any nation in the world except Denmark; and 45 percent of this money comes from the federal, state, and local governments. Congress cannot allow athletic corruption to jeopardize the taxpayers' investment in the future. . . .

Congress now realizes that sporadic federal involvement will not work. What is needed from Congress is not short-term grandstanding, but a full-court press for systemic, fundamental reform. . . .

I have introduced the . . . Collegiate Athletic Reform Act. The purpose of this act is to restore education as the primary goal of our institutions of higher learning by assisting college presidents in reining in the money-hungry monsters on their campuses.

I do not make great claims for the originality of my bill. Instead I take comfort in the realization that many of its components have been around for years or even decades. . . .

The structure of my bill is simple. Upon its passage the NCAA will be granted an antitrust exemption for five years to negotiate and approve all major TV and radio contracts for college football and basketball (to the exclusion of individual schools or conferences, which would be dropped from the organization if they insisted on striking their own TV deals). The antitrust exemption is necessary to overcome [a] 1984 Supreme Court decision.

My bill would place a presidentially controlled NCAA in charge of broadcasting, as opposed to the present situation in which TV executives can pit the schools and conferences against each other. The Federal Communications Commission will conduct a study to determine the extent to which college sports programs are migrating from free TV to cable and pay-per-view systems. It is doubtful that the NCAA can presently stop or even regulate the migration of college sports from free TV. But under my bill, the NCAA will be empowered to control it.

In return for the antitrust exemption granted by my bill, the NCAA is required to enact various reform measures, including the establishment of a more powerful Board of Presidents to set major policy, which can be overruled only by a two-thirds majority of the organization's membership; the formulation of a more equitable revenue distribution plan, which does not depend on the win-loss record of an institution but takes into account the school's efforts to downsize its athletic programs and facilities, the academic performance of its student-athletes, and its compliance with Title IX [a law mandating gender equity in college athletic programs]; and the provision of due process protections to athletes, coaches, and institutions. If the NCAA fails to enact the reform measures within a year of the passage of my bill, the IRS will be authorized to tax the revenues produced by intercollegiate athletics. . . .

Protecting Student-Athletes

Finally, my bill furnishes greater protection for student-athletes. Schools are authorized to pay student-athletes a stipend of up to

$300 a month. And athletic scholarships will no longer be renewable on a year-to-year basis but will be extended to cover up to five years and cannot be withdrawn by the school as long as the student-athlete is enrolled in good standing at the institution. . . .

In supporting my bill, the chancellor of the Regency Universities System in Illinois [Rod Groves] concluded:

> By addressing the root cause of the problem, the McMillen legislation will enable us to take effective steps to restore public confidence in higher education and intercollegiate athletics. As such, it deserves our support. There's a time to fight your critics and a time to join them and this is the latter.

But I do not exaggerate my bill's potential effect for good. Sports reform is necessary at all levels of our educational process, not merely at our colleges. And even at the college level, Congress cannot achieve fundamental reform on its own. Only through a concerted, long-term effort by Congress, the NCAA, college officials, athletes, the media, and the public can we redress the present imbalance between academics and athletics.

> *"The leaders and members of the NCAA now have a framework for meaningful reform."*

Colleges Can Reform Their Own Programs

Knight Foundation Commission on Intercollegiate Athletics

The Knight Foundation Commission on Intercollegiate Athletics was created on October 19, 1989, by the John S. and James L. Knight Foundation to propose a reform agenda for intercollegiate athletics. The commission was co-chaired by Theodore M. Hesburgh, former president of the University of Notre Dame, and business executive William C. Friday. In 1991 it produced a report entitled *Keeping Faith with the Student-Athlete* in which it proposed reforms designed to strengthen university presidents' control over athletic programs. Two years later the commission produced a follow-up report, *A New Beginning for a New Century*. In that document, from which this viewpoint is excerpted, the commission describes what it calls successful reforms within the universities and the National Collegiate Athletic Association (NCAA). It concludes that academics and sports can successfully coexist on college campuses with such efforts at reform and that federal government action is not necessary.

As you read, consider the following questions:

1. What positive aspects of college sports do the authors argue must be preserved?
2. What are some of the problems facing college sports, according to the commission?
3. What are the elements of the authors' proposed "one-plus-three" structure of reform?

From *A New Beginning for a New Century* by the Knight Foundation Commission on Intercollegiate Athletics, 1990-1993, William C. Friday and Rev. Theodore M. Hesburgh, C.S.C., co-chairs. Reprinted by permission.

"As our nation approaches a new century," the Knight Foundation Commission observed in 1991, "the demand for reform of intercollegiate athletics has escalated dramatically." Today [March 1993], that escalating demand is being matched by accelerating reform. College and university presidents, along with the leaders and members of the National Collegiate Athletic Association (NCAA), have taken advantage of a swelling chorus for reform to make a new beginning in college sports. Although barely implemented today, the full effects of recent reforms will be visible as the 21st Century dawns.

The distance college sports have traveled in three short years can be measured by developments in public opinion. In 1989, pollster Louis Harris asked if big-time intercollegiate athletics were out of control. Across the United States, heads nodded in agreement: 78 percent of Americans thought that the situation was out of hand. In 1993, 52 percent of the public continued to agree. This significant 26-point decline represents how far college sports have come. The fact that about half of all Americans remain troubled represents the distance yet to go. Nevertheless, a new air of confidence is measurable and can be seen in other findings of the Harris survey: In 1989, nearly two-thirds of Americans believed state or national legislation was needed to control college sports; less than half feel that way today. Earlier negative views of the NCAA have turned into positive marks for its efforts to control excesses in college sports.

What accounts for the impressive turnaround in perceptions? The improvement is no accident, but a response to the highly visible pace of reform in recent years. Since 1989, college and university presidents, the members of the NCAA, and athletics leaders have addressed a single goal with singular concentration: restoring integrity to the games played in the university's name. They have created a structure of reform that can reshape the conduct, management and accountability of college sports. The new Harris poll tells us the American people are paying attention.

Reforms of Recent Years

In 1991, this Commission proposed a new model for intercollegiate athletics, a kind of road map entitled "one-plus-three," in which the "one"—presidential control—would be directed toward the "three"—academic integrity, financial integrity and independent certification.

Such a model, this Commission believed, represented higher education's only real assurance that intercollegiate athletics could be grounded in the primacy of academic values. NCAA legislation in recent years has put this model in place.

These changes promise to reshape dramatically the environment for intercollegiate athletics. In 1989, the NCAA's Presidents

Commission was tentative about how best to challenge the *status quo* in intercollegiate athletics. Established in 1984 as a compromise to a more ambitious effort to ensure presidential control of the NCAA, the Commission found itself five years later on the defensive. But by 1993, the Presidents Commission was in firm control of the Association's legislative agenda. Presidents Commission recommendations have dominated three successive NCAA conventions. With majorities of 3-1 or better, the Commission has pushed through preliminary cost reductions, new academic standards and an athletics certification program. Of even greater long-term significance, the 1993 legislation created an NCAA Joint Policy Board, made up of the Association's Administrative Committee and officers of the Presidents Commission, with authority to review the NCAA budget and legislative agenda and to evaluate and supervise the executive director. Presidential leadership is the hallmark of today's NCAA.

"VERY IMPRESSIVE... NOW LET'S SEE HIM READ IT."

Henry Payne reprinted by permission of UFS, Inc.

In 1989, student-athletes could compete in their first year of college if they had finished high school with a "C" average in 11 core academic subjects, along with combined Scholastic Aptitude Test scores of 700. This weak foundation, combined with lack of attention to academic progress, meant that, five years later, many student-athletes found themselves far short of a college degree. By 1995, eligibility to play in the freshman year will require a 2.5 high school grade point average ("C +" or "B-") in 13 high school academic units. One year later the 13 units must include four years of English and one year each of algebra and geometry. Meanwhile, graduation rates for student-athletes are published annually and . . . student-athletes must demonstrate continuous, satisfactory progress toward graduation: They are now required to meet annual benchmarks in both grades and coursework applicable to a specific degree. Academic integrity is being restored; student-athletes will now be students as well as athletes.

An Athletics Arms Race

In 1989, athletics finances were escalating beyond reason. Colleges and universities were in the midst of a kind of athletics arms race: Deficits mounted . . . the costs of grants-in-aid mushroomed . . . athletics budgets ballooned beyond institutional reach . . . and it was unclear who employed some "power" coaches, since their outside income often dwarfed university compensation. In 1993, the number of grants-in-aid for men in Divisions I and II of the NCAA has been reduced 10 percent; coaching staffs have been trimmed; athletics budgets are reviewed as part of a new certification process; cost containment is the subject of a major new study; and coaches must have annual written approval from their presidents for all athletically related outside income. Universities have made a start in restoring order to the financial side of the house of athletics.

Finally, in 1989, too many big-time athletics programs had succeeded in imposing on universities a great reversal of ends and means. They had, this Commission found, become self-justifying enterprises in which winning-at-all-costs had pushed aside the educational context of athletics competition. Beginning in 1993, each NCAA Division I institution will have to participate in a certification program once every five years. This program requires each institution to examine four key areas—institutional mission, academic integrity, fiscal integrity, and commitment to equity—and (the most important factor) permit an external jury of academic and sports peers to evaluate and verify its findings. The new program promises to align means and ends.

The certification process is the capstone of the reform movement and will remain one of the movement's genuine legacies. Because it involves the entire campus community in a detailed examination of athletics policy issues, certification embodies the standards and values befitting higher education. By calling for regular self-examination of every corner of big-time programs under the bright light of outside peer review, certification should curb abuse before it starts, instead of after the damage has been done.

Meanwhile, on campuses and in conferences across the country, athletics and academic leaders have drawn new energy from the reform movement. Often using the "one-plus-three" model as their lens, presidentially appointed task forces, trustees and athletics boards have examined again the goals and operations of their athletics programs.

Challenges Ahead

This progress is encouraging, but the struggle for reform is far from won. Winning that struggle is what the "one-plus-three" model is all about. Academic and athletics officials now possess a new framework within which to tackle the many problems of college sports:

- abuses in recruiting, the bane of the college coach's life;
- the compulsion of boosters to meddle in athletics decision-making;
- the search for television revenues and the influence of the entertainment industry on intercollegiate athletics;
- the relationships among high school, junior college, college and professional sports;
- the need to respect the dignity of the young men and women who represent the university on the playing field;
- the obligation to further strengthen academic standards so that the profile of student-athletes matches that of other full-time undergraduates in admissions, academic progress and graduation rates; and
- the imperative to meet the needs of minority student-athletes, particularly those from backgrounds of inner-city or rural poverty.

As this Commission's tenure draws to a close, two great issues, cost containment and gender equity, dominate athletics policy discussions. These are first-order questions, significant problems requiring the best thinking of the nation's university and athletics leaders. Part of their complexity lies in the fact they are intertwined: Costs should not be controlled at the price of rebuffing women's aspirations. Opportunities for women must be provided in the context of controlling outlays for athletics programs that already cost too much. The cost control and equity dilemmas have to be addressed together. . . .

Reforms Must Continue

Tempted to believe the battle for reform has been won because the framework is in place, presidents may turn their attention to other demands. That must not be allowed to happen. Presidential neglect of these issues is a sure formula for giving ground on the progress already made.

This Commission believes the reforms enacted to date represent some of the most encouraging developments in intercollegiate athletics since the NCAA was established in 1906. But optimism about the reforms and their potential must be tempered with realism. Reform is not a destination but a never-ending process, a race without a finish. That is why the new NCAA certification program is so significant. By requiring presidents, trustees, faculty members, athletics administrators and coaches to examine the integrity of their sports programs every five years, certification keeps the process alive.

College Presidents Must Be Involved

Above all, college presidents must become more actively involved in running their sports programs. Too often, a president and his or her athletic director have a kind of perfunctory relationship typical of many bureaucracies. The president assumes things are going well in the athletic department; therefore, they are. That is not active management. At best, it's wishful thinking, a bit like putting off a physical checkup because you're afraid to find out if you have cancer.

Only when college presidents involve themselves directly in their athletic programs—in the details of policy, budget, and recruiting—will they have a true grasp of what's really going on. Until then, they will be operating at least partly in the dark. If presidents devoted the same proportion of their time to sports programs that those programs occupy in the public consciousness, many of the current problems might not exist.

E. Gordon Gee, *USA Today*, November 1990.

Maintaining the momentum for reform is important. The reforms . . . remain a promise yet to be kept: They will be implemented fully in 1995-96. . . . Making judgments today about the effects of these changes is premature; their real effects will appear at the end of the decade.

Moreover, no matter how deep-rooted reform is, it cannot transform human nature. Even with the new changes fully in place and working effectively, no one should be surprised when some institutions continue to be embarrassed by revelations about their athletics departments. People in college sports are like people everywhere: Most want to do the right thing; but some will try to skirt the rules, inevitably getting themselves, their associates and their institutions into trouble because, sooner or later, they will ignore the line dividing the acceptable from the unacceptable.

But realism should not give way to pessimism or cynicism. Cynics may dismiss the reform effort, but they do so at their own risk. Something fundamental has changed in college sports. It is perhaps best illustrated by support for the Presidents Commission reform agenda from coaches, athletics directors, conference leaders and faculty representatives. Because not everyone is ready for reform, this support is far from universal; nevertheless, it is impressive.

What has changed fundamentally is the following: The institutional indifference and presidential neglect that led to disturbing patterns of abuse throughout the 1980s have been replaced with a new structure insisting on institutional oversight and depending on presidential leadership backed up by trustee support. The leaders and members of the NCAA now have a framework for meaningful reform if they have the will, the courage and the perseverance to use it.

Along with that framework come new responsibilities. It was once possible for college sports administrators on the one hand, and university presidents and trustees, on the other, to evade responsibility for the difficulties of intercollegiate athletics. Each side could plausibly claim the other possessed the authority to act. That claim no longer holds water. The "one-plus-three" model places authority exactly where it belongs both in the councils of the NCAA and on individual campuses. Presidents today possess the power they need and, with the backing of their trustees, the responsibility to act.

A New Beginning

The presidents of the nation's colleges and universities have reached a kind of Rubicon, a point of decision, with regard to their athletics programs. They face a choice about how to proceed, a choice between business as usual and making a new beginning.

Business as usual in college sports will undermine American higher education. It leads inexorably to regulation of intercollegiate athletics by the courts or Congress. That is a consequence no one wants, but many, unwittingly, may invite.

The second choice strengthens American higher education. The Harris poll convincingly demonstrates that the American people respect college sports when they are grounded in the larger mission of the university. As the United States approaches a new century, the new beginning represented by a strong "one-plus-three" model promises to restore higher education's moral claim to the high ground it should occupy.

These choices and their consequences are what is at stake in the athletics reform movement. The final words of the members of the Knight Foundation Commission on Intercollegiate Athletics to the leaders of the nation's colleges and universities are an echo from long ago. In 1929, the Carnegie Foundation for the Advancement of Teaching published a landmark study taking presidents to task for their failure to defend the integrity of higher education. There can be no doubt that presidents today have the opportunity to put that long-standing criticism to rest. A genuine assessment of the value of the current reform movement cannot be made by today's observers. The true test will be applied by historians of the future, because they will ask whether today's presidents employed their power wisely and chose well.

Periodical Bibliography

The following articles have been selected to supplement the diverse views presented in this chapter.

Wayne M. Barrett	"Curb Campus Corruption," *USA Today*, May 1990.
Ira Berkow	"Might John Dillinger Crack the Lineup?" *The New York Times*, July 26, 1993.
Charles S. Farrell	"Black Collegiate Athletes Are Being Doublecrossed," *USA Today*, November 1990.
E. Gordon Gee	"Greed and Avarice: The Crisis in College Athletics," *USA Today*, November 1990.
Richard Grenier	"Money Game Cheats Sport of Its Power to Build Men," *Insight*, February 1, 1993. Available from 3600 New York Ave. NE, Washington, DC 20002.
Constance Johnson	"The Rules of the Game," *U.S. News & World Report*, April 13, 1992.
D.G. Myers	"Why College Sports?" *Commentary*, December 1990.
Joe Paterno	"Exploiting Student-Athletes Defeats Colleges' Purpose," *USA Today*, November 1990.
William F. Reed	"It's the Rules, Stupid!" *Sports Illustrated*, May 24, 1993.
William C. Rhoden	"Engaged in a Great Civil War for Change," *The New York Times*, October 19, 1993.
William C. Symonds	"March Madness Is Getting Even Crazier," *Business Week*, April 2, 1990.
Phil Taylor	"Players Have Rights, Too," *Sports Illustrated*, November 23, 1992.
James M. Wall	"When Colleges Become Sports Training Camps," *The Christian Century*, May 8, 1991.
George F. Will	"College Football Coaches Are Not Cheering," *Conservative Chronicle*, October 13, 1993. Available from Box 11297, Des Moines, IA 50340-1297.
Alexander Wolff	"Finders, Keepers, Losers, Sleepers," *Sports Illustrated*, February 15, 1993.
Raymond Yasser	"Athletic Scholarship Disarmament," *Journal of Sport and Social Issues*, April 1993.

How Should Professional Sports Be Reformed?

Chapter Preface

Spectator sports are a big business in the United States, generating billions of dollars in revenues. Even people who are not directly involved with sports can be economically affected. Because a major league sports franchise can provide a community with financial benefits and prestige, the demand for sports franchises can often lead to "bidding wars," as cities try to hold on to a local team or to entice another city's team to relocate there. The bidding chips include such incentives as stadium financing with public funds, financial concessions, and other lucrative arrangements for team owners. These arrangements are costly for taxpayers, however. "We must be conscious of the absurdities of subsidizing some of the most wealthy of our society, literally putting taxpayer money into their pockets," argues attorney Peter Gruenstein.

One ongoing example of such "sportmail" began when St. Petersburg, Florida, built a domed stadium in the hopes of luring a team. In 1988, when the owners of the Chicago White Sox baseball team threatened to move to St. Petersburg, the state of Illinois and the city of Chicago responded by building a new $150-million stadium at public expense for the White Sox to play in, charging the team minimal rent. More recently, St. Petersburg also narrowly failed to persuade baseball's San Francisco Giants to relocate; this time San Francisco officials promised to help the Giants owners obtain land for a new stadium there, again costing taxpayers millions of dollars.

Defenders of such public expenditures argue that major league sports teams provide economic benefits to the surrounding community. A 1985 University of Pennsylvania study attributed $300 million of the state's economic growth to the presence of major league sports teams. In addition to economic benefits, defenders of public support for major league sports cite the increased prestige and recognition sports can give a community.

The controversy over public subsidies is but one of many that surround the often complex economics of professional sports. Whether the public should have greater control over sports franchises, whether greater regulation of the sports marketplace is required and, if so, how the business of sports should be reformed are some of the subjects addressed by the authors in this chapter.

97

> *"Professional sports management has contributed greatly to the increased accessibility, enjoyment and vitality of American sports."*

Business Management Has Helped Professional Sports

Jeremy M. Jacobs

Jeremy M. Jacobs is owner of the Boston Bruins, a team that competes in the National Hockey League (NHL). In the following viewpoint, he defends professional sports against charges that it is run too much like a business, to the detriment of the game. Jacobs asserts that modern business practices have benefited professional sports and their fans by building successful sports franchises and by enabling more people to enjoy professional sports.

As you read, consider the following questions:

1. What belief lies behind many complaints about sports, according to Jacobs?
2. What factor has been most responsible for changes in sports since the 1960s, according to the author?
3. How have business management practices benefited sports fans, according to Jacobs?

"Sports Must Employ Business Practices to Maintain Vitality" by Jeremy M. Jacobs, *The Sporting News*, July 13, 1992. Reprinted with the author's permission.

"Times have changed. Today it's a business."

In the past 25 years, this lament has become an increasingly common reference to professional sports in America.

A Sense of Loss

For some, the comment expresses a sense of loss, a feeling that something of value that existed in the past has somehow been forsaken. It also reveals a belief that the evolution of professional sports in this country has been a movement away from the fun and innocence of a game to a singular concern for the bottom line of a business.

But making polar opposites of "sports as a game" and "sports as a business" overlooks the tremendous changes in professional baseball, basketball, football and hockey in the past 50 years. In reality, professional sports in America simply could not have evolved to their current positions of extraordinary popularity without adopting contemporary business practices. Professional sports management has contributed greatly to the increased accessibility, enjoyment and vitality of American sports.

Certainly, there has been change. More than any other factor, electronic mass media are responsible for altering America's perception of sports. It began with radio and reached maturity with television, which expanded audiences at an exponential rate. In all of the 1948 season, for example, about 21 million people were able to see major league baseball games by going to ballparks. Contrast that with the TV audience of 90 million for one game, the final game of the 1991 World Series.

Television and the Fan

Television also brought with it a tremendous impact on the financial aspects of professional sports and helped to push the price of sports contracts sky-high. But these heights, we are beginning to learn, are unsustainable. With few exceptions, pro sports contracts are not profitable for national TV networks and likely will not be renewed under current conditions. Sports are keying on the idea that there is no mass market anymore, but rather a multiple-option society that must be approached market by market. That can only help the fan.

The shift in perceptions about sports may be traced to the 1960s. During this time, the expansion and maturation of major league sports gave rise to a need for much better management.

In an earlier era, baseball chose Kennesaw Mountain Landis to be the first commissioner to repair the sport's tarnished image after the Black Sox scandal. Decades later, the NFL [National Football League] turned to Pete Rozelle for his organizational skills.

[In the 1990s], . . . baseball's Fay Vincent, the NBA's [National Basketball Association] David Stern, the NFL's Paul Tagliabue and the NHL's Gil Stein [have brought] solid business management skills to their leadership posts.

Ideas for Encouraging Entrepreneurship

• Allow complete free agency for the players. It's simple economics. By increasing the supply of players, the amount of compensation they could command would be reduced. It's hard to believe that [NFL player] Reggie White would have gotten a $17 million contract from the [Green Bay] Packers had Bruce Smith, Russell Maryland, Lawrence Taylor and the other top defensive players in the league all been unrestricted free agents.

• Allow teams to change location at will. This would bring pro sports to those cities that can best support them and would reduce the need for government subsidies in those cities that cannot, or will not, back a team. It would also mean franchises would make more money because of higher attendance.

• Permit more corporate ownership, which is allowed only in hockey and grandfathered in baseball. After all, corporations, through advertising and the sponsorship of sky boxes, finance the vast majority of sports teams anyway. Media companies such as Turner Broadcasting, Tribune and Paramount Communications have all had success with the synergies of athletics and broadcasting. So can entertainment companies such as Walt Disney, which recently bought a hockey franchise.

• Eliminate Major League Baseball's antitrust exemption. This would allow for greater competition among cities for professional teams and make the player draft illegal. By allowing athletes to play for whichever team they wanted to, only well-managed teams would survive.

• Remove the salary caps. If owners can make as much money as the free market allows, players should be permitted to do the same.

• Reduce revenue sharing to national TV revenues only. This would encourage more entrepreneurs, like [Dallas Cowboys owner] Jerry Jones, to buy teams. It's not surprising that such owners field the most entertaining teams for the fans.

Michael K. Ozanian et al., *Financial World*, May 25, 1993.

Similarly, the evolution of pro sports into large and complex endeavors has brought changes in the way owners must organize the management of their teams. Major sports teams must have a cadre of specialized professionals and solid executive management. Teams require a solid financial foundation and sound management principles to remain viable economic entities. Across all sports, franchise success is built on commitment and talent, on the field and in the front office.

In the end, the most-often voiced criticism of professional sports is directed at something that actually has a beneficial impact. Sports have not lost their souls because they are run more like a business. Instead, the necessary muscle of business disciplines allows sports to maintain vitality.

"Business interests dominate the teams and players, and threaten the development of a new generation of fans."

Business Management Has Harmed Professional Sports

Bob McCabe

Bob McCabe is a staff member of the Center for the Study of Sports in Society at Northeastern University in Boston, Massachusetts. He is also an adviser for Sports Fans United, a fan advocacy group. In the following viewpoint, he decries many of the changes business interests have wrought in professional sports, including the dominance of business values, the increased price of tickets, and the influence of television. Treating professional sports as an entertainment business, McCabe concludes, has made them inaccessible to the average sports fan.

As you read, consider the following questions:

1. What differences does McCabe describe between attending a Boston Celtics game in the 1960s and attending one in the 1990s?
2. How has sports been damaged by corporate business practices, according to the author?
3. What predictions concerning sports does McCabe make?

"Business Interests Threaten New Generation of Fans" by Bob McCabe. Reprinted with permission from *Fan Advocate*, the quarterly newsletter of SPORTS FANS UNITED, Summer 1993.

When I was a youngster in Boston in the sixties, my father would occasionally take me to a Celtics game. Supporting a family of seven on a postal clerk's salary, he did not have a lot of money.

Boston Garden

Nonetheless, we could head to the Boston Garden, purchase two balcony tickets the night of the game and watch brilliant basketball featuring the likes of Bill Russell and John Havlicek. We were blue collar fans, the bread and butter of the franchise.

Of course, affordable tickets and easy access to the games was not the goal of the Celtics' owners. Even then, the top brass must have dreamed of consecutive sellouts and premium ticket prices.

How Times Have Changed

Today, the Celtics and their brethren in professional sports are realizing their fantasy of riches. But this magical success story that has transformed sport in our popular culture has a down side as well. As a sporting nation we have lost our innocence, and professional sport may never recapture the traditional qualities that spawned our passion.

In December 1992 a co-worker offered me a pair of Celtic tickets. My wife and I were excited about the opportunity to attend what would be our only game of the year. The cost was $18 per ticket plus a service charge.

We found our seats in the rafters and stared eye level at the much vaunted championship banners.

Understand that I love the Celtics. I played college ball and professionally in Europe, and the Celtics were an inspiration.

But forty bucks for a good look at the roof didn't seem fair. Committed to getting through the evening with some semblance of fiscal dignity, we abstained from the $3.50 beers and $2.00 hotdogs.

Of course I realize this is a market driven phenomenon. However, I bear witness to the cultural loss associated with these capitalist rights.

Loss of Heroes

Since the turn of the century, spectator sports have enthralled millions of Americans. The popularity of teams and individual athletes made sport one of our most cherished shared experiences.

We found heroes, icons for the ages like Babe Ruth, Jim Thorpe, Jesse Owens and Wilma Rudolph. Their legends were rooted in the thrill we experienced when watching them perform.

Today, business interests dominate the teams and players, and threaten the development of a new generation of fans. The athletic feats of today's superstars like Michael Jordan are rivaled only by their commercial endeavors.

By contrast, other tremendous athletes, particularly those in baseball, find themselves out of the marketing loop, scandalized by their own fame and resented for their wealth. This dichotomy is less a result of athletic attributes than a marketing strategy.

Corporate America

Fans may play a role in crowning today's sports heroes, but corporate America will make the final decision. The evolving marriage of sport to commercial interests has broad implications for anyone interested in athletic events.

Fan Manipulation

Professional sports management often means fan management, fan manipulation and exploitation of the fans' fantasies. Professional sport management has made viewing the game, in person or on television, less accessible, less affordable and less enjoyable. . . .

Professional sports management has successfully adjusted to the demands of TV by orchestrating what, when and how we view professional sports. The marriage of sports management to television, players to agents and the games to show business are the result of economic decisions that have sidelined the fan, discarded him like a ticket stub after a home-game loss.

The scenario runs like this: Make the "product" so desirable that ticket prices are unattainable for the average family. Introduce mismanagement scenarios such as strikes, lockouts and collective bargaining. Demand higher TV rights fees, send player salaries up and increase the cost to the fans, regardless of the quality of the game. And when TV revenue decreases, make sure pay-per-view is forced down fans' throats so the bottom line remains intact.

That is what professional sports management has done. And the American sports fan is tired, disgusted and wants a change.

Nicholas F. Filla, *The Sporting News*, July 13, 1992.

Attendance at games will require lots of cash. Watching at home will also be expensive as premium cable and pay-per-view continue their assault on spectator access.

As for myself, I'm at a crossroads. I won't be going to the

Boston Garden anymore. I understand the new "Garden" won't be a garden at all but rather a megaplex called the "Shawmut Center" (named after a bank). And in my case, attendance will depend in part on my ability to pay, but more importantly, on my willingness to stomach sport as a corporate expression.

I'm not a blue collar fan anymore. I can't afford to be one, and neither can you.

"How can fans relate to these athletes? How can they embrace heroes who have so much money and so little loyalty?"

Athletes' Greed Has Marred Professional Sports

Dick Schaap

One of the most dramatic and widely discussed developments in professional sports within the past few decades has been the sharp rise in salaries paid to many professional athletes. In the following viewpoint, Dick Schaap argues that such high pay has robbed professional sports of its special charm for the American people. While professional athletes and sports in general may be flush with money, Schaap writes, they are missing something fundamental to the game. Schaap is a sports commentator with ABC News, and has written numerous sports books, including *Bo Knows Bo*, written in collaboration with football and baseball star Bo Jackson.

As you read, consider the following questions:

1. In what respects are athletes better than ever, according to Schaap?
2. Why has the increased money paid to athletes made it harder for fans to appreciate sports, according to the author?
3. What does Schaap find admirable about some athletes?

From "So Much of the Joy Is Gone" by Dick Schaap, *Forbes*, September 14, 1992. Reprinted with the author's permission.

Athletes are better than ever. They are taller, heavier, faster, stronger, smarter. In every sport in which achievement can be measured objectively, their progress is stunning.

A girl barely into her teens swims more swiftly than Johnny Weismuller swam in the Olympics, or in his loincloth.

A high school boy jumps farther and sprints faster than Jesse Owens jumped and sprinted in front of Adolf Hitler.

A 30-year-old married woman surpasses Jim Thorpe's best marks in a variety of track and field events.

Even a man over 40 runs a mile faster than Paavo Nurmi ran in his prime.

The performances are so much better.

But so much of the joy is gone. Sports has too often been called a microcosm of society, yet its present state certainly reflects the uneasy prosperity of the times, the suspicion that, despite encouraging facts and heartening figures, something is fundamentally wrong. The cheers may be louder than ever, but they ring a little hollow.

It is almost impossible to overstate the pervasiveness of sports in American society, the breadth and strength of its special appeal, to bricklayers and novelists, accountants and comedians. "Have you met Mr. Nixon yet?" the future President's press secretary once asked me. "You'll like him. He reads the sports pages first."

Then when I did meet Richard Nixon, he phrased his political thoughts in sports terms, spoke of hitting home runs and getting to first base and striking out. Sports is a language and a diversion and sometimes an obsession, and more than ever, it is a business.

High Stakes

The stakes are so high now. The *average* major league baseball player earns more than a million dollars a year. Losing pitchers and feeble hitters, men with stunningly modest statistics, demand much more. Steve Greenberg, the deputy commissioner of baseball, used to be an agent, negotiating players' contracts. He once told his father, Hank Greenberg, the Hall of Famer, who was the first ballplayer to earn $100,000 in a season, that he was representing a certain player. "What should I ask for?" Steve said. "He hit .238."

"Ask for a uniform," Hank said.

Steve shook his head. "Dad," he said, "you just don't understand baseball any more."

Nobody understands baseball any more. No one relates to the salaries. Not even the players themselves. They earn so much more than they ever dreamed of.

They also throw pitches Cy Young never dreamed of. (Ever see Cy Young's glove? Small. Very small. Now they have big hands,

hands that can wrap around a ball and deliver a palmball.) They swing bats with muscles Babe Ruth never dreamed of. They sprint from home to first, or first to third, with incredible speed. That's the biggest difference, the way they run these days. They fly.

Q: Guess who went on strike again over salaries

But they don't know how to bunt. They don't know how to hit and run. They don't know which base to throw to. They didn't spend childhoods in cornfields playing baseball 10 or 12 hours a day, absorbing the nuances of the game. They may have developed terrific hand-eye coordination playing video games, but that didn't teach them how to hit the cutoffman.

Baseball players earn up to $7 million a season. So do basketball players. Football players are embarrassed. Their ceiling is a few million dollars lower. Golfers and tennis players only go up to a million or two a year in prize money, but they can quadruple their income by wearing the right clothes, wielding the right clubs, advertising the right corporate logos on their visors and their sleeves.

Even athletes who are officially amateurs, runners and skaters and skiers, earn hundreds of thousands of dollars a year. How can anyone afford to have fun?

Once there was a camaraderie among athletes. They competed on the field, but afterward they were friends, sharing a common experience, a common attitude, bonded by their love for their game. Tennis players, for instance, traveled together, roomed together, partied together, exchanged advice and rackets. Now each has a coach, and an agent, and a father or brother, and a fistful of sponsors, walling them off, separating them. They can face each other across the net for years and never get to know each other.

Even in team sports, team spirit is, for the most part, gone, rekindled only occasionally by victory. "We are family," in sports terms, means: "We won." It doesn't mean we worry about each other, bolster each other, counsel each other.

How can fans relate to these athletes? How can they embrace heroes who have so much money and so little loyalty? Players change teams now as casually as they change jockstraps. Once you could fall in love with a lineup, commit it to your heart and your memory, and not have to learn more than one or two new names a year.

"The names, just to say the names, you could sing them," the playwright Herb Gardner once wrote, lamenting the Dodgers' move to Los Angeles. "Sandy Amoros, Jim Gilliam, Hodges, Newcombe, Campanella, Erskine, Furillo, Podres, gone, gone . . . even the sound is gone. What's left? A cap, I got a cap, Dodgers, '55, and sometimes on the wind I hear a gull, and Red Barber's voice. . . ."

Now the Dodger lineup changes every day, millionaires come and go, succumbing to minor injuries, whining about imagined slights, and even the manager, Tom Lasorda, who loves the team so much he says he bleeds Dodger blue, can't call all his players by name.

Once Dodgers were Dodgers for decades, and Cardinals Cardinals, and Red Sox Red Sox, but now they're L.A. Kings for a day, or maybe a month or a season, and if an athlete puts in a full career with one team, in one city, he isn't a hero, he's a monument.

Learning from the Owners

It's easy to fault the players for earning so much money, for displaying so little loyalty, but it isn't fair. They didn't invent greed, or ingratitude. They learned from their mentors, the owners. The baseball players of the 1950s, the football players of the 1960s, had little idea of how underpaid they were. Soon after the salaries started to soar, a baseball player named Ken Singleton told me, "The owners screwed the players for one hundred years. We've been screwing them for five. We've got ninety-five more years coming."

The owners came up with the idea of moving for the money, too. The Braves went from Boston to Milwaukee to Atlanta, strip-mining stadia along the way. The Dodgers and the Giants traveled west hand in hand, with the other hands, of course, thrust out. They left shattered fans behind.

"They went, and the city went with them," Herb Gardner wrote. "The heart went with them, and the city started to die. Look what you got now, look what you got without no heart. What's to root for? Duke Snider! He went away! How many years in the stands hollering? A lifetime in the afternoon hollering, 'I'm witcha, Duke, I'm witcha,' never dreaming for a moment that he wasn't with *me*!"

Teams, and owners, and athletes, have disappointed us in so many ways. The disappointment goes beyond the greed, beyond the selfishness. How can you put athletes up on a pedestal who flaunt fast cars at illegal speeds, who succumb to the lures of social drugs and performance-enhancing drugs, who maltreat women as spoils, who lose gambling fortunes that would change most people's lives? How can you pick a hero any more and count on him?

Sports has let us down. . . .

Sports could be forgiven its flaws, at least some of them, if it had compensating strengths, if it taught the heroic lessons that Homer once sang of, if it emphasized positive values, if it truly rewarded perseverance and teamwork and similar virtues.

But these days sports preaches greed above all else. Bad enough that the status of all professional athletes is determined, to a considerable extent, by their income; in golf, pretense is stripped away and the players are ranked, officially, by their earnings. Worse, the sports world also glamorizes hypocrisy and deception and corruption. . . .

Finding Inspiration

I still find individual athletes who lift my spirits: Bonny Warner, America's best female luger in the 1980s, a graduate of Stanford, a reformed sportscaster, now a United Airlines pilot; Jim Abbott, one of the few baseball players ever to leap straight from college to the major leagues, a man who expects neither sympathy nor attention for the fact that he was born with only one hand, yet a man who quietly offers time and hope and encouragement to children with physical differences; Mike Reid, first an All-American football player, then an All-Pro tackle, from Altoona, Pa., a town in which it is easy to play football but takes courage to play piano, now a Grammy Award-winning songwriter and singer of sensitive ballads.

In all sports, I find stars with the ultimate saving grace, the ability to laugh at themselves; stars who rose to great wealth from the meanest streets without forgetting their roots; stars whose intellect contradicts athletic stereotypes; stars whose values are the decent traditional ones that start with family and loyalty. "When I was growing up," Bo Jackson recalled, "my mom cleaned people's houses during the day and cleaned a motel at night. She also raised ten children by herself. And people try to tell me that playing two sports is hard." Bo Jackson's wife is a counseling psychologist; their three children are his most prized trophies.

Some athletes are better than ever.

Even off the field.

When I was a graduate student at Columbia, the school had a very good basketball team.

The best player on the team became a degenerate gambler, a convicted criminal.

The second-best player became president of the Ford Foundation.

I still see both of them, on infrequent occasion, and they remind me of the potential of sports, and the peril. Sports can inspire greatness, but, too often these days, it inspires only greed.

> *"Owners justify the maximizing of profits because they say that sports is business. . . . But sports is also sports."*

Team Owners' Greed Has Marred Professional Sports

Frank Dell'Apa

Frank Dell'Apa is a staff writer for the *Boston Globe*. In the following viewpoint, he criticizes the owners and league executives of professional sports, particularly baseball, basketball, and football. He argues that the actions of the owners have raised the costs of attending games to prohibitive levels for the average fan, and that owners have used their monopoly positions to extract concessions from taxpayers. The values of sport, Dell'Apa concludes, are being perverted by the greedy actions of team owners.

As you read, consider the following questions:

1. Why is Dell'Apa skeptical of claims of team owners that they are losing money?
2. How does public tax money subsidize team owners, according to the author?
3. Why have groups representing the fans' interests been trivialized in the past, according to Dell'Apa?

"Do Pro Sports Take Advantage of Their Fans?" by Frank Dell'Apa, *Public Citizen*, May/June 1993. Reprinted by permission of the author.

In 1983, Wall Street investors Alan Cohen, Paul Dupee, and Don Gaston purchased the Boston Celtics franchise for $18 million. Today, this National Basketball Association franchise is worth about $120 million. The owners made $50 million by selling stock in the team. They also have floated a selling price of $200 million for a package that would include the Celtics franchise, a radio station valued at $6 million, and a television station that cost them $10 million.

Cohen, Dupee, and Gaston have been praised by the investment community for their acumen. While they profited immensely, the sports fans are really paying the bill. Celtics ticket prices have increased from a range of $6 to $17 in 1983 to a range of $19 to $45 in 1993. This represents a nearly 300 percent increase, well above the national inflation rate of 45.8 percent over the same period. . . .

A family of four will spend an average of $201.30 on food, merchandise, parking, programs, and tickets at each Celtics game, according to the Chicago-based *Team Marketing Report*.

Such price increases and profits in recent years have marked much of professional sports in the United States. Not only have sports become bigger business than ever, but because of their monopolistic nature the sports leagues also have gripped the free enterprise system in a virtual stranglehold.

The Sports Industry

The sports industry, with a gross domestic product of more than $65 billion, is among the nation's top 25 industries. The industry generates revenues such as the $850,000 per 30-second commercial that NBC charged in January 1993 during the Super Bowl. Major league baseball, the National Football League (NFL), and even the National Collegiate Athletic Association have billion-dollar television network contracts.

The sports industry portrays itself as an energetic, healthy success story, symbolized by strong, young athletes, sparkling new stadia, and swaggering franchise owners. Meanwhile, only the affluent can take anyone out to the ball game, and many communities wanting a major league team cannot get one.

"Pharmaceuticals and professional sports franchises are the two biggest ripoffs in American industry, and for much the same reason—both are monopolies," said Peter Gruenstein, an attorney in Anchorage, Alaska, who directed the now-defunct consumer advocacy group Fight to Advance the Nation's Sports (FANS) in the 1970s. "The pharmaceutical industry develops a product, gets a (17-year exclusive) patent, and sets a price. You can get that product only from that company, so the price goes up dramatically."

Because sports franchise owners control the supply of their

product, the public pays extravagant sums for the privilege of attending their events. According to the *Team Marketing Report*, the average cost for a family of four to attend an NFL game is $163.19, an NBA game costs $158.17, and a major league baseball game costs $85.85.

Reprinted by permission: Tribune Media Services.

Owners and league spokesmen protest that professional sports franchises lose money because of rising operating costs and salaries. Few NFL franchises report profits, according to testimony in a 1992 suit filed by NFL players against the league in federal district court in Minnesota. Bud Selig, Milwaukee Braves owner and acting commissioner of major league baseball, testified in February 1993 before the Senate Subcommittee on Antitrust, Monopolies, and Business Rights that professional baseball franchises are break-even enterprises.

Losing Money?

Analysts insist that such assertions are misleading. The major expense of an NFL franchise, for instance, is player salaries—about $28 million, much of which can be amortized. These salaries are more than covered by average gate receipts of more than $1.5 million per game and revenue from a national television contract worth $34 million per team and scheduled to increase to $38 million in 1994.

Added to those figures is residual revenue, especially from marketing ventures. The value of licensing fees for major league baseball in 1992 was $2.4 billion, but owners do not have to declare royalties for these fees in franchise operating statements. Each franchise received a net return of more than $3 million from those fees in 1992, according to Andrew Zimbalist, an economics professor at Smith College in Northampton, Mass. Zimbalist also warns of the franchises' ability "to trade with themselves."

As an example, he noted that The Tribune Company—which owns the *Chicago Tribune*, WGN-TV, and the Chicago Cubs—reduced revenues $30 million by paying itself a $10 million broadcasting fee on a deal that was worth $40 million to televise Cubs baseball games to 40 million homes.

"Under generally accepted accounting principles, I can turn a $4 million profit into a $2 million loss, and I can get every national accounting firm to agree with me," a Toronto Blue Jays executive is quoted as saying in Zimbalist's 1992 book, *Baseball and Billions*.

Professional team sports in the United States have been able to conduct the business side of their operations largely outside of governmental control and public scrutiny. Major league baseball is actually an adjudicated monopoly.

A Legal Monopoly

Baseball is the only sport with a legal monopoly, but the NFL takes its cue from baseball and conducts business in the manner of a monopoly. The NBA has had to be more resourceful, but has controlled its costs with a salary cap restriction tied to revenues.

Baseball's exemption from antitrust statutes has been subjected to extreme pressure in 1993, however, especially from Florida Senators Bob Graham (D) and Connie Mack (R). Their constituencies have been unable to secure a baseball franchise to inhabit the $135 million Sundome in St. Petersburg.

In early March, Senator Howard Metzenbaum (D-Ohio), chairman of the Senate subcommittee on antitrust, introduced S. 500, the Professional Baseball Antitrust Reform Act of 1993 to remove the exemption. "Baseball is a $1.5 billion a year business, and many of its teams are owned by or affiliated with some of America's largest corporations," Metzenbaum said in introducing the bill. It has nine co-sponsors, including Graham and Mack.

"The business deals of baseball's barons don't just affect the price of a ticket or the cost of a hot dog at the stadium," he continued. "They also affect things like the taxes paid by the public, the economic well-being of local communities, the size of a consumer's cable bill, and the educational and career choices of thousands of young men in this country. And yet these deals, even if they hurt consumers or harm competition, are completely exempt from scrutiny under our nation's fair competition laws."

Defenders of legislated antitrust exemption believe it is essential for the preservation of a highly profitable, sophisticated sports industry. Others believe that the wealth should be more widely dispersed.

Community Exploitation

The exploitation of entire communities by a relative handful of adroit bottom-liners, whose actions in almost any other context would be preceded by words like "gimme your wallet," is now commonplace. Pro sport is a high-stakes game of making a pawn (and a shambles) of the public trust, with owners . . . making consistent good use of two now-standard operating ploys: the threat to transfer the beloved home team out of town or the threat to the targeted city of not moving *into* town.

In either case, taxpayers are counted on to spring for every favor a pro team thinks it needs to maximize profits. And faced with the potential loss of a "valuable community asset," public officials can be counted on to cave in.

John Underwood, *The New York Times*, October 31, 1993.

"We must be conscious of the absurdities of subsidizing some of the most wealthy of our society, literally putting taxpayer money into their pockets," Gruenstein said. "These people are already phenomenally rich, and they are getting richer selling a monopoly product at monopoly prices. If Congress were to give Ross Perot a $50 million subsidy, they would be sent to the psychiatric facility for something so ludicrous. But that is what we do with owners of sports franchises." Municipalities consider it is so important to have a professional team that they "are fighting against each other and bribing teams with subsidies."

The dispute that could finally trigger the end of baseball's antitrust exemption began when the city of San Francisco initially refused to subsidize construction of a new stadium for the Giants baseball team. Giants owners, angered at this refusal, began shopping the team, which already had moved from New York City where the Giants had been for decades. Franchise owners discovered a willing, even desperate, buyer on the other side of the country in St. Petersburg—a city without a team but currently paying $12 million a year in local taxpayer money to service the debt on the Sundome Stadium.

Giants franchise owners, however, were only using St. Petersburg as leverage to stimulate support for the team in San Francisco. Eventually, San Francisco retained the Giants when a new group of private investors agreed to buy the team. City officials also agreed to help the new owners shop for land in the Bay Area to relocate the team's home stadium—at a cost of millions that local taxpayers will pay.

Baseball, operating as a monopoly, has not experienced direct competition. In 1993 two new teams were introduced in Miami and Denver, major league baseball's first expansion since 1977. Critics of baseball's antitrust exemption believe that opening baseball to direct competition will benefit the game and its fans.

Organizing the Fans

The FANS group, which Ralph Nader founded in 1977, attempted to hold professional leagues accountable in its year of existence.

"The problem was that FANS got trivialized," Gruenstein said. "There has always been a bias in sports journalism toward the conservative, a bias that was pro-owners. Things have changed in the last 20 years. But then it was easy to denigrate FANS as focused on minor issues such as cold hot dogs."

FANS attracted as many as 3,000 members, who paid dues of $15 a year to join. FANS critically evaluated the business operations of sporting franchises and insisted that the public have something to say about the affairs of the teams it supported. FANS was received apathetically by the fans, and with hostility by the establishment and the mainstream media. But the issues that FANS raised then remain largely unresolved today.

"There has been an acceleration of what was happening then," Gruenstein said. "The most obvious concern to the sports fan at that time was the movement from free television to cable and pay-per-view, and that clearly has been happening. The idea that teams would actually sell their rights to cable, at a time when a lot of people didn't have cable, was hard to conceive for a lot of people. We did studies on the prices, and they were extraordinarily high, but nothing like what they are now. We were railing against $12 and $14 a seat."

For now, ticket prices appear to be holding steady, according to Alan Friedman of the *Team Marketing Report*.

"It appears that in baseball in 1993, there will be fewer discounts, special deals, and promotions," Friedman said. "So baseball will be able to increase gross ticket receipts without increasing prices. There is a threshold to how high you can go with ticket prices without alienating the fans. But concession prices have increased at a higher rate than ticket prices. I don't think we are at the point where they are not going to increase prices."

Exploiting the Fans

Indeed, some observers believe that prices have only started to rise. Prices for Celtics games at the new Boston Garden could double by the end of the 1990s. The only exceptions are the 104 luxury boxes, each priced between $700,000 and $1.4 million. These boxes gross $100 million every five years.

"I don't think the leagues care about the fan," said Adam Kolton, a founder of Sports Fans United, a New York City-based organization that continues in the spirit of FANS. "The leagues are doing a lot of things for themselves. Corporations buy up tickets to games, and that doesn't leave a whole lot of room for the average fan or inner-city fan.

"Fans haven't seen themselves as activists," Kolton continued. "But they are more upset than they were in the 1970s. If you listen to the talk shows, the fans are fed up. They are ready to get behind something if they think it can make a difference."

Americans are becoming less rhapsodic about their sports, and more aware of the cold impersonality of big business. There is a feeling that essentially the same product is being offered in the 1990s as before, with distractions and sideshows to justify the greatly inflated prices.

In fact, the average consumer can afford to attend only a limited number of games. So the American spectator's main experience with professional sports is becoming increasingly restricted to watching games on television. That makes the spectator a sitting duck for pay-per-view schemes, which means consumers will pay to watch events even when they are in their own homes.

Baseball has increased television revenues by reducing the amount of free broadcast, such as Game of the Week, and by switching broadcasts to cable networks and pay-per-view. Soon only the fan with extensive cable connections will be able to see any games on television.

"By dividing the country into exclusive 'home television territories,' the league ensures that teams can shift television rights from over-the-air stations to cable networks without fear that a local broadcaster would compete by importing another team's games," said Gene Kimmelman, legislative director of the Consumer Federation of American, located in Washington, D.C. "These territorial restrictions allow major league teams to maximize television revenue by maintaining a monopoly on local baseball viewing options."

Owners justify the maximizing of profits because they say that sports is business, or sports is entertainment. But sports is also sports, as much a manifestation of culture as dance or music. As sports becomes increasingly perverted by greed, its fabric is ripped apart and few of the values it should embody are left.

Until the early 1970s, sports were accessible to youngsters receiving allowances of 50 cents a week and gas station attendants making $2 an hour. They watched games in which athletes often earned only marginally more than the fans themselves. Like their fans, some major league baseball players commuted to the stadium on public transportation. Fans and athletes interacted, and they often returned home enriched by the experience. All that has changed radically. Today, enrichment comes with a prohibitive price tag.

"If the public does not benefit, then the exemption should be restricted or repealed."

Baseball's Antitrust Immunity Should Be Repealed

Howard Metzenbaum

The 1890 Sherman Antitrust Act prohibits large business entities from using monopolistic powers to suppress competition. A 1922 decision of the U.S. Supreme Court ruled that antitrust laws as written do not apply to baseball. In the decades since that ruling, Congress has periodically debated whether to place baseball under antitrust law. The following viewpoint is taken from a U.S. Senate hearing held December 10, 1992— shortly after baseball's owners blocked an attempt by St. Petersburg, Florida, to obtain the San Francisco Giants franchise. Howard Metzenbaum, Democratic senator from Ohio from 1976 to 1994, chaired the hearings. In his opening statement Metzenbaum questioned the fairness of baseball's antitrust exemption.

As you read, consider the following questions:

1. Why is there intense interest in the issue of baseball's antitrust exemption, according to Metzenbaum?
2. What does Metzenbaum find disturbing about actions by baseball team owners?
3. How are many cities victimized by professional baseball team owners, according to the author?

From the Opening Statement of Sen. Howard Metzenbaum, chairman, to the Subcommittee on Antitrust, Monopolies, and Business Rights, Committee on the Judiciary, December 10, 1992.

This morning, the Antitrust Subcommittee holds an oversight hearing on the validity of major league baseball's exemption from the antitrust laws. All of us recognize that today's hearing does not involve one of the critical problems facing the new President and the new Congress, but there is, nevertheless, intense interest in this subject among the public, the press, and my colleagues.

The reason for this interest is simple. Baseball has been a special part of American life for over a century. It provides millions of fans with a well-deserved break from the rigors of everyday life. Americans from all walks of life and from all parts of the country have grown up with this game. It has been a bridge of tradition and nostalgia that connects the past with the present and parents with their children.

But while the game of baseball remains a simple pleasure, the business of baseball has become complicated and, at times, cutthroat. As a consequence, there has been a certain element of disenchantment as to the fans. Major league baseball is not just a sport. It is also a billion-dollar big business, and it is a big business which enjoys unique treatment under the law.

A Legalized Cartel

Unlike any other big business in America, major league baseball is a legally sanctioned, unregulated cartel. The Supreme Court conferred that extraordinary privilege upon baseball 70 years ago when it granted major league baseball a complete exemption from the antitrust laws. Justice Holmes reasoned that the antitrust laws did not apply because baseball could not be considered interstate commerce. Although the soundness of this ruling has often been questioned even by the Court itself, it has never been overturned. Instead, the Court has tossed the ball to Congress, which is why we are here today.

While Congress did not create baseball's blanket antitrust immunity, we do have the authority to remove it. Many in this body now believe that it is time to repeal the exemption. The burden is on major league baseball to demonstrate that the exemption is in the public interest.

Baseball's antitrust exemption is a privilege that the baseball owners may be abusing. I am particularly concerned that their ouster of [former major league baseball commissioner] Fay Vincent . . . and their plans to weaken the commissioner's powers invites more abuse of that privilege. Fay Vincent understood that the antitrust exemption placed a special obligation on the commissioner to govern the sport in a manner that protected the public interest. Vincent had independent authority to put the interests of the fans and the interests of the sport of baseball ahead of the business interests of the team owners. That is no longer the case.

Jerry Reinsdorf, the owner of the Chicago White Sox, and one of the key participants in Vincent's ouster, has stated that the job of the next baseball commissioner will be to "run the business for the owners, not the players or the umpires or the fans.". . .

Baseball and Other Sports

Federal antitrust law prohibits businesses from taking actions that "unreasonably" constrain interstate commerce. However, in a 1922 decision that I can only term "capricious," the U.S. Supreme Court exempted professional baseball from these federal antitrust laws as an "amusement" and not a business. . . .

I am a great fan of the game, . . . but . . . I do not find many of the actions of the Major League Baseball owners amusing these days.

Their treatment of the fans, the players, host cities and cities seeking that opportunity . . . militates against them.

No other professional sport enjoys this kind of blanket exemption. What possible standard can be advanced to support such a circumstance in this day of multi-million-dollar player salaries and telecommunications contracts? What possible difference sets Major League Baseball's owners apart from their peers in other professional sports? I maintain that there is none.

Michael Bilirakis, statement before Congress, December 10, 1992.

It appears that the owners don't want a strong and independent commissioner who can act in the best interests of the sport or act as a potential check against abuse of their monopoly power. Instead, they want a commissioner who will function as the cruise director for their cartel. If decisions about the direction and future of major league baseball are going to be dictated by the business interests of team owners, then the owners should be required to play by the same antitrust rules that apply to any other business.

Even if the owners give the next commissioner a fig leaf of authority, Vincent's ouster sends a clear signal that he or she should not cross them. It also raises questions about whether baseball can respond credibly and effectively to allegations of misconduct by an owner or league official. . . .

There are other issues that need to be explored aside from the question of the commissioner's authority. The other three major professional sports—football, basketball, and hockey—function quite well without the blanket exemption from the antitrust laws enjoyed by baseball. Why should baseball be treated differently?

A number of commentators assert that baseball uses its privileged status to maintain an artificial scarcity of franchises. The recent tug of war between Tampa Bay [St. Petersburg] and San Francisco is a perfect illustration. It is clear that the number of cities which can support baseball franchises greatly exceeds the number of franchises established by the owners.

A scarcity of franchises inflates the resale value of existing teams and increases each owner's share of baseball's national broadcasting revenue, the total of which is about $380 million annually. It also enables owners to squeeze concessions and subsidies from their home cities by threatening relocation to another city. Many cities badly in need of revenues for schools, hospitals, their police and fire forces, and other vital projects have been forced to obtain public funding of elaborate new stadiums or risk having their team move to another city. This blackmail game is unseemly and a disservice to the fans.

The baseball owners trumpet their commitment to franchise stability even though they routinely threaten to abandon their home city whenever it suits them financially, and the owners reportedly have refused to permit municipal ownership of teams, which is probably the most effective way to protect fans from franchise relocations. When Joan Kroc tried to give the Padres to the city of San Diego, baseball's barons said no.

For decades, the owners also used their antitrust exemption to suppress players' salaries and stifle player mobility through the use of the reserve clause. As it now stands, the reserve clause can bind a player to a single team for 6 years. Players have gained a limited amount of movement through the collective bargaining process, but the reopening of the labor agreement means that the players will once again have to bargain for some semblance of a free market. Moreover, minor league players who constitute the vast majority of professional ballplayers still labor under conditions reminiscent of indentured servitude.

Hurting the Fans

Baseball's special treatment under the antitrust laws also has helped to inflate the value of its TV contracts. The baseball owners have agreed among themselves to impose territorial restrictions on the broadcasting of games by local TV stations. These restrictions can facilitate the movement of games to pay TV and hurt fans who can't afford or don't have access to cable.

The sport of baseball is a national treasure, and both Congress and the team owners must be careful not to take actions that would hurt the game and alienate fans. But if the antitrust exemption does provide some benefit to the fans and the game, the owners are going to have to prove it. If the public does not benefit, then the exemption should be restricted or repealed.

"Baseball . . . deserves to retain its current status under the antitrust laws."

Baseball's Antitrust Immunity Should Not Be Repealed

Allan H. Selig

Many people have called for the repeal of baseball's unique exemption from antitrust laws. Antitrust suits have been used against leagues of other professional sports; for example, in the National Football League these suits have had such diverse effects as granting free agency to players and restricting the NFL's power to prevent franchise relocations. Baseball's exemption from such antitrust suits (derived from a 1922 Supreme Court ruling) makes the owners less accountable to the players and the fans, some people argue. In the following viewpoint, Allan H. (Bud) Selig argues that baseball's antitrust exemption has been beneficial to the sport by enabling it to preserve franchise stability and prevent team owners from deserting cities for greater profits elsewhere. Selig, testifying before Congress, cites his own experiences as president of the Milwaukee Brewers baseball organization to support his views.

As you read, consider the following questions:

1. What point does Selig make in describing the history of the Milwaukee Braves and their move to Atlanta?
2. What is special and unique about baseball that makes it deserving of antitrust exemption, according to the author?

From the testimony of Allan H. Selig to the Subcommittee on Antitrust, Monopolies, and Business Rights, Committee on the Judiciary, U.S. Senate, December 10, 1992.

I understand that this hearing was called . . . [because of] the concern of some over the National League's decision not to approve the relocation of the Giants from San Francisco to Tampa Bay/St. Petersburg. . . .

Let me first say to the many, many loyal baseball fans in the Tampa Bay/St. Petersburg area that I genuinely understand and appreciate the disappointment and the anger that you feel as a result of the National League's decision not to approve the relocation of the Giants to your fine city. As I will explain, I was in your shoes on several occasions in the 1960's when it took me 6½ years to bring a baseball team back to Milwaukee. But the National League's decision to keep the Giants in San Francisco, where they have successfully operated with loyal support from millions of fans for the past 35 years, was simply a reaffirmation of Baseball's long-established policy against the relocation of franchises that have not been abandoned by their local communities. So although I understand the disappointment of the people of Tampa Bay/St. Petersburg, my vivid memory of the devastation caused in Milwaukee when the Braves went to Atlanta leaves me firmly convinced that Baseball's preference for franchise stability is not only an appropriate policy, but the only policy that is in the public interest.

The Milwaukee Braves

The Boston Braves moved to my hometown of Milwaukee in 1953. Ironically, this was the first franchise relocation permitted in Baseball since the 1903 Agreement between the National and American Leagues. The Braves' stay in Milwaukee was, until their abrupt departure 12 years later, one of the great success stories in Baseball. Though a small town compared to most other Major League cities, the Milwaukee community immediately embraced the Braves and supported them spectacularly. Immediately, the Braves became a part of the basic fibre of the Milwaukee community. The Braves drew 1.83 million fans in their inaugural season in Milwaukee, which was an all-time National League record. . . .

But despite our best efforts, the Braves did move to Atlanta at the end of the 1965 season. I was personally heartbroken and I can tell the Subcommittee that the city of Milwaukee and the state of Wisconsin were traumatized by the loss of that franchise. The people in my town felt hostility, bitterness and a deep sense of betrayal towards Major League Baseball for allowing the Braves to abandon us. Our loyal financial and emotional support of Baseball was rewarded with a slap in the face. The years of drawing more than 2 million fans per season were forgotten. The Club simply got up and moved to what it considered to be an even greener pasture and no one from Major League

Baseball stopped them.

The void left in the community by the Braves' departure drove me to devote the next 6½ years of my life to trying to bring Major League Baseball back to Milwaukee. . . .

Unpredictable Results

The value of eliminating the baseball antitrust exemption (which is more appropriately called the "baseball antitrust *exclusion*") depends on how baseball would be affected and constrained if it did not exist. Ascertaining this requires an exploration of how antitrust law would likely be applied to baseball. My conclusion is that while it is in theory unjustified to treat baseball differently from other sports, and while there are certainly problems in baseball of concern to the public and Congress, abolishing the exclusion would be unlikely to further the public interest.

Although baseball is treated differently under antitrust law than the major leagues in football, basketball, and hockey, the conduct of those leagues is not discernably more pro-public than that of Major League Baseball. Furthermore, the application of antitrust law to these other major sports leagues over the years by the federal courts has been inconsistent, often unjustifiable, and generally counterproductive. Subjecting baseball to the vagaries of this confusing enforcement process cannot predictably result in benefits to the public interest.

Gary R. Roberts, statement before Congress, December 10, 1992.

By the end of the 1969 season, the ownership group of the Seattle Pilots concluded that it could not successfully operate a franchise in Seattle and so they began looking to sell the team. I led a group that signed a contract to buy the Pilots in October of 1969. But for the next six months, Baseball, acting responsibly and properly in my view, did everything it could to keep the Pilots in Seattle. It was not until the Pilots' owners put the team into bankruptcy and the bankruptcy judge ordered the sale of the Club to my group that Baseball reluctantly allowed the Club to move to Milwaukee. We actually purchased the Club on March 31, 1970, just days before the opening of the 1970 season. After 6½ years of heartbreak, the people of Milwaukee finally got back something that should never have been taken from them in the first place.

And that is the abridged version of how I became involved in Major League Baseball. The moral of my experience in Milwaukee is, to my mind, that the professional sports leagues in general and Baseball in particular should vigilantly enforce strong policies prohibiting Clubs from abandoning local communities which have supported them. The Milwaukee experience confirms for me that the appropriate policy of every professional sports league is to prohibit franchise relocations except in the most dire circumstances where the local community has, over a sustained period, demonstrated that it cannot or will not support the franchise. This, I am happy to report to you, is precisely Baseball's policy. It is also the reason why the loyal supporters of the San Francisco Giants will continue to enjoy the performances of Will Clark and his teammates next year and for (we hope) many years after that.

The Antitrust Exemption

But if Baseball were not exempt from the antitrust laws, a decision protecting franchise stability such as the one made in San Francisco would have certainly subjected Baseball to a costly and unpredictable treble damage lawsuit. Indeed, without its exemption, Baseball might not have even attempted to save the Giants for the people of San Francisco. Ever since a court concluded that the antitrust laws left the NFL powerless to stop [football team owner] Al Davis from abandoning the remarkably supportive (and profitable) Oakland market for greener pastures in Los Angeles, no professional sports league other than Baseball has been able to stop a franchise from abandoning its local community for what the owner perceives to be greater riches elsewhere.

This misguided application of the antitrust rules is why Oakland is today without its famed Raiders, although it does still have the publicly financed stadium it built for the team with its annual debt service of $1.5 million through the year 2006. It is also why Baltimore no longer has its beloved Colts, the football Cardinals now play in Phoenix rather than St. Louis, the basketball Clippers are in Los Angeles rather than San Diego and the basketball Kings play in Sacramento rather than Kansas City. From a purely personal standpoint, I feel for all the loyal fans in those cities who lost such important parts of their communities because of the Davis decision. I think it is a sad commentary that the NFL and the NBA [National Basketball Association] could not prevent the hurt that these communities have had to endure. . . .

Those who suggest that Baseball's problems would be solved by subjecting the Game's decisionmaking to the antitrust principles developed in the other professional sports simply ignore the undeniable fact that the application of antitrust laws has been the *cause* of the many problems, including franchise instability, that exist in the other professional sports today. . . .

Although the effects of eliminating Baseball's exemption cannot be thoroughly anticipated by anyone, it seems inevitable to me that the most immediate consequence would be that a number of teams in small markets would attempt to abandon some of Baseball's existing cities for what they think are better economic conditions elsewhere. This is particularly likely today because Baseball has moved into an extremely difficult economic time. As more and more small market Clubs continue to lose money year after year, the temptation to move to a city that appears to offer a "quick fix" is likely to become overwhelming. Indeed, Baseball could be faced with Clubs jumping from town to town to take advantage of the "honeymoon" period that relocated teams enjoy in their first few years. It would obviously not be in the public interest to render Baseball impotent to stop such conduct. . . .

Baseball's Covenant

Club owners and the governments and communities in which Baseball currently operates have all relied on Baseball's antitrust immunity which has now existed for 70 years. Nothing has happened recently to suggest that Baseball has abused its exemption so that Congress should reverse its long-held position on this issue. If anything, recent events such as Baseball's decision to preserve the National Pastime in Seattle and San Francisco make it all the more clear that Baseball's status should remain as it has for the last 70 years. Baseball's critics who have advocated for the removal of Baseball's exemption have consistently failed to describe the ways in which the performance of Baseball would better serve the public interest if it operated under the antitrust rules which the courts have unfortunately applied to the other professional sports leagues. The same is true today. The fact of the matter is that the threat of antitrust liability has caused nothing but confusion and instability in the other professional sports for both the franchises' investors and the communities in which they operate. Baseball has continued to uphold its unique covenant with its fans and it deserves to retain its current status under the antitrust laws.

Periodical Bibliography

The following articles have been selected to supplement the diverse views presented in this chapter.

Jerry Adler — "Good Field, No Pitch," *Newsweek*, April 12, 1993.

Jonathan S. Cohn — "Divided the Stands," *The Washington Monthly*, December 1991.

Frank Dell'Apa — "City Loyalty for Franchise Owners Is a Sometime Thing," *Public Citizen*, May/June 1993.

David Gelman — "The Most Dangerous Game," *Newsweek*, December 14, 1992.

David A. Kaplan — "Congress Takes a Schott," *Newsweek*, December 14, 1992.

Jay P. Lefkowitz — "The Baseball Business," *Commentary*, September 1993.

Erle Norton — "New Game Plan to Sell Baseball Is Pitching Stars," *The Wall Street Journal*, October 25, 1993.

David Rapp — "Saving the States from the Gambling Impulse," *Governing*, August 1992.

William C. Rhoden — "Gambling Away a Sense of Values," *The New York Times*, July 21, 1993.

Curt Smith — "Where Have All the Children Gone?" *Reader's Digest*, October 1993.

Mark Starr — "Big Men, Bigger Money," *Newsweek*, November 1, 1993.

Paul D. Staudohar — "McNeil and Football's Antitrust Quagmire," *Journal of Sport and Social Issues*, December 1992.

Leigh Steinberg — "Agents and Agency: A Sports Agent's View," *Journal of Sport and Social Issues*, December 1992.

David E. Thigpen — "Is Nike Getting Too Big for Its Shoes?" *Time*, April 26, 1993.

John Underwood — "From Baseball and Apple Pie, to Greed and Sky Boxes," *The New York Times*, October 31, 1993.

Mortimer B. Zuckerman — "It's Only a Game—or Was," *U.S. News & World Report*, August 23, 1993.

Is Discrimination Against Minorities a Serious Problem in Sports?

SPORTS
IN AMERICA

Chapter Preface

On April 15, 1947, Jackie Robinson played first base for the season opener of the Brooklyn Dodgers baseball team and became the first black to play in a major league team sport. Although Jack Johnson and Joe Louis gained fame as heavyweight boxing champions, and Jesse Owens captivated Americans with his track-and-field exploits in the 1936 Olympics, blacks who wished to play professional football, basketball, or baseball were unable to or were forced to play in segregated all-black leagues. Robinson, who went on to a distinguished baseball career despite resistance and abuse from teammates, fans, and others, was the first to cross this racial barrier.

Today blacks constitute approximately 20 percent of major league baseball players, roughly half of the football players in the National Football League (NFL), and over three-quarters of the players of the National Basketball Association (NBA). Many of the best known and wealthiest sports stars are black. Some observers have argued that this dramatic change from total segregation shows that sports has become the great equalizer where a person can succeed solely on ability rather than social connections or background—an ideal example of the American dream of achievement without racial obstacles.

This favorable view of sports is contested by many critics, including sociologist Richard E. Lapchick and political leader Jesse Jackson. They and others point out that while blacks have certainly excelled as athletes, relatively few have achieved coaching, managerial, or front-office positions. They argue that blacks and minorities are also discouraged from playing certain key positions—such as quarterback in football and catcher in baseball—that demand leadership and intelligence. They assert that true power comes from the ownership of sports franchises—an area where blacks and other minorities remain virtually shut out. For these and other reasons, critics conclude that racism and minority discrimination are still serious problems in sports, just as they are for American society as a whole.

The viewpoints in this chapter examine several aspects of the experiences of minorities in sports and provide a look at the problems that remain to be solved.

"Do we want a society in which a racial division of labor governs the roles of blacks and whites? Obviously not. But it happens in sports."

Racism Is a Serious Problem in Sports

Jim Myers

In December 1991 the national newspaper *USA Today* published the results of an intensive survey on racial attitudes in sports. The study, which formed the basis for a series of articles in the newspaper, concluded that racial stereotypes and attitudes remain a factor in determining what opportunities blacks, Hispanics, and other minorities receive in sports. The following viewpoint is taken from three of those articles written by Jim Myers, a reporter for *USA Today*. Myers examines the results of a *USA Today* poll on racial attitudes, investigates the stereotype that blacks have innate speed and athletic ability, and exposes the phenomenon of "stacking"—the practice of confining blacks and other minorities to a few select sports and positions.

As you read, consider the following questions:

1. What racial stereotypes regarding race and sports exist in America, according to Myers?
2. What is problematic about the belief that blacks have more natural athletic ability than whites, according to the author?
3. How does "stacking" harm minority athletes, according to Myers?

From "Race and Sports, Myth and Reality," a series of articles by Jim Myers published in *USA Today*, December 16-20, 1991. Copyright 1991, *USA Today*. Reprinted with permission.

DECEMBER 16, 1991—Fact: 90% of the running backs in the National Football League are black, and 92% of the quarterbacks are white.

Why?

A *USA Today* poll finds the answer might be linked to the way we think about race: Many of our beliefs about sports are based on classic racial stereotypes.

Black and white respondents agree that black athletes are fast runners, and white athletes are slow. More significantly, both agree white athletes are leaders and thinkers; blacks excel physically.

If applied to overall society, such views would have disturbing implications: Do we want a society in which a racial division of labor governs the roles of blacks and whites?

Obviously not. But it happens in sports. . . .

Racial Stereotypes

From sports come some of the nation's most familiar images in black and white. Sports almost begs the drawing of conclusions about race. For example, that whites should be quarterbacks, coaches, managers, and blacks should be running backs, sprinters, basketball stars.

"In sports, we've set up a system of who plays what," says Richard Lapchick of Boston's Northeastern University. "We've built a thought process here that blacks have more physical abilities, and for decades we've been trying to concoct theories that would prove this scientifically. But none of them has ever held up to rigorous scientific test."

Results of the *USA Today* poll show how well defined the stereotypes are. When asked to rate athletes on five skills black and white respondents rate white athletes highest for "leadership," followed by "thinking," "instincts," "strength" and "speed."

The skills of black athletes are rated in the exact opposite order.

Athletes may confront these stereotypes almost daily.

"People (say), 'What's he doing out there? He's in the wrong event,'" says Kevin Little, the USA's top white sprinter.

Says Alabama quarterback Danny Woodson, who is black: "The first thing most people think is that a black quarterback is a runner and not that sharp on the passing. You even have black guys who think that."

Kelvin Askew, 18, a Spring Valley, Calif., high school honor student, says that gives black players a special reputation. "I don't mind the stereotype for basketball. I'm proud of it because I play."

Evidence shows "leadership" stereotypes favor whites: Only one of the 105 major-college football coaches is black; one of 28 NFL coaches and two of 26 big-league baseball managers are black.

Sociologists say the results of the *USA Today* poll show whites tend to endorse a social order that keeps whites in the leadership and thinking positions. And blacks might accept the order because it recognizes the proven successes of blacks in one area—sports.

Both races "will buy into stereotypes as long as they don't impact on fundamental interests," says University of California sociologist Harry Edwards. "Stereotypes are a shortcut to thinking."

Science, meanwhile, has not provided compelling evidence that racial stereotypes represent biological facts.

Still, many in the USA believe the races are physically different: Half of poll respondents agree that "blacks have more natural physical ability."

Other findings:

• White athletes abandon sports and events in which blacks are perceived successful, and this contributes to the overall impression that blacks must be better at these sports or events.

• The energies of black athletes are channeled to so few sports or specific positions in team play that the overall opportunities for whites for college scholarships or pro careers still vastly outnumber those for blacks.

• With the exception of baseball, sports that once operated under restrictive "Caucasians only" rules remain virtually as white as they ever were.

In follow-up interviews with respondents to the poll, whites frequently cite physical or psychological advantages they believe black athletes might have:

"I feel (blacks) do work a bit harder," says Colin Kelley, 33, of Chelmsford, Mass. "I also believe they have more physical ability . . . but I think socioeconomic influences are more important."

Many black respondents dispute the idea that blacks are born with a physical edge. "A lot of people think that because you're black you're a natural athlete and you don't have to work hard," says Anthony Markum, 27, of Queens, N.Y. "But you do have to work hard."

Blacks and Whites Disagree

On other poll issues, blacks and whites disagree more sharply: A majority of blacks say prejudice remains a factor in sports. Most whites disagree.

A majority of blacks say prejudice favors whites in glamour positions like quarterback or pitcher. Again, whites disagree. In follow-up interviews, whites often cite evidence that the world has improved on racial matters.

"In the old days they never gave the black athlete a chance," says Herb Budd Jr., 55, of Woodbury, N.J., "and now he has the opportunity."

"I think there's equal opportunity, if you're good—whether you're black, white or green," says Donald Coyle, 69, of Johnstown, Pa.

Blacks, however, see evidence that the world still is far from racial equality.

"Stereotypes still exist," says Dwight Robbins, 34, of Washington, D.C. "In pro football, the quarterbacks are white because they're supposedly smarter (and) blacks can't be team leaders."

Who's right?

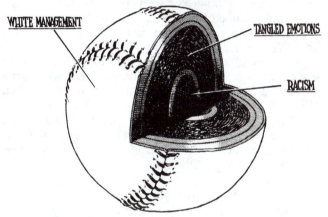

BillDay Detroit Free Press

THE CONTROVERSIAL LIVELY BALL
OF BASEBALL MANAGEMENT:

WHITE MANAGEMENT

TANGLED EMOTIONS

RACISM

Reprinted by permission: Tribune Media Services.

Progress can be seen in the general disappearance of unwritten quotas governing the number of black athletes on pro teams and in the successful entry of black athletes in sports that previously had no black participants.

But blacks are underrepresented in coaching and management. Researchers say pay discrimination sometimes arises in pro sports because white fans still want to see whites on teams they support.

"A lot of (problems) are still out there," says poll respondent James Simon, 48, of Los Angeles. "It's a shame America hasn't grown up."

DECEMBER 16, 1991—Half the respondents in a *USA Today* poll say blacks bring more natural physical ability to sports than whites.

What's the truth?

Most experts say the idea is nonsense—no biological proof exists, and the sports performances of members of any group can be explained in other ways. Others say there might be relevant physical differences among the races that just haven't been found yet—or proved.

The contributions of science in these matters have not always been objective, accurate or even relevant. Various 19th century studies attempted to rank intelligence by race but subsequently were found rife with scientific quackery, errors in method and outright prejudice. Incidentally, the studies, done by whites, usually found whites superior.

Stephen Jay Gould, Harvard professor of paleontology, says many of these efforts depended on "the finagle factor," the manner in which allegedly objective science can be manipulated to produce desired results. "No subject . . . has been more congenial to finagling than scientific ideas about human races and their status," Gould has written.

That anyone should argue that blacks are biologically superior as athletes is, at the least, a historical irony: Blacks were systematically excluded from baseball under the argument that blacks lacked the skills to play.

Several attempts to find race-linked, biological explanations for athletic excellence followed the early successes of African-American sprinters and jumpers—especially after Jesse Owens' victories at the 1936 Berlin Olympics.

An Oddity

Critics say there's an oddity in this: Why is an explanation for black athletic success necessary, when white successes beg no explanation? "The Swiss and Austrians do very well in World Cup skiing," says Jay Coakley, professor of sociology at the University of Colorado at Colorado Springs. "But nobody has felt compelled to take muscle biopsies of Swiss and Austrian skiers. Everybody says no wonder they're good skiers. They come from countries with wonderful mountains and they start when they're very young. But soon as athletes show up with black skin people started asking why they succeed."

Not all studies have claimed that black athletes have a biological advantage. After claims made about Owens' Berlin triumphs, the late W. Montague Cobb, a Howard University physical anthropologist, used preserved skeletons to measure black and white leg, heel and foot bones. He concluded the differences too small and the evidence too contradictory to say that runners of either race had an advantage.

136

Cobb also measured Owens and Frank Wykoff, a white sprinter who finished fourth behind Owens in the 100 meters at Berlin. Owens, he found, had the long calf muscles traditionally associated with whites; Wykoff had the short-bellied calf traditionally associated with blacks.

"Cobb said all you need to say," says Michael Blakey, a Howard University anthropologist. "He showed there was no relation between race and athletic ability in that case."

Other studies have produced odd or puzzling results. A study that involved measuring athletes at the 1960 Rome Olympics found black sprinters on average had longer legs, narrower hips, wider bones than white sprinters.

But what did it mean in 1960? White runners finished 1-2-3 in the 100-meter final and first in the 200 meters.

The study also found sprinters tended to have shorter legs than middle-distance runners, which seems to indicate that coaches, presumably whites, might have entered the long-legged black athletes in the wrong events.

Stacking

DECEMBER 17, 1991—Stacking is a sports phenomenon hidden in plain sight.

Certain positions in team sports—most markedly at the pro level—tend to be played by white athletes; others tend to be played by black athletes.

In the National Football League, 95% of defensive backs and 89% of wide receivers are black.

In major league baseball, 86% of pitchers and 88% of catchers are white, while 51% of outfielders are black. Indeed, 58% of blacks in baseball are outfielders; 54% of white players are pitchers.

Stacking exists in other sports: It has been found in British soccer, where black West Indians and Africans are overrepresented in the wide forward position; in Australian Rules Football, with Aborigines overrepresented at wide positions; and in college women's volleyball, where, at the time of a 1989 study, only 6% of players were black. . . .

What causes stacking? Several theories exist:

• Traditional stereotypes. Black players tend to be found at positions where "speed" and "quickness" are thought necessary; white players at positions where "intelligence" and "leadership" are considered important.

In hockey, an ethnic stereotype is at work: French Canadians are presumed to lack the toughness and aggressiveness to play good defense.

• Coaches, who tend to be white, consciously or otherwise put white players at positions pivotal to the outcome of games.

They put black players at "reactive" positions.

Stacking patterns also tend to be most pronounced at a sport's highest levels, less pronounced at lower ones. Studies of NFL players find that black players were more likely than white players to have changed positions. "Whites tended to stay in the positions they started at in high school," says Stanley Eitzen, professor of sociology at Colorado State. "But blacks tended to move away from the central positions towards the peripheral ones."

Coaches frequently deny race has anything to do with the positions their players play. When your job depends on winning, they say, you make sure you've got the best player possible at each position, regardless of race.

Critics reply that when race is involved, coaches don't always play the best players. Example: In the 1960s, unwritten rules dictated the number of black players NBA [National Basketball Association] coaches put on the court at one time, meaning coaches weren't always necessarily playing the best players.

Zakhour Youssef, professor of psychology at Eastern Michigan University, and his colleague Roger Williams, professor of physical education, studied the attitudes of football coaches toward race and positioning in the late 1970s.

Focusing on three predominantly "white" football positions (center, guard, quarterback) and three predominantly "black" positions (running back, defensive back and wide receiver), they found that coaches:

• Have developed stereotypes about skills and personality traits required at each position.

• Have developed stereotypes about mental, physical and personality characteristics of black and white players.

• Match the racial stereotype to the positional stereotype, producing teams on which positions tend to be predominantly white or black.

"Consciously or unconsciously," Youssef says, "they may believe that a position like wide receiver requires an exhibitionistic quality, and that black athletes have more of that. Or they may assign leadership qualities to white players and assign them to positions requiring leadership."

"U.S. athletics . . . offer an inspiring display of
American racial amity."

Racism in Sports
Is Exaggerated

George Gilder

George Gilder is a prominent conservative writer and social
commentator whose books include *Wealth and Poverty*, *Sexual
Suicide*, and *The Spirit of Enterprise*. In the following viewpoint,
he disputes claims of widespread racism in American sports. He
argues that physical differences between blacks and whites, especially in the area of speed, account for patterns in athletic employment that others have interpreted as racist. Gilder concludes
that sports provide a display of the American dream in which a
person can achieve performance goals regardless of race.

As you read, consider the following questions:

1. What obvious fact about black athletes does Gilder argue the
   media ignore?
2. Why are there few professional black quarterbacks or
   baseball catchers, according to the author?
3. What evidence does Gilder cite to support his belief that
   whites in America want blacks to succeed?

In early September, in nearly every city and town in America, football coaches perform a rough sort on their charges. Without any notion that they are performing a sinister act that will beget a cascading series of effects angrily denounced as racist in the U.S. media, the coaches line up their recruits for a 40-yard dash. And in almost every town, the result is the same. If there are any black boys in the group, they usually win the race.

Claims of Racism

This ritual has many consequences. Among them are black dominance of most of the more glamorous running roles in football, and U.S. global dominance in sports requiring leg speed. Another result is the regular investigative report on racism in American athletics conducted by reporters professionally blind to the obvious facts of black superiority in running speed.

The latest example is *USA Today*'s four-part series on Race and Sports, which ran from December 16 to 20, 1991. Like previous series in *Sports Illustrated* and the *New York Times*, the reporters begin and end by doggedly denying the totally obvious black genetic advantage in sprint speed. Ignoring this crucial factor and artfully probing the paranoia of blacks taught from childhood to see racism everywhere, the reporters can build up a shocking and sensational case for widespread discrimination in sports.

USA Today tried to deny the sprint speed difference by citing the occasional white sprint star and by arguing that racist white American athletes avoid the dashes out of aversion to blacks. But blacks dominate the dashes everywhere they compete, including countries such as France, Britain, and Canada, which have few blacks for whites to avoid. For two decades now, some 95 percent of the world's dashmen listed in the *Track and Field News* Top 100 rankings have been black. History's top ten 100-meter times are all by blacks, including a black Briton and a black Cuban.

Speed and Discrimination

Recognize this fact of life and nearly all the claims of racism in sports collapse. Sprint speed, for example, explains relatively low black representation at quarterback in football. Because sprint speed is so valuable and cannot be much enhanced by training, coaches cherish their sprinters. Sprinters are not "stacked" on the bench for years awaiting their chance to play quarterback. Indispensable at several key positions, they get to play right away. If an athlete with sprint speed fails to win the quarterback slot, he can play an array of other prestigious positions; without sprint speed, a white quarterback sits. With no alternative role, the non-sprinter will struggle harder to master the array of skills at quarterback than the sprinter will.

On Yale's unbeaten football team in the mid-1960s, the slow Brian Dowling (B.D. of "Doonesbury" fame) was picked for quarterback over Calvin Hill, who weighed 220 pounds and could run 100 yards in 9.6 seconds. Despite Hill's complaints of racism, the coach's decision to shift a big 9.6 sprinter to fullback had no more to do with racism than Hill's later success as a fullback in the NFL [National Football League], where Dowling failed. In the Canadian league, where quarterback is more a running position, blacks do better at quarterback than in the U.S., where it is a throwing position. The "leadership stereotyping" blamed by *USA Today* has nothing to do with it. This pattern prevails in other sports: in baseball, superior sprint speed explains higher black batting averages and stolen base records and only proportionate representation in positions where throwing or agility is the key. People gifted with sprint speed have less motive to undergo the arduous and specialized training required to pitch or play catcher.

Positions by Race in the National Football League

	% of White Players				% of Black Players			
	1983	1990	1991	1992	1983	1990	1991	1992
OFFENSE								
Quarterback	99	92	92	94	1	8	8	6
Running Back	12	7	8	7	88	90	90	92
Wide Receiver	23	14	10	11	77	86	89	88
Center	97	87	89	76	3	13	10	19
Guard	77	76	67	62	2	24	31	35
Tight End	52	49	49	39	48	51	51	59
Tackle	68	71	60	50	32	29	31	46
Kicker	98	97	88	83	2	0	0	7
DEFENSE								
Cornerback	8	4	4	2	92	96	96	98
Safety	43	17	20	12	57	83	80	88
Linebacker	53	31	29	28	47	66	68	71
Defensive End	31	28	28	26	69	72	70	73
Defensive Tackle	47	50	44	30	53	50	54	67

This table compares the racial composition of the NFL by position for four seasons. Some observers believe the disparities found in some positions are caused by racism; Gilder believes they derive from racial differences in sprinting speed.

Source: Center for the Study of Sports in Society, 1993.

USA Today tried to find racism even in track and field, a sport ruled entirely by objective standards of performance. Track and field shows the same black dominance in events based on sprint speed and the same merely proportionate representation elsewhere that is ascribed to racism when found on football and baseball teams. In track and field, sprinters have less motive to master the intricacies of pole vaulting or javelin throwing.

Ever alert to bizarre evidence of racism, *USA Today* claimed that declining white performances at 800 meters were attributable to "white flight" in the face of the rising dominance of blacks in the event. But similar declines have occurred in several other track events with few American blacks. If the reporters want to know the reasons for the decline, perhaps they might begin by considering that the American media covers track and field chiefly as an extension of the drugs and steroids beat.

Finding Racism Everywhere

The ingenuity of the American media in discovering and promoting racism knows no bounds. In their analysis, whites are racist because they lose to blacks in the 100; whites are also racist because they succeed against blacks at quarterback. Basketball is racist because it is dominated by blacks; golf is racist because it is dominated by whites. College teams are racist because they "exploit" black athletes and fail to educate them; the NCAA [National Collegiate Athletic Association] is racist because it insists that blacks unqualified for higher education be excluded from college teams.

It is obvious that whites in America desperately want blacks to succeed. From Michael Jordan to Bill Cosby, from Magic Johnson to Eddie Murphy, from Whitney Houston to Toni Morrison, from O.J. Simpson to Arsenio Hall, blacks who excel whites in important fields win the most sincere votes of all: the unimpeachable vote of the marketplace. Conclusively refuting the idea that white Americans resent black athletes is the ever-increasing popularity of professional basketball and football during the very period that blacks have moved to dominance. Despite constant charges of racism, whites still flock to watch black athletes perform; whites continue to invest in mostly black teams.

Americans even supported affirmative action until it became obvious that its chief beneficiaries were not deserving blacks but litigious whiners, black and white, male and female, and their obnoxious lawyers. . . . Now the media seem determined to make athletics, too, an arena of racial bitterness and litigation.

Athletes and the American Dream

Nonetheless, U.S. athletics still offer an inspiring display of American racial amity—a continual enactment of the American dream. Today, sports are inherently a worthier field to cover, more valuable morally and aesthetically than most contemporary art, music, films, and drama chiefly because these other fields have been befouled by leftist politics and nihilism. The best way for sports reporters both to defend their beat and to fight racism is by spurning the phony sanctimony and cynicism of the front of the paper—by merely telling the dramatic stories of athletic achievement by multiracial teams performing before enthusiastic multiracial crowds.

"Concedes one team owner: 'Of course there is racism.'"

Minority Coaches and Executives Face Discrimination in Hiring

Joshua Hammer

In 1987 Al Campanis, a Los Angeles Dodgers baseball team executive, made headlines when he stated on national television that blacks "may not have some of the necessities" to become coaches or front-office personnel for professional sports teams. The relative scarcity of minorities in positions of leadership in professional sports has remained a controversial issue. In the following viewpoint, Joshua Hammer, a reporter for *Newsweek* magazine, writes that racial prejudice still plays a role when it comes to the hiring of managers, coaches, general managers, and other sports executives. He argues that blacks and other minorities, despite their success on the playing field, still face significant racial barriers in attaining leadership positions in sports.

As you read, consider the following questions:

1. What examples of discrimination against blacks does Hammer cite?
2. What steps have some professional sports leagues and teams taken to improve their record in minority hiring, according to the author?
3. What factors besides racial prejudice create barriers for minorities seeking coaching and other jobs, according to Hammer?

Dave Shula didn't exactly dazzle his peers in his accelerated rise through the National Football League. The Dallas Cowboys demoted the 32-year-old assistant coach after he'd become the target of criticism for the team's inability to assemble an effective offense. But Shula had one big advantage—he's the son of Don Shula, who compiled one of the most successful records in NFL history. And that, some say, gave him the edge over other contenders for the job of Cincinnati Bengals head coach, including Jim Anderson, 43, the black assistant who had directed the Bengals' running game for eight seasons. "All [Shula] had was the right complexion and the right connections," wrote Greg Logan, a *Newsday* columnist, after Shula became the youngest NFL coach ever. The Bengals defended him—though hardly in ringing terms. "He has pretty good credentials," says publicity director Al Heim. (Shula wouldn't respond to calls from *Newsweek*.)

Lack of Progress

Shula's hiring breathed new life into a controversy that won't go away: professional sports' abysmal record promoting minorities to head-coaching and major front-office positions. With eight head-coaching jobs open in the NFL following the 1991 season—the most in any year since 1983—only one job . . . has gone to an African-American, Stanford University's Dennis Green, hired by the Minnesota Vikings in mid-January 1992. Despite years of jawboning about reform, critics point to numerous factors, from endemic racism to the "old-boy network," to explain the lack of progress. "It should not take courage in 1992 to hire a black coach, [but] not much has changed in [decades]," says Richard Lapchick, director of the Center for the Study of Sport in Society at Northeastern University. NFL vice president for labor relations Harold Henderson, the highest-ranking black in league history, says: "There is definitely [still] a barrier."

The barrier has eroded slightly since 1987, when Los Angeles Dodgers executive Al Campanis made his infamous remark on "Nightline" that blacks "may not have some of the necessities" to become head coaches or executives. Following the controversy, Baseball Commissioner Peter Ueberroth hired a consulting firm, Alexander & Associates, to address the minority-hiring problem. . . . [But] owners still have autonomy over whom they hire, and they've done little to expand minority recruitment. For example: despite more than two dozen managerial openings in 1991, only one black, Hal McRae, got a job. (Bill White, an African-American, became the National League president in 1989.) McRae, manager of the Kansas City Royals, joined the Toronto Blue Jays' Cito Gaston as one of two major-league pilots. "Baseball [isn't] the national pastime," says consultant Clifford Alexander. "It's white America's pastime."

145

The NFL has improved somewhat under Commissioner Paul Tagliabue, who appointed blacks to top positions in the NFL office. Yet Green was the first black hired as head coach since Art Shell took the top field job with the Los Angeles Raiders in 1989. Green is "young, motivated, a leader, a builder, [with] a good record at Stanford and Northwestern," says Vikings president Roger Headrick. In the National Basketball Association, where nearly three quarters of the players are black, 9 percent of front-office management jobs are held by blacks, the highest of the three sports. (In the NFL, the figure is 7 percent; in major-league baseball, 4 percent.) But only three of 27 NBA coaches are black. "Management has to be reminded not to rely on its normal contacts," says Deputy Commissioner Russ Granik.

Persistent Factors

While attitudes among many owners have changed (since 1987), certain factors persist in preventing minorities from getting hired:

Team owners recycle. Owners often pass over qualified blacks and recycle the same white faces. For instance, baseball manager John McNamara compiled an overall losing record with six teams in 17 years, most recently the Cleveland Indians. While many recycled white coaches are winners, critics charge that owners too often fall back on tired veterans. "You don't hear people saying, 'I'm not going to hire the black guy,'" says NFL vice president Henderson. "But the way the system works, it's status quo." Owners discount charges of favoritism, saying they hire people who they think can bring victories. "The teams are trying to run a business and be successful," says Lamar Hunt, owner of the Kansas City Chiefs.

The "old-boy network" is white. Many blacks say they lack the social, business or family connections that give a boost to whites such as Dave Shula. By January 1992, Tony Dungy had been waiting for the call for three years. He served three years as a Pittsburgh Steelers defensive back, eight years as a Steelers assistant coach and defensive coordinator and three as defensive back coach with the Kansas City Chiefs. The media have touted him as a potential coach since 1989—but . . . his phone hasn't rung once. "I had two strikes against me—I was young and black," he says. "Mean" Joe Greene, the legendary lineman with the Pittsburgh Steelers, now the team's defensive line coach, looked like the favorite to replace coach Chuck Noll, who resigned after 23 years. But some published reports now suggest the top candidates are whites. Greene says he lacks support within the owners' network. "It's a question of familiarity," Greene told the *Philadelphia Inquirer.* . . .

Blacks don't get stepping-stone jobs. Although the number of black assistant coaches in the NFL has risen from 14 to 51 [since 1981], there is only one black coordinator out of 56. Owners haven't facilitated black mobility. In 1990, when Atlanta Falcons coach Jerry Glanville offered Indianapolis Colts assistant coach Milt Jackson the offensive-coordinator position, owner Robert Irsay refused to release Jackson from his contract. "Milt's too important to our coaching staff," Irsay said. Jackson, a 12-year NFL veteran, remains a Colts assistant and was passed in 1991 for the interim head-coaching job; Irsay picked Rick Venturi, another longtime Colts assistant. The Colts say the issue was seniority, not racism. "Irsay felt more comfortable with Venturi," says a Colts official.

Baseball's Sorry Record

On the field, baseball generally offers opportunity to those who have the skills to play. But off the field, plantation rules apply. As the Rainbow Commission for Fairness in Athletics has detailed, baseball's front offices have systematically locked out people on the basis of sex or race.

For example, at the beginning of the 1993 season only 21 of 534 top executives and department heads were Latino or African American. Forty-six years after Jackie Robinson, baseball still has hired only two black umpires. For 28 teams, only one chief financial officer is black; and there is only one director of public relations. Otherwise, in its power positions, baseball throws a shutout: zero owners, zero presidents, zero chief scouts, zero general managers, zero play-by-play announcers, zero directors of player personnel are black or Latino.

Jesse Jackson, *Liberal Opinion*, July 19, 1993.

White owners aren't the only culprits. Henry Aaron, vice president of the Atlanta Braves, has been an outspoken executive on minority hiring. But the *New York Times* pointed out that in the 13 years Aaron ran the Braves' farm system, he hired only two minority managers. (Aaron declined to talk to *Newsweek*. A Braves spokesman disputed those numbers but said he "doesn't know" how many Aaron had hired.)

Plain old bigotry still exists. "The perception is that blacks can run the ball, can make the jumper but just can't do the mental work," insists Charles Farrell, a lobbyist for college and pro athletes. Concedes one team owner: "Of course there is racism. But it will change by virtue of whites and blacks being together, and the passage of time."

Some experts aren't optimistic about the pace of progress.

Lapchick remembers that when Frank Robinson was made baseball's first black manager in 1975, pundits predicted blacks would pour into those jobs. Thirteen years later, although others had come and gone, Robinson was still the only black manager. There are more hopeful signs, including the NFL front office's new coach-scouting program and internships to prepare black athletes for the business side of sports. "To me the glass is half full," says Bernie Bickerstaff, the Denver Nuggets general manager. Bickerstaff himself is a promising case: he rose from Washington Bullets assistant coach at 29 to Seattle SuperSonics head coach at 41 and landed the front-office job in 1990. "It's a question of people creating an opportunity," he says. But until owners make a concerted effort to change practices they've followed for years, successes like Bickerstaff could remain a token exception.

"With few exceptions, sports entities are dying to hire minorities."

Racism Should Not Be Blamed for the Lack of Minority Coaches and Executives

Wayne M. Barrett

Nearly five decades after Jackie Robinson became the first black baseball player in the major leagues in 1947, charges of racism continue to haunt baseball and other professional sports. One recent example of controversy is Marge Schott, owner of baseball's Cincinnati Reds, who was fined and suspended for one year by National League officials for uttering racial slurs. Some critics have said her remarks exemplify racial prejudice that prevents blacks and other minorities from gaining jobs as managers and front-office personnel. In the following viewpoint, Wayne M. Barrett questions the argument that racism prevents minority hiring. He argues that a scarcity of minority applicants with the necessary experience and willingness to take entry-level management jobs better explains the relative rarity of minorities in management positions.

As you read, consider the following questions:

1. What observations does Barrett make about Marge Schott?
2. Why does Barrett believe there are few minorities in the front offices of sports teams?

"Baseball Becomes Raceball" by Wayne M. Barrett. Reprinted from *USA Today* magazine, March 1993. Copyright 1993 by the Society for the Advancement of Education.

Racists screaming racism makes for an ugly feeding frenzy. Cincinnati Reds majority owner Marge Schott has uttered ethnic and religiously inflammatory remarks, as well as the ultimate killer word, "nigger." There has been a much-deserved uproar over her comments, which earned her a one-year suspension and a $25,000 fine. Trouble is, much of the reaction is wrong-headed and as ignorant as the woman who caused it all.

Marge Schott is a baseball owner, and a successful one. She took over a struggling franchise—the Reds were one of only two National League teams that failed to make the playoffs in the 1980s, and the club lost $4,000,000 the year before she assumed control—and turned it around. The Reds won the 1990 World Series and have produced a $40,000,000 profit over the last three seasons.

In other words, Marge Schott is a power broker—and a *minority*. Name another woman who runs a baseball franchise successfully. Powerful people like Schott, and the other 27 baseball owners, are intent on keeping their power. All threats, real and imagined, are treated as such. Businessmen, and women, are calculating cutthroats. So what? This doesn't abridge their right to free speech and free thought—no matter how appalling their outlook may be.

Same Old Arguments

Nevertheless, the same old arguments are trotted out every time some high-profile person is pinpointed as a designated bigot. Then the usual black rabble-rousers—the Jesse Jacksons, the Al Sharptons, even the Charles Rangels—start screaming to the media. Remember, Rangel called independent presidential candidate Ross Perot a "white cracker." Sharpton's black power abuses are too numerous to list. Jackson, meanwhile—even considering his New York "Hymietown" crack—does make sense sometimes, but not this time. He invaded baseball's winter meeting with high-handed boycott threats, demanding that more minorities be given front-office positions on big league clubs. What Jackson, and all those who demand quotas, refuse to understand is that, with few exceptions, sports entities are dying to hire minorities. But don't equate *qualified* with intelligence. Blacks aren't stupid, but they are inexperienced.

"Jackson does a disservice to young blacks when he tells them that blacks are not being hired to work in sports' front offices because they're black," writes *New York Post* columnist Phil Mushnick. "For Jackson to demand that sports businesses pass on the opportunity to hire a marketing exec with marketing experience in favor of an experience-less person because of skin color is to demand that people hire to the detriment of their business. That not only benefits no one, it hurts everyone.

150

"Rev. Jackson is demanding change while preaching wishful, self-serving theory instead of studied pragmatics. Change should be demanded, beginning with his message. He should demand that all minorities who show up to be interviewed for big-time front-office positions in sports come armed with a resume that points to their hard-won qualifications, and not the color of their skin."

Making Progress

Commissioners David Stern and Paul Tagliabue have been active in taking leadership roles on issues regarding race. During their respective tenures, the league offices of the NBA [National Basketball Assocation] and NFL [National Football League] have had continual increases in the number of minorities hired. Both have been active in appointing minorities for key positions within their respective offices. . . .

Of the three league offices, the NBA is leading the way in minority representation. Presently there are five vice presidents (19 percent) who are Black and three female vice presidents (12 percent). Nearly 27 percent of all management positions are held by minorities. The 44 percent of management positions held by women is by far the highest percentage in any league. Forty percent of all support staff in the league office of the NBA are minorities.

Center for the Study of Sport in Society, *1993 Racial Report Card*.

The first stop in such a corporate climb is an entry-level position, a poorly paid go-fer willing to be the first to arrive in the morning and the last to leave at night, assuming every menial task imaginable along the way. These are the young and hungry who will not be denied, and there are practically no African-Americans working in these positions, not because they were refused employment, but because they haven't applied.

Baseball has its racists, but that hasn't stopped talented black ballplayers from cashing their multi-million-dollar paychecks signed by their "racist" bosses. Admittedly, baseball has a good-old-boy buddy system, and most of the buddies are white males. So white managers are recycled, being fired by one team and eagerly hired by another. But it's the same for blacks and other minorities. Hall of Famer Frank Robinson, who is black, has managed three teams, none a first-place finisher. He'll probably manage three more. Yet, Davey Johnson, a white manager fired by the New York Mets a few seasons back, hasn't been able to land another managerial job despite the most successful reign in that team's history. His 1984-90 tenure produced a World Series title, two N.L. [National League] East Division crowns, and a club that never was eliminated from any pennant race before the final week of the season. Gee, sounds like a case of reverse discrimination. . . .

A Double Standard

The double standard is more pervasive than racism. "It is ironic that Colorado is being applauded for hiring Don Baylor, [a black] who has no managerial experience, by the same people who lambasted the Brewers when they hired Phil Garner [who is white] over Baylor last year, saying Garner had no managerial experience. [Garner took the Brewers to within a whisker of first place in his rookie campaign.] That no-experience whine also isn't being heard in Cincinnati over the hiring of [Hispanic] Tony Perez," writes baseball columnist Peter Pascarelli in *The Sporting News*.

No one is claiming that all is right on baseball's racial front. But neither should anyone be crying "foul on everyone" by maintaining there is a systematic plot afoot to keep minorities out of baseball. Salem witch hunts aren't the answer. Not to make too light of what indeed is a situation with grave overtones, recall that, during the McCarthy era of blacklisting and commie-bashing, the Cincinnati club actually was pressured by anti-Soviets to change its name from Reds, a monicker the club has carried since forming baseball's first professional team in 1869. Replied one Cincinnati executive: "Let the Communists change their name. We had it first."

Periodical Bibliography

The following articles have been selected to supplement the diverse views presented in this chapter.

Laurel R. Davis	"Protest Against the Use of Native American Mascots: A Challenge to Traditional American Identity," *Journal of Sport and Social Issues*, April 1993.
Ebony	"What's Behind the Shrinking Number of African-American Players?" June 1992.
James B. Goodno	"Fields of Broken Dreams," *Dollars & Sense*, October 1992.
Jet	"Jackson Convenes Commission to Discuss Fairness in Sports," March 22, 1993.
Sharon Richardson Jones	"Race and Baseball: Getting Beyond Business as Usual," *Journal of Sport and Social Issues*, April 1993.
Richard E. Lapchick	"Discovering Fool's Gold on the Golden Horizon," *The World & I*, October 1988.
Merlisa Lawrence	"The Silent Minorities," *Sports Illustrated*, April 5, 1993.
John Leo	"Baseball Takes a Schott," *U.S. News & World Report*, February 15, 1993.
Mike Lupica	"The Righteous Rage of Arthur Ashe," *Esquire*, October 1992.
Diane McWhorter	"The White Man's Last Stand," *The Nation*, October 8, 1990.
Scott Ostler	"Simply Black and White?" *Sport*, January 1993.
Gary A. Sailes	"The Myth of Black Sports Supremacy," *Journal of Black Studies*, June 1991. Available from Sage Publications, PO Box 504, Thousand Oaks, CA 91359-9924.
Mark Starr et al.	"Baseball's Black Problem," *Newsweek*, July 19, 1993.
Lois Tomas	"Nobody's Mascot," *Third Force*, July/August 1993.
Miki Turner	"White Girls Can't Jump: Racism in Sports Hurts Women of All Colors," *Women's Sports & Fitness*, October 1992.
Steven Waldman and Clara Bingham	"Sports, Race, and Politics," *Newsweek*, August 17, 1992.

Is Sexism a Serious Problem in Sports?

SPORTS
IN AMERICA

Chapter Preface

Women in America have historically been discouraged from participating in sports. Assumed physical limitations and questions of social impropriety once made women seem less suitable for sports than men. One example of such thinking is found in a 1929 article in *School and Society* by educator Frederick R. Rogers, who writes: "Men are more animal-like, mobile, energetic. . . . Intense forms of physical and psychic conflicts . . . tend to destroy girls' physical and psychic charm and adaptability for motherhood." Successful women athletes, such as 1932 Olympic star Babe Didrikson, were often described in unflattering terms that questioned their femininity. Teachers Jane Curry and Marjorie Bingham note that "by and large, sport has been defined as a male arena. Women's participation in sport has therefore led some to fear either the feminization of sport or the masculinization of women."

Whether women athletes still face prejudice is a matter of debate. Undeniably, however, the number of women in sports has greatly increased in the past quarter century. The number of U.S. female high school athletes rose from 294,000 in 1971 to nearly 2 million by 1991. One-third of all college athletes are women. Women athletes pursue lucrative professional careers in sports ranging from golf and tennis to beach volleyball. A major factor behind the growth of women's sports is Title IX, a 1972 law banning sex discrimination in all schools receiving federal funding. Title IX forced many high schools and colleges to take steps to equalize the support they gave to men's and women's athletic programs, which usually meant increasing the latter.

Such progress indicates to some that barriers against women in sports are falling. But sports in America "is still a right for little boys and a privilege for little girls," charges Donna Lopiano, director of the Women's Sports Foundation. Female athletes, some argue, still face barriers to social acceptance. Psychologist Mary Jo Kane found that only ten of the more than one hundred high school girls she surveyed "wanted to be remembered as a star athlete" because of fears of seeming unfeminine. Meanwhile, continued unequal funding of many men's and women's school athletic programs, despite Title IX, raises charges of a stubborn bias. "Discrimination has gone underground," argues Peggy Kellers of the National Association for Girls and Women in Sport. "No one's talking about it, no one's raising questions."

The viewpoints in this chapter examine the rise of women's sports and debate whether sexism is still a serious problem in both women's and men's sports.

"College and university presidents are [trying] . . . to ensure that our women students have opportunities to compete that meet both the spirit and the letter of Title IX obligations."

Discrimination Against Female College Athletes Is Decreasing

Thomas K. Hearn Jr.

Thomas K. Hearn Jr. is president of Wake Forest University, a private university in Winston-Salem, North Carolina, that is a member of the National Collegiate Athletic Association (NCAA). The following viewpoint is taken from a statement made before Congress in hearings held in 1993 to determine whether greater federal enforcement of Title IX was needed to ensure equality between men's and women's athletic programs. Title IX is the name for a federal law passed in 1972 which prohibited sex discrimination "in any educational program or activity receiving federal financial assistance." Hearn argues against greater government involvement, arguing that since the passage of Title IX colleges and universities have made significant progress in promoting women's athletics, and that strict enforcement measures might unfairly harm men's athletic programs.

As you read, consider the following questions:

1. How does Hearn describe the progress made toward gender equity in athletic programs at his own university?
2. Why does Hearn oppose further federal intervention?

From the testimony of Thomas K. Hearn Jr. to the Subcommittee on Commerce, Consumer Protection, and Competitiveness, Committee on Energy and Commerce, U.S. House of Representatives, February 17, 1993.

The moral issue of gender equity and its legal expression through Title IX have been given high priority by the NCAA, the Presidents' Commission of the NCAA, and other national organizations with an interest in collegiate athletics, most notably the Knight Foundation Commission on Intercollegiate Athletics. . . .

I want to affirm emphatically that college and university presidents are dealing every day with strategies to ensure that our women students have opportunities to compete that meet both the spirit and the letter of Title IX obligations. It is a leading national agenda item for the NCAA convention next January [1994]. People want to do the right thing. There is consensus on the matter of principle.

A Complex Challenge

Having affirmed the importance of the issue, we all recognize that this effort is complex and expensive in its implementation. We are faced generally with changes in opportunities for women in every segment and sector of society. Higher education and collegiate athletics must also face these changes and find solutions to open opportunities. I am convinced that colleges and universities are taking seriously their responsibilities to women student-athletes. All of us are being asked to assume the responsibility for a change involving the entire culture. Higher education must take a leadership role in that change. But changes of this magnitude are lengthy and unpredictable processes, and it is especially difficult at any point to say how much effort is enough. I hope that this does not mean that this issue will be in litigation for the future yet unforeseen, but it may.

At Wake Forest, for example, we are celebrating in 1993 the fiftieth anniversary of the admission of women as full-time students. Our enrollment is evenly balanced between women and men. Among other curriculum opportunities, we have a superb women's studies program which regularly enrolls both male and female students. Our men and women students are equally well qualified and compete evenly for academic achievements and honors. . . .

Gender equity is not just a matter of money, it is a matter of access to opportunity. This is true in sports as well as academics. However, the fact is that creating and increasing opportunities do require money, and those of us who lead universities are grappling with financial questions of crisis proportions.

Collegiate athletic programs have been in fiscal distress for some time. Of the 107 institutions in NCAA Division 1-A, 40 percent had athletic program operating deficits in 1989, which was the last reporting period. According to Ted Tow, associate executive director of the NCAA, the situation has deteriorated since that time.

Compounding this dilemma is the serious and deteriorating economic climate in which virtually all colleges and universities operate. Across the country, tax revenues have fallen, and public universities have seen major erosion of their tax support. Presidents are under mandate from State legislatures to cut costs. Almost every major public institution has had its resource base diminished, some drastically. One need only look at the huge deficits being posted by distinguished private institutions—many who have a low percentage of total budget committed to intercollegiate athletics—to know that diminishing dollars for higher education must serve a widening range of academic demands, from technology to the salaries needed to put professors in classrooms to the grim specter of deferred physical plant maintenance. In academics and athletics, what we should do forms a priority list for what we can do as funds become available.

Money Problems

The lesson here is radically at odds with the public perception of athletic departments awash in money. We built, in an environment of expanding resources, an athletic gorilla we cannot feed. This problem is complicated by the effects of recession on higher education. Television has given, and now television is taking away. How can there be new dollars for any purpose in athletics when faculty have lost salaries or jobs and the library budget has been slashed?

College and university campuses are, of course, affected in differing degrees by the quandary of allocating shrinking funds. At Wake Forest, our tuition is $12,000 annually, a relatively low figure among private schools. Because we have a historic commitment to students of less than affluent means and a need-blind admissions policy, we have been cautious about raising tuition and generous with student aid. In February 1993, our trustees approved a tuition increase of 8.3 percent, about $1,000. That increase to a still relatively low tuition figure, however, translates to $200,000 that our athletic department must add to its budget expenditures even before addressing the issues of salary increases and other operational increases. Every full athletic scholarship at Wake Forest in 1993-94 means $19,020 of revenue that must be generated by our athletic department. Obviously, at public institutions that figure is lower because tuition is lower, but because of public university budget cuts, funding full athletic scholarships remains difficult. When other educational needs are unmet, the athletic issue takes on a different cast.

Unless Wake Forest supplements athletics from academic resources, which we have not done, the athletic department must increase its revenues to cover the tuition increase, not to mention any staff salary increases or other operating increases. It means our fund-raisers must find more money from private sources. It means that we must find ways to cut costs in athletics. This comes at a time when we have just added women's field hockey scholarships at a cost of $88,000 per year and are about to add a women's soccer program at a $90,000 annual expense. Every addition of every sport requires expenditures not only for scholarships, but also for recruiting, travel, equipment, supplies, and personnel.

The questions in this fiscal climate are whether Title IX compliance can be fully realized with new revenues or by reallocating from men's programs without diminishing the quality of men's programs. The answer is a qualified "no." The qualification is added because of football programs. Some schools—those which award no athletic scholarships and those which do not have large, expensive football programs—have realized or are approaching gender equity. At Wake Forest, our athletic scholarship awards without football would approach parity, with 60 percent going to men and 40 percent to women.

Men's Football

Another widespread mistaken perception is that football, because it is a major and highly visible revenue sport, generates large profits. Unfortunately, this perception is wrong. It is an enormously expensive sport, so that profits—where they exist—are insignificant in all but a fraction of NCAA Division I-A schools.

Because of the effect of football on all sports and on the scholarship balance in particular, women advocates for progress are placed in the unwelcome position of being critics of men's sports programs. Most women with whom I have spoken about this issue don't want it to be cast in terms of reduced opportunity for men to provide opportunities for women. University presidents and athletic directors, therefore, in the councils of the NCAA, must speak up and say how we will effect cost reductions and other efficiencies to support women's athletics.

The reform movement has and will have both academic and financial concerns. We have sought to provide college sports with academic principles and fiscal responsibility. Our premise is simple: that universities must educate student athletes, all of them. Perhaps the most visible—and, I might add, controversial—changes we have advocated affect football. Spending disparities between men and women are created by Division I-A football, for which there is no comparable women's sport and in which there are comparatively large average squad sizes, huge capital investment, and daunting operating costs. We have advocated smaller squad sizes in football, reduction in the size of coaching staffs, and other changes, which can lead to expanded opportunities for other students.

Since 1964, the last year of one-platoon football, limits on football scholarships have been implemented. The first limit came in 1973, with a cap of 105 [football scholarships per school]. From 1988 to 1993, the limit went from 95 to 88, and in 1994 it will be 85 scholarships. Theoretically, these reductions should enable us to apply the needed funds to women's athletics, and in many places, including Wake Forest, that has happened. However, with the example I cited earlier regarding our tuition increase, you can see that the reduction in football scholarships doesn't even offset a moderate tuition increase. So reducing football costs alone cannot enable Division I-A institutions to meet the obligations of gender equity and Title IX.

Forces for Change

While I agree that the college athletic community will not meaningfully address sex discrimination unless it is forced to do so, [there are] many external "forces" making colleges and universities address Title IX and gender equity. One of the key factors that is "forcing" change at many institutions is simply the public scrutiny and debate over gender equity and opportunities for women. The creation of the NCAA gender equity task force and the emphasis on practical ideas for promoting Title IX compliance are making members of the college community think about the nature of the intercollegiate athletics program on their campus and ways in which opportunities for women can be enhanced, without eliminating existing opportunities for men.

In addition, student interests and demands, congressional oversight, agency enforcement of Title IX, and court orders all operate to "force" colleges and universities to address ways in which to improve the quality and offerings of their women's intercollegiate athletic programs. . . .

Whatever it once may have been, college athletics no longer is a "boys' club." Shrinking financial resources and increasing operating costs, not some effort to maintain intercollegiate athletics as an entrenched boys' club, constitute the greatest single obstacle to achieving gender equity.

Grant G. Teaff, statement before Congress, February 17, 1993.

There are efforts under way nationally, through the leadership of the NCAA, to address the issue of how we cut costs and reallocate funds to open opportunity for women in collegiate sports. There are appropriate pressures toward compliance, including the fact that gender equity will be a required standard for the NCAA certification program just adopted. The outcome will be change.

These recommendations will need to be joined with those of the Special NCAA Committee to Review Financial Conditions in Intercollegiate Athletics. Bringing down expenses is vital for all sorts of reasons including gender issues.

Cultural Change

The NCAA Gender Equity Task Force, for example, is also examining other recommendations which go deeper into the cultural change required. These will include better marketing and publicity strategies for women's revenue sports, so that those programs can pay for themselves and provide additional revenue. Only women's basketball is currently approaching the kind of success we envision. In 1993, for example, I am told that the University of Virginia sold 8,000 season tickets for its women's basketball program. Women's volleyball holds a realistic prospect of becoming a revenue sport, along with soccer.

But as American industry has learned, this is an era of restraint. . . .

These efforts are good faith evidence of our intent to allocate resources to open opportunities to women. People in higher education want to do what is right.

There are, of course, ways to help open opportunity that are cost-free. The scheduling of practice times in arenas or fields shared by men's and women's teams can become a battleground between and among coaches. Leadership from athletic directors and presidents can ensure that use of facilities is allocated fairly. Marketing and publicity dollars can be reallocated, and a new distribution of existing resources can be made without new expenditures.

You asked me to answer three questions. . . .

1. Is the fight about gender equity in sports just a matter of money?

Gender equity is much more than a matter of money. It is a matter of opportunity and a moral issue. However, to open the opportunities required by Title IX, major funding is necessary. Because of the recent recession, many colleges and universities face the most devastating fiscal conditions experienced since the Great Depression. Athletic department budgets were already in a crisis situation before the recession.

Forty percent of NCAA Division I-A athletic programs reported operating deficits in 1989, and the situation has deteriorated since then. The costs of ensuring gender equity are therefore a matter of serious concern to those who lead institutions of higher education. "Just a matter of money" implies a quick fix. Finding the money is an issue that requires careful and well-planned actions.

Are there enough revenues to provide increased opportunities for women athletes without a negative effect on men's sports funding levels?

The answer is a qualified "no." At institutions without major football programs or without athletic scholarships, compliance is somewhat easier to achieve, and many of those institutions have achieved it.

But for other colleges and universities, especially those with expensive major football programs, considerable additional revenues will be required. Reducing opportunities for men might be viewed as the only viable option.

By NCAA ruling, men's programs must already reduce scholarships by 10 percent across the board by 1994, with the intent of having the money saved designated for women's sports. Reductions in men's sports are already being made and further changes will doubtless be considered.

2. Have college and university presidents played a strong enough role in bringing about equal opportunities for women in college sports? . . .

At the institutional level, many schools, under the leadership of their presidents, have already assured equitable opportunities for women. At other institutions, presidents are searching for the best ways to bring about gender equity. I believe that, yes, college and university presidents are giving strong leadership in this issue.

3. The executive director of the NCAA testified at the April 9, 1992, Title IX hearing that gender equity would be placed on the front burner. In your opinion, has this happened? Is further Federal intervention needed to make gender equity a reality?

Yes, gender equity is a primary issue in the NCAA. The priority given to Title IX in the task forces and committees attest its importance. Gender equity will be a required standard for the NCAA certification program just adopted.

Federal Intervention Is Unnecessary

No, Federal intervention is not the answer to making gender equity a reality. Athletic departments that are now working hard to cut costs so that dollars can be reallocated to support women's athletic programs would probably have to add personnel and would incur other costs if such intervention occurred. State legislatures, too, are bringing pressures to bear on university presidents, so that Federal intervention would be redundant.

What is needed is the appropriate time to study the issues and formulate recommended action plans. . . .

The process for change is already under way. Federal intervention now would be redundant.

"Glaring inequities between women's and men's school sports are common—and illegal."

Female College Athletes Still Face Widespread Discrimination

Kathleen Sharp

The passage of Title IX by Congress in 1972 prohibiting sex discrimination in educational institutions has greatly affected college and high school women's athletics. The money and support for women's athletic programs has risen sharply, and the number of females participating in organized sports has exploded. However, many critics charge that women's athletic programs still receive less support than men's programs. In the following viewpoint, Kathleen Sharp maintains that women athletes face a struggle in enforcing the provisions of Title IX. In response, a growing number of them are suing schools and athletic departments for sex discrimination. Sharp is a special correspondent for the *Los Angeles Times*, and has written for *Elle*, *Parade*, and other magazines.

As you read, consider the following questions:

1. What examples of sex discrimination does Sharp describe?
2. How have women responded to discrimination in recent years, according to the author?
3. What points does Sharp make about men's football programs?

"Foul Play" by Kathleen Sharp, *Ms.*, September/October 1993. Reprinted by permission of *Ms.* Magazine, © 1993.

The game is tied and Cori Close dribbles the ball, racing for the basket while searching for an open teammate. Her players close in instinctively, but each is covered by defense. Then, like a lazy eye, teammate Sasha Scardino wanders to the side. Without a glance, Close passes to Scardino, who sinks a three-pointer.

When the buzzer signals the game's end, the small, rabid crowd goes bonkers. Close, Scardino, and the women's team at the University of California, Santa Barbara, have won yet another game, despite a skeleton staff, a sliver of a budget, and a low profile. Although the men's Gaucho team is richer, and more visible, the "Lady" Gauchos rely on an uncanny, extrasensory style.

"With us, it's not about how much one person can score," said Close. "It's about working together. The more we rely on all parts of our bodies—our legs, our eyes, our hearts—the better we get."

In the 1992 season the team was among the best in the West. In four years, it climbed from the bottom of the league to the top, winning the prestigious Big West Tournament in 1992 and 1993. It has gone on to win the first round of the National Collegiate Athletics Association (NCAA) Tournament—the nation's top play-offs.

Off-Court Challenges

Off the court, the team's challenges are more daunting. The women ride buses to most games—some of which are 12 hours away. On one grueling weekend during final exams, as the women traveled 350 miles to play the first of three games, their bus broke down on a snowy mountain pass. By contrast, the male Gauchos, who have never won the Big West championship and haven't made the NCAA play-offs for three years, fly to many of their games and stay comfortably in hotels.

The women's coach, Mark French, is paid about $33,000—less than half the salary of Jerry Pimm, the head coach of the male Gauchos. French's full-time assistant works additional jobs to eke out a living. The men's team is coddled by five well-paid staff members.

Glaring inequities between women's and men's school sports are common—and illegal. Two decades after Title IX of the Education Amendments was passed to eliminate sex discrimination, the women's field is riddled with potholes. In the last three years [since 1990], a growing corps of women have complained to deans, filed formal complaints with the Office of Civil Rights, and exhausted all "proper" channels to uphold the law. Now, these women are suing Ivy League schools, big college football powers, and respected state universities. In almost every case women are winning. Said Judy Sweet, former NCAA president: "Women are getting fed up."

Title IX prohibits schools that receive federal funds from discriminating against students on the basis of gender. Under the law, female athletes are required to receive the same opportunities extended to men. That means if female students make up 50 percent of the student body, they must make up 50 percent of varsity slots, or the school must demonstrate that it is meeting the level of interest of women athletes or has a history of expanding women's programs.

Open Discrimination

In my professional opinion, intercollegiate athletics in our nation's universities are openly discriminating against women in participation opportunities, the provision of educational opportunities via athletic scholarships and the employment of coaches and administrators. Few if any institutions of higher education, or high schools for that matter, are complying with Title IX of the 1972 Education Amendments Act.

Donna A. Lopiano, statement before Congress, February 17, 1993.

The nation's schools had six years to comply with the new standards. At first, the number of women's teams exploded, so that by 1978 women accounted for 33 percent of the nation's college athletes. "Unfortunately, that's where we've remained for the last fifteen years," said Donna Lopiano, executive director of the Women's Sports Foundation (WSF). Although 53 percent of college students today are female, they occupy only 34 percent of athletic slots. When Lopiano testified before Congress, she didn't mince words: "Intercollegiate athletics in our nation's universities are openly discriminating against women."

Violating Title IX

In fact, from kindergarten to college most schools are currently in violation of Title IX. "You pick a school and I'll bet it's in violation," said Kathryn Reith, WSF assistant director. But school administrators tend to resist addressing their Title IX problems. "There's a lot of fear out there, especially in athletic departments where men's sports are sacrosanct," said Diane Henson, a lawyer who litigates sex discrimination cases. Added Ellen Vargyas, senior counsel of the National Women's Law Center: "There's a firm conviction that women's sports are not as good, lucrative, or important as men's. Somehow, men's teams are more valuable, financially and cosmically."

Female athletes have long understood this reality. But it wasn't until 1992, when the NCAA released its benchmark study of gender equity, that the rest of us started to understand the extent of the problems. The survey found that:

- Men make up nearly 70 percent of students who play in top-level college sports.
- Female athletes receive less than a third of all college scholarships.
- Women's teams receive only 23 percent of school athletic budgets.
- Men's teams receive five times more money to recruit new members.
- Coaches of men's teams are paid 81 percent more than coaches of women's teams.

With fewer resources and opportunities, it's more difficult for women to succeed in college sports, said Vargyas. Male sports directors argue that the numbers are imbalanced because few women want to play college sports. According to Vargyas: "That's like a Southerner in the 1950s saying African Americans don't like to ride in the front of the bus."

Cultural Stereotypes

Indeed, the resistance to Title IX goes to the heart of our cultural stereotypes regarding the proper roles of women and men. Nowhere is this concept more entrenched than at schools with large football programs. Take the University of Texas, where women make up 47 percent of students but only 23 percent of the athletes. "And this is for a school that's known for its top women's varsity teams," said Henson, who represented female plaintiffs at Texas.

In July 1992, athletes on the Texas women's crew, gymnastics, softball, and soccer clubs sued the school and asked it to upgrade their teams to varsity level. The school objected, claiming that it was meeting women's interest in sports and that female athletes were underrepresented because the men's football program is so big and popular. By law, that excuse is no defense. Yet it underscores one of the great myths in the Title IX debate. "Men like to claim that football makes money, so they can't possibly cut those programs," said Henson. "But more often than not, football loses money." Still, nostalgic alumni tend to treat college pigskin programs like a golden goose, when it's more of a white elephant.

Texas' football program makes money, although it depends heavily on university funds and alumni donations. "These guys spend money like there's no tomorrow," said Henson. Country club dues, cars, and other perks are given to the football team's staff. The men's athletic department spent $167,000 on mahogany office furniture and redecorating. That money probably didn't contribute much to athletic performance and it could have funded a women's soccer team, said Henson. The men's athletic department also has a $5 million "rainy day" account. "I told them their rainy day was about to arrive," she said. Henson won a settlement that will double women's sports participation over the next three years.

The Slighting of Women's Sports

At the university level, equity in sports is regarded as something of a joke. Nationwide, female college athletes routinely get a third of the team spots, less than a third of the scholarship dollars and a mere fifth of the total athletic budget. . . .

Fewer than ever female student athletes enter careers in physical education, and leadership ranks are shrinking. In 1972 women coached more than 90 percent of college women's sports teams and headed nearly all women's college athletic programs. Female coaches today head less than a quarter of all teams. Female athletic directors, at 16 percent, are practically an endangered species.

Susan L. Morse, *CQ Researcher*, March 6, 1992.

Most of the Title IX cases involve women's club teams simply seeking varsity team status, which would mean the school would devote substantial resources to their teams. In 1992, however, the Supreme Court ruled that women can also sue for monetary damages as part of their Title IX rights. In June 1993, a Washington, D.C., jury awarded Howard University basketball coach Sonya Tyler $2.4 million (later reduced by a judge to $1.1 million) in her sex discrimination suit against the school. Now, the specter of large financial penalties hangs over offending institutions, many of which are already strapped for cash. Still, based on pending Title IX litigation, it appears most schools would rather fight than comply:

• In April 1990, female hockey players sued Colgate University because it had repeatedly denied the club team varsity status. Women paid for their own gear, uniforms, and transportation—unlike the varsity men. In September 1992, U.S. magistrate David N. Hurd ordered Colgate to elevate the women's team to varsity status. "The men's hockey players are treated as princes while the women are treated as chimney sweeps," he said. Colgate appealed. This spring [1993], the appeals court declared the case moot because all the female plaintiffs were about to graduate.

• In June 1992, Colorado State University cut its NCAA Division I women's varsity softball team, along with men's baseball. The women sued, claiming that Colorado didn't give women equal opportunities. In February 1993, the court ordered Colorado to reinstate the women's team, a decision that was upheld on appeal.

• After Brown University cut its women's gymnastics and volleyball teams, players sued to restore their teams to varsity status. In December 1992, the court ordered the Ivy League school to reinstate the teams. Brown got a temporary stay, which delayed implementation of the court's order. Brown then appealed. In April 1993, the appeals court upheld the stay and remanded the case to lower court for trial.

• At Auburn University, the women's soccer club has for years requested varsity status. The women must practice on a half-sized, poorly kept field they share with a rugby team. "Two players have already suffered injuries because of holes in the field," said plaintiffs' attorney Nancy Ryan. Auburn, located in rural Alabama, has plenty of fields for men's baseball and football, but the school won't let the women play on them, added Ryan.

In October 1992, one of the women filed a complaint with the Office of Civil Rights, which found Auburn in noncompliance after a lengthy investigation. In April the club filed a class action suit, which was settled the following month when the university agreed to institute a varsity soccer program in the fall of 1993.

Legal Battles

These legal cases reflect poorly on educators and officials, who waste thousands of dollars to thwart the legal rights of young female athletes, say Title IX advocates. "These 18-year-old women are not only attending school and succeeding in sports, they're taking on the most powerful institutions in their lives," said Patricia Flannery, an attorney who has worked on Title IX cases. Added Ryan, "Enforcing the law is falling on the shoulders of these young women."

The Auburn women have enjoyed widespread campus support, but that's not the case on all campuses. For example, after publicly voicing her concerns about Title IX problems, Harvard lacrosse coach Carole Kleinfelder found her car tires slashed. At California State University (CSU) at Fullerton, women's volleyball coach Jim Huffman lost his job after he successfully sued to reinstate his varsity team. At CSU's San Diego campus, women's volleyball coach Rudy Suwara was fired when he lobbied for more money for all school women's programs. His wrongful termination suit seeks $1 million in damages.

Perhaps Title IX problems wouldn't be so rampant if more women headed big athletic departments. Yet, of the 107 schools in the NCAA's top division, only two employ a female athletic director who oversees both men's and women's athletics. Employment discrimination in college athletics is strong but subtle, said Lopiano. "Single women are assumed to be lesbians or women with children are thought to have too many responsibilities."

Lately, Title IX has reverberated beyond the university walls. In February 1993, the California chapter of the National Organization for Women sued the entire CSU system, claiming that the system has "actually regressed from gender equity since 1978." But for every suit filed by women, there are legions of girls fighting for the chance to play on a team. In small grammar and high schools, few students even know about Title IX, let alone understand their rights.

One Story of Perseverance

One exception is Misty Allen of Alabama. She attended a rural, predominantly black high school in Talladega County that funded boys' football, track, basketball, and baseball teams but nothing for girls. On her own, Allen formed a girls' basketball team, which was funded and coached by volunteers and parents. After its first season, the principal, John Stamps, cut the team, complaining he had to pay for referees.

Through Allen, the WSF explained the law to Stamps. In short order, he reinstated the team, which eventually placed in a regional tournament. However, weeks before the play-off, he gave the wrong game date to the coach, which caused the team to forfeit its game and lose the championship, said WSF's Reith. On top of that, Stamps made the girls pay the $500 forfeiture fine. Who can explain such meanness to girls who fought for a chance to learn a game their brothers take for granted?

Despite their geographic distances, the girls in Alabama share much with the women in Texas, New York, and California. They are being squashed by mostly male teachers and administrators who don't seem to understand what it really means to be a sport: to value honor, fairness, and graceful acceptance of results—win, lose, or draw. "It benefits all of society to teach both men *and women* about teamwork, competition, and cooperation," said basketball player Cori Close. "That's the only way to play." To instill that lesson in only half of our society is to hobble us from participating fully in life's larger contests. And that way, we all lose.

"In contemporary Western culture . . . sport . . . ritualizes aggression and allows it to be linked with competitive achievement and . . . masculinity."

Sport Promotes Negative Male Values

David Whitson

Sport has been criticized by some for fostering negative social values, including values that define male/female roles. One such critic is David Whitson, a professor of the sociology of sport at the University of Alberta in Edmonton, Canada, and author of numerous articles on gender and sport in academic journals. In the following viewpoint, he describes how sport is used in the socializing of boys to teach concepts of masculinity. Some of the socializing sport engenders involves the denigrating of women, Whitson asserts, which he believes is the reason many men strongly oppose the rise of women's athletics.

As you read, consider the following questions:

1. How is the link between sports and masculinity made, according to Whitson?
2. Why are some men threatened by the growing presence of women in sports, according to the author?
3. What suggestions does Whitson make concerning boys, girls, and sports?

From "Sport in the Social Construction of Masculinity" by David Whitson. In *Sport, Men, and the Gender Order: Critical Feminist Perspectives* (pp. 19-29), M.A. Messner and D.F. Sabo, eds. Champaign, IL: Human Kinetics Publishers. Copyright 1990 by Don Sabo, Ph.D. and Michael Messner, Ph.D. Adapted and reprinted by permission.

Sport has become, it is fair to suggest, one of the central sites in the social production of masculinity in societies characterized by longer schooling and by a decline in the social currency attached to other ways of demonstrating physical prowess (e.g., physical labour or combat). Indeed, demonstrating the physical and psychological attributes associated with success in athletic contests has now become an important requirement for status in most adolescent and preadolescent male peer groups. Boys who are good at sports have happily profited from this fact and often come to think of it as natural. Meanwhile, other boys—small or awkward boys, scholarly or artistic boys, boys who get turned off from sports (or who never develop any interest in sports)—have to come to their own terms with sport and find other ways to stake their claims to masculinity. . . .

This viewpoint seeks to explore the place of sport in the social construction of masculinity. Two main lines of argument will be developed. The first emphasizes connections between manliness and the body. . . . Second, it will be argued that sport . . . has served as an important site in the construction of male solidarity, an institution that encourages men to identify with other men and provides for the regular rehearsal of such identifications. It is proposed that together, these dynamics point to a powerful role for sport in the reproduction of male hegemony.

Masculinity, Manliness, and the Body

Our concern in this section is with how masculinity is constructed in a society and how the particular way of being male that we know as manliness has achieved and maintained its privileged position in Western societies. Arguably, sport has played an important part in this, at least since the middle of the 19th century. Analyses of the prominent place of sport in the programmes of the elite English boys' schools are replete with references to manliness and to official belief in the capacity of sport to "turn boys into men.". . . Meanwhile, in America, the founders of the playground movement were making a somewhat different but not dissimilar case for organized sports in teaching boys (this time working-class boys) to be appropriate kinds of men.

Several themes recur in this literature that are appropriate to our own discussion. The first is the equation of physical prowess with moral strength. In the "muscular Christianity" espoused by the leading English headmasters and their counterparts abroad, athletic fields were places where the development of physical presence, stoic courage in the endurance of pain, and judgement under pressure was portrayed as simply part of the achievement of manhood. The second theme is a clear concern to maximize and (among men) to celebrate the differences between men and women. This underlines Ian Craib's observation that masculinity is often organized not as a positive construct but rather as that which is "not feminine, or, more bluntly, not effeminate.". . .

Finally, it is important to register just how much time, effort, and institutional support is given over to *masculinizing practices*. It is also important to understand just how much urgency is usually attached to the success or failure of such projects—by parents and indeed by the boys themselves. What such effort and concern immediately belie is any notion of biological destiny. If boys simply grew into men and that was that, the efforts described to teach boys how to be men would be redundant. We can suggest, then, that "becoming a man" is something that boys (and especially adolescent boys) work at. We can also suggest, however, that although this work takes place in the context of considerable pressures from adults and peers alike, a personal way of being a man must be constructed out of each boy's own body and desires. Indeed, R.W. Connell suggests that for some years, as the adolescent tries out different ways of being himself, there is much unsettled about the kind of man he will become. . . .

Sport and Feminist Ideals

Although participation in sport may possess the potential to empower women, many scholars have argued that sport is male-dominated and perpetuates patriarchal power and privilege. Uncritical acceptance of these male structures and values contributes to the oppression of women participants. Moreover, feminists associate the form of competition found in male-controlled sport settings with such patriarchal values as aggression, power, and domination. An overemphasis on competition and winning may instill values in women that run counter to feminist ideals.

Elaine M. Blinde et al., *Journal of Sport and Social Issues*, April 1993.

This leads us, then, to the importance of the body (and how we come to know our bodies) in the formation of gender identity, and from there to the importance of sport, especially in the childhood and adolescent years. Maurice Merleau-Ponty has presented the fullest argument that our experiences of our bodies are central to our senses of who we are and how we relate to the world and thereby to other people. However, Connell, in an important argument that body sense is crucial to the development of male identity, suggests that to learn to be a male is to learn to project a physical presence that speaks of latent power. He argues that sport is empowering for many young males precisely because it teaches us how to use our own bodies to produce effects and because it teaches us how to achieve power through practiced combinations of force and skill.

Certainly Michael Oriard's discussion of the importance of football in his (and his friends') learning to be a man illustrates the force of the belief that "what it means to be masculine is, quite literally, to embody force, to embody competence." Especially among adolescent males, for whom other sources of recognized masculine authority (based on earning power, adult sexual relations, or fatherhood) are some ways off, the development of body appearance and body language that are suggestive of force and skill is experienced as an urgent task. This explains boys' embarrassment at weakness or lack of coordination as well as the energy they invest in many forms of exercise, in cults of physicality and martial arts, and especially in sport.

The Empowerment Experience

It is worth observing that the experience of force and skill coming together, however briefly, in the long home run, the perfectly hit golf shot, the crosscourt backhand, or "flow" in a cross-country run, is a great part of what makes sport so popular. Such moments afford enormous satisfaction and pleasure, even to the normally moderate athlete, and indeed to the spectator who understands and appreciates what has been achieved. The experience of empowerment, however temporary, is captured by former hockey player Eric Nesterenko as quoted by Studs Terkel:

> You wheel and dive and turn, and you can lay yourself into impossible angles that you never could walking or running. You lay yourself out at a forty-five degree angle, your elbows virtually touching the ice . . . Incredible! It's beautiful! You're breaking the grounds of gravity.

Nesterenko is talking here about how much he loved the physicality of sport, and arguably it is precisely this physicality, this potential for the sensuous experiencing of strength and skill, that makes many kinds of sport (including the noncompetitive pursuit of sports like swimming and skiing) so appealing, especially among those whose daily lives do not otherwise afford such experiences of completeness and competence.

If Merleau-Ponty and Connell are right, then, in contending that our sense of who we are is firmly rooted in our experiences of embodiment, it is integral to the reproduction of gender relations that boys are encouraged to experience their bodies, and therefore themselves, in forceful, space-occupying, even dominating ways. It may be suggested that masculinizing and feminizing practices associated with the body are at the heart of the social construction of masculinity and femininity and that this is precisely why sport matters in the total structure of gender rela-

173

tions. We are suggesting that assertiveness and confidence, as ways of relating to others, become embodied through the development of strength and skill and through prevailing over opponents in competitive situations. Conversely, I. Young argues that the exclusion of women from sport has historically denied girls these kinds of formative experiences, with the result that their embodied senses of self were more likely to be awkward, fragile, and diffident.

Certainly the movement of women into many kinds of sports (though not so much into confrontational sports like football) has rendered this now less true as a description of women. However, arguably, even though there are today many women who achieve particular combinations of force and skill much more effectively than do many men, the persistence of "normal" differences in empowerment remains "one of the main ways in which the superiority of men becomes 'naturalized,'" writes R.W. Connell. Moreover, the regular opportunities for the celebration of male superiority that are afforded by "Monday Night Football" or by "Hockey Night in Canada" may be especially important for men who feel threatened by contemporary changes in gender relations.

This comment leads us finally to the question of why men have been so defensive about the entry of women into sport.

Exclusion and Membership

A male cliff diver quoted by Lois Bryson explained, "This is a death-defying activity—the men are taking a great gamble to prove their courage. What would be the point if everyone saw that a woman could do the same?" At one level, the refusal of Mexican cliff divers to compete in an Acapulco competition unless an American woman (who had qualified for the final in preliminary competitions) was forced to withdraw is self-explanatory. A proving ground for masculinity can only be preserved as such by the exclusion of women from the activity. Yet the adamant, almost desperate quality of some men's reactions requires further exploration.

One starting point is to suggest that such reactions simply reproduce the Victorian concern with maximizing the differences between men and women; little has changed, in other words. The realities, of course, are that much has changed on the terrain of gender relations and that male dominance has been and is being challenged on a great many fronts. Eric Dunning has proposed, in this respect, that male hegemony is strengthened to the extent that fighting skills and physical prowess are honoured in a society and that men have their own social institutions whereas women do not. Conversely, he argues, male advantages are eroded when society is pacified and when segregation of the

174

sexes breaks down. If this analysis is astute, and I suggest that it is, it becomes easy to see why men who are threatened by these larger changes in gender relations talk loudly about the importance of all-male institutions and defend the importance of confrontation in "men's games.". . .

Erosion of Male Companionship in Sport

However, another aspect of the breakdown of segregation in sport invites fuller consideration. This is the significance of the erosion of sport as a site of specifically male companionship, which allows boys to be with boys and men with men and which allows men to initiate boys into traditions men have shared and enjoyed. The latter occurs in the conscious and institutionalized ways captured in Gary Alan Fine's account of the "specifically didactic roles" that some Little League coaches see for themselves. It occurs, of course, in the masculinizing practices of schools. . . . All such efforts, as masculinizing projects, would be scrambled by the presence of girls on boys' teams.

Sports, Machismo, and Violence

Some experts point out that violence in sports is almost exclusively a male behavior. They associate it with *machismo*, the exaggerated sense of masculine pride. Defeat is seen as a severe blow to *machismo*, and resorting to violence in athletic contests is thought to be a way of protecting one's pride and manhood.

Many athletes have a double standard as regards morality in sports and in everyday life. As one high school basketball player put it, "In life . . . there are so many people to think about. . . . In sports you're free to think about yourself." This self-centeredness is considered necessary in athletes who are playing to win.

While competing, some athletes tend to think of the opposing team members as not merely opponents who are human beings just like themselves but as enemies. This reduces their sense of responsibility; it releases them from the usual demands of morality. Hurting the "enemy" to get him out of the game or using intimidation to interfere with his performance becomes acceptable behavior. In any other area of life, those same athletes would consider such acts as immoral. But in sports, they feel, anything goes—as long as it helps to win the game or to come in first in the race.

Gilda Berger, *Violence in Sports*, 1990.

Yet initiation also occurs in more personal and warmly remembered ways, which are alluded to in Bryson's analysis of the messages of a popular Australian commercial in which a father is taking his son to an important match. The father and son are depicted as doing something male together, and the boy, it is suggested, is especially delighted that his Dad is taking him, however briefly, into the world of men. That such a commercial resonates with the experiences of many men and boys is attested to by Oriard's discussion of what it meant to him to watch football with his father and by Fred Inglis's discussions of fathers sharing sports talk with their sons and other men. Inglis suggests that what is happening in such exchanges is the sharing of men's emotional responses and judgements and the initiation of the boy into a male language and into male traditions. In these traditions, however, heroism and community are rendered concrete in ways that encourage male bonding and encourage the exclusion of women from the brotherhood of those who can understand.

With respect to the bonding that can occur among male teammates, many have written lyrically about the comradeship and intimacy that can develop as men come to depend upon one another in a shared quest. Certainly, this kind of solidarity and companionship is a rare enough experience in modern life. Nesterenko, described in Studs Terkel's book *Working*, suggests that the intimacy he experienced on a successful team is not something he has been able to find elsewhere; men who have known this naturally treasure such memories and are uneasy about that which might alter or threaten the possibilities of such intimacy. What is really threatened by the entry of women into male preserves is opportunities for men to rehearse their ties as men and reaffirm their differences from women. For certainly women have forged strong bonds with one another in their own athletic quests, and men and women have known solidarity together when other struggles (e.g., labor strikes) have underlined their common interests rather than their differences.

Effects of Social Practices on Sport

It is important, in this respect, to recognize the effects on men (as well as women) of some of the social practices that surround sport, for these social practices as well as the physical practices described previously together constitute sport as a social institution. Professional athletes' accounts of the practice of "shooting beaver" and other similar antics in this all-male subculture, as well as Dunning's more scholarly account of the misogynist and homophobic songs and jokes that are part of the tradition surrounding English rugby, serve as pointed reminders that much that is described as male comradeship has its darker side. It demeans and objectifies women, and it enforces and reinforces a certain standard of masculinity (i.e., aggressive, dominating, or "macho") among men.

John Thompson has pointed, here, to the role that humour can play in rehearsing in-group solidarity, in objectifying and demeaning "the other," and in deterring potential deviants or sympathizers. It would be difficult to deny that locker-room humour, and indeed the sexist humour that dominates many all-male environments, has served all of these functions. Certainly the accounts of Dunning, Fine, and others all suggest that sport as a male preserve remains a bastion of reaction, in which traditional masculinity is celebrated and other kinds of masculinity are disparaged and deterred. In such circumstances, Don Sabo suggests that we need to ask ourselves the following:

> Does the risk of ridicule lead some males to develop a more exploitative attitude toward dating, sex, and women? . . . Do male athletes learn to downplay love and relationships and how much they need and care about women? What sort of customs or rituals serve to put women down while solidifying male supremacist bonds? . . .

In contemporary Western culture, arguably, sport (and especially confrontational team games) ritualizes aggression and allows it to be linked with competitive achievement and, in turn, with masculinity. Following both Connell and Dunning, we can suggest that sport has become one of the most important sites of masculinizing practice in cultures (and within classes) in which other kinds of physical prowess have become devalued and in which direct aggression is officially illegitimate. Yet two points need to be noted.

Sports and Power

First, the promotion of other sports ranging from racquet sports to running and swimming to wilderness sports and even skateboarding affords many new opportunities for the development of strength and skill—in other words, for empowerment. These opportunities are open, moreover, to people who do not typically shine in confrontational team games, to smaller men, and to women; this has broadened the recognized boundaries of masculinity (e.g., to include the boy whose claim to masculinity is asserted through achievement as a diver or a climber). Beyond this, the demonstrable achievements of women in such sports, indeed the presence of women in sport, have helped to weaken the popular association between sport and masculinity pointed to by Bryson.

At the same time, though, the continued place we accord to confrontational team games in our hierarchy of sports, and the continued acclaim we accord to the men who shine in them, mean that these games continue to offer important opportunities for masculinizing practices, in the politicized sense outlined here.

The major games, in other words, continue as institutions through which the reproduction of hegemonic masculinity, and through this, male hegemony, are actively pursued. To apply

Dunning's framework, these games are typically institutions in which physical strength and fighting skills are celebrated, in which male solidarity (and especially solidarity among aggressive, dominating males) is also celebrated, and which therefore reinforce constraints on boys' experimenting with other ways of being male.

What are the implications of all of this for men? To begin with, it is necessary to affirm the value of sport and to celebrate the sense of confirmation and empowerment that is afforded by the embodiment of strength and skill in a perfectly executed dive, as well as the mutual understanding and teamwork that are experienced in a good team. These things are too widely known among men for us to deny them, even if we wished to. However, if we want to open a constructive dialogue with the many men for whom sport has been a formative (and positive) experience, it is important not to come across as "sport bashers."

At the same time, though, it is necessary to insist that these positive experiences are not for men alone and that sport not be used as a kind of initiation into a male tribe. This will make the kinds of empowering experiences that sport affords more readily available to women, at the same time that men will come to appreciate the companionship of women in task-oriented situations. Most importantly, though, I. Young writes, "the mere entry of women into sport in greater numbers—even into masculinist sport—will begin to break down the masculinist meaning of sport." And this is something that will benefit many (though not all) men, as well as women. A corollary of this, though, is that it is necessary to deconstruct the connection between empowerment and domination. We need to introduce boys and girls alike to the empowering experiences of skill and strength that are offered in many kinds of nonconfrontative sports, and we need to celebrate these more than we do fighting skills.

"Sport participation [has] tremendous potential for being self-actualizing, self-empowering . . . and greatly enjoyable. This is . . . especially true for [women]."

Sport Promotes Positive Social Values

Gail Whitaker

Some critics of sport have castigated it for promoting violence, a win-at-all-costs attitude, and other negative social values. Some feminists, equating sport with the worst aspects of masculinity, have questioned whether women should even attempt to achieve equality in this area. In the following viewpoint, Gail Whitaker, a professor of physical education at San Francisco State University, argues that sport can be pursued in ways consistent with humane and feminist values, and that sport has many positive characteristics, including the empowerment of women.

As you read, consider the following questions:

1. What are some of the positive dimensions of sport that Whitaker describes?
2. Between what two opposing views of women and sport does Whitaker try to find a middle ground?
3. What should be the primary focus of sport, according to the author?

The traditionally male-dominated world of sport has recently begun attracting larger numbers of girls and women than ever before. Youth sport programs, secondary school and collegiate programs, adult recreational programs, and Olympic and professional competition are all experiencing an increase in female participation. Some feminist observers have viewed this trend with suspicion, citing the tendency of contemporary American sport to exhibit and reflect values that are inconsistent with feminist principles. It is all too common in today's sport world for physical aggressiveness to escalate into violence, psychological aggressiveness into hostility toward opponents, and competitiveness into a callous preoccupation with outcome, or "winning at all costs." In our lust for success and our covetousness of the physical prowess that we associate with it, we Americans often tolerate brutality and idolize savage bullies. Moreover, our money-brokers have succeeded in capitalizing on the spectacle of cruel conquest and tragic defeat, turning much of the sport world into the big business of public entertainment, which benefits a few by exploiting many more.

Dimensions of Sport

If we accept the notion that participation in sport automatically implies complicity with hostile, dehumanizing, even violent attempts to dominate and subdue other people at all costs, it will be difficult at best to promote such participation by women or indeed anyone with any degree of social, much less feminist, consciousness. My contention, however, is that sport participation need not involve deplorable human behavior. Rather, I argue that sport also lends itself to a more humanistic approach that is consistent with feminist values of self-actualization and empowerment, mutual respect and affirmation, and emotional and expressive freedom. Inherently, "generically" if you will, sport has dimensions that offer exciting possibilities for self-enrichment without exploitative side effects. Following are some of these dimensions.

Competence   The ability to do something well—through talent or hard work or simply a lot of repetition to accomplish a level of skill at something that we are proud of—is pleasurable, fulfilling, maybe even necessary. Performance excellence engenders a sense of personal excellence that in large part defines our self-concept and our self-worth; we view ourselves largely as functions of what we can do. Competence, then, is vital to a strong self-concept.

Sport involves challenging skills and provides opportunities to develop, exercise, and demonstrate competence in those skills. Furthermore, it does this in a wide range of settings. In sport one can cultivate competence on ice, under water, on a mountainside, or in free fall if one wishes. This variety in sport permits the development of a medley of skills, so that it is a potential source of competence for virtually everyone.

Limitation   Rarely in the everyday world are we pushed to the limit either physically, intellectually, or emotionally. We can easily go through most of our lives without locating—much less extending—the boundaries of what we can do. Sport is attractive in that it allows us to test ourselves, to define and expand our personal limits. It pushes us to the edge; it asks us to give, and allows us to discover, our best efforts. It provides a realistic assessment of what we can and cannot do, and a means of experiencing and overcoming the forces that act to restrain us.

The 10 Most Popular Girls' Sports

Sport	*Number of participants*
Basketball	387,802
Track and field (outdoor)	320,763
Volleyball	300,810
Softball (fast-pitch)	219,464
Tennis	132,607
Soccer	121,722
Cross-country	106,514
Swimming and diving	88,122
Field hockey	48,384
Golf	41,410

Source: *National Federation of State High School Associations*, 1990-91 Sports Participation Survey.

As Warren Fraleigh points out in his discussion of necessity, we are limited in sport not only by the laws of physics, but also by forms of motor inability and by artificially imposed restrictions on movement choices. Many children enjoy experimenting with swings, seesaws, sliding boards, and bicycles as they learn how to work with momentum, leverage, friction, and gravity. Even without knowing the words, they can experience the physical causes and effects dictated by those laws. In addition, in sport we encounter the limits imposed by fatigue, stress, injury, and insufficient skill, as well as by narrowed ranges of allowable movement patterns due to restrictive rules. Everywhere there is limitation coupled with opportunity, and this affords us a measure of ourselves that is available in precious few of life's arenas.

Personal Expression   Our need to be unique and to express that uniqueness runs deep, whether the medium of expression is words, music, clothing, art, or movement. Sport serves as such a medium in two ways. First, it provides us with the opportunity to express sides of our personality that we have little chance to reveal elsewhere. A clear example is our instrumentalism. Although sport need not, I believe, be exclusively instrumental, it certainly holds appeal for those who wish to be more instrumental, and its instrumentality need not be carried to exploitative extremes. It also allows us in an otherwise nonphysical life to be physical, in a noncompetitive life to be competitive, and in a routine life to be adventurous and strategic. In short, it can compensate for what we may find missing elsewhere in our experiences.

A Chance to Be Different

Second, sport provides us with a chance to be different, to express our individuality by placing the personal stamp of our own style on our activities. Our uniqueness is expressed in our choice of sport—tennis or softball, mountain climbing or bowling, volleyball or surfing. It also comes through in our style of play—power or finesse, drop shot or smash, front running or charging from the pack. It makes Martina Navratilova's tennis different from Chris Evert's, Debi Thomas's skating different from Peggy Fleming's, your softball different from mine. Everywhere in sport we can find ways to be ourselves, to exercise our individuality and celebrate our specialness.

Physical and Emotional Tenderness So much of sport involves rough physical movements and steely emotional control that we tend to forget the other side of it. In fact, success at sport often requires mastery of highly delicate, precise skills. The putt in golf, the bunt in softball, the set shot in volleyball, the free throw in basketball, the lateral pass in football—these are all examples of sport skills that require great physical sensitivity rather than brute power. The execution of such skills is at least as satisfying for many participants as are attempts to dominate by sheer force.

Sport also involves a wealth of emotional tenderness. Camaraderie among teammates and even opponents is what most firmly binds many athletes to their sport. Mutual encouragement, shared victories, consolation in defeat, and comfort in injury are all features of the compassionate side of sport. It is a realm of experience that is rich in affection, and this emotional warmth is a large part of its allure for many people.

Risk Taking Some degree of physical, strategic, and emotional risk characterizes most sports. Physically, a softball batter risks being hit by a wild pitch, and the pitcher risks being drilled by a line drive. A scuba diver could pass out under water, a skier might lose control and hit a tree, a surfer could "wipe out." Strategically, stealing bases in softball is risky, as is rushing the net in tennis, attempting a three-point shot in basketball, or blitzing in football. Emotionally, all sport participants risk the embarrassment of a poor performance, the anguish of losing, and the sense of personal failure when confronted by a greater challenge than they can handle.

Some people reluctantly tolerate the physical risks of their sport, play conservatively to minimize the strategic risks, and avoid pressure situations that create emotional risks. Others find those risks to be highly attractive, even intoxicating. Risk-takers may even seek out sports that build in a high degree of risk. Sky diving, ski jumping, mountain climbing, and tightrope walking are fulfilling for the thrill-seekers who need high levels of arousal and find it in such sporting activities.

Cooperation   Dynamic relationship with another or others is an integral part of the sport experience. It offers the participant an array of potentially fulfilling cooperative challenges. In one sense it is related to teamwork, the coordination of one's own efforts with those of teammates in order to create a co-functioning whole. For the team sport participant especially, being part of such a whole is a source of great satisfaction. In another sense, cooperation may involve external objects, as when the sailboat feels like an extension of the sailor rather than something to be controlled by the sailor, or when the skier seeks to commune with the mountain rather than conquer it.

In yet another sense, cooperation refers to one's attitude toward the opponent in a contest. It is an interrelationship based on the coordinated efforts of kindred spirits who serve to bring out each other's best performances. It is an acceptance of the opponent as an other who is like oneself rather than the alienation of hostile, antagonistic enemies. When one's approach to sport is characterized by this kind of cooperative relationship, the focus of the participation tends to be on excellence rather than on conquest.

The Sports Experience

Drama   Sport competition features two essential elements that make for excellent suspenseful drama. First, it involves purposeful human beings who are striving for something that is important to them in some sense. (This is not necessarily a winning score—it could be a personal best or simply a satisfying performance.) Second, the outcome is uncertain. For the participant as well as for any audience that may be present, these dramatic qualities can be very enjoyable. Like any good suspense story, the drama is especially high when the competition is close and/or historic (e.g., the first all-female climb up Mount Everest), when a lot is at stake (e.g., qualifying for the Olympics), when there is adversity to overcome (e.g., conquering one's fear), or when a participant is heroic in some way (e.g., disabled). The suspense and drama in sport are available to all participants at all levels, and they certainly enrich the activity overall.

Sensuousness   Sport participation offers an abundance of sensuous experiences. Everywhere are things that look and sound and smell and taste and feel delicious. The visual poetry of a well-turned double play, the sound of a tennis ball on the "sweet spot" of a racket, the smell of a good leather fielder's mitt, a salty spray on a windsurfer's tongue, the cool buoyancy of a swimming pool on a hot day—these are just a few of the sensual delights in sport. Many sport participants also take pleasure in the personal experience of speed, rhythm, power, artistry, and control that is akin to the enjoyment felt by a dancer. Pleasures such as these are widely sought, intensely felt, and deeply appreciated by many a sport enthusiast.

Cognitive Complexity   The strategic side of sport is a source of great challenge for participants and spectators alike. Volumes have been written and whole careers have been made in the attempt to master the complexity of a single sport. General strategies as well as cunning responses to opponents' strategies require concentration, quick perception, and the comprehension of a multitude of interrelated situational factors. Sport requires a rapid-fire series of decisions based on the processing of diverse and fleeting bits of information. The permutations of possible choices for action in any given situation can paralyze, and each situation presents itself only briefly before metamorphosing into a newly challenging situation. This kind of complexity provides for a tough but rewarding exercise of cognitive skill.

Transcendental Experience   Sport participants at all levels of skill have reported experiences of uncommon states of being. Elusive, rarely sustained, and difficult to explain, such experiences are nevertheless highly attractive and remarkably pleasant. They have been described using such terms as "peak experience," "perfect moment," "athletic high," "flow experience," and "being in the zone." They are frequently characterized by feelings of total control or invincibility, of floating, of time slowing, of otherworldliness, or of supernatural ability to influence external objects and events. The sport world seems somehow to engender such transcendental experiences, and sport participants, although often embarrassed by them, tend to cherish them as well.

Torn Between Two Extremes

Such experiences, along with the others listed above, give sport participation tremendous potential for being self-actualizing, self-empowering, mutually affirming, and greatly enjoyable. This is not just additionally or marginally true for women, but rather especially true for us. Historically we have been torn between two extreme and equally debilitating views of our embodiment. On the one hand, for too long we have been defined and identified in offensively physical terms—that is, both as mindless and as exclusively sexual beings. On the other hand, our frequent response to those characterizations has been to disconnect ourselves from our physicality altogether by retreating into a world that values only intellectual pursuits (and denounces sport as vulgar and excessive). We desperately need a middle ground between these two approaches, a way of exploring, developing, and celebrating our embodiment without abandoning our intelligence or prostituting our feminist convictions. I maintain that sport can provide such a middle ground if we go about it conscientiously, making the personal growth and enrichment of every participant our central and primary focus.

"Sports is the last great bastion of male chauvinism."

Male Chauvinism Obstructs Women's Sports

Kate Rounds

Women's sports, especially team sports, have not achieved the visibility and economic success of men's sports such as football and baseball. In the following viewpoint, Kate Rounds blames the resistance to professional women's sports on men's deep-seated prejudices as well as on the dominance of men's sports in media coverage and public attention. Rounds is a sports and fiction writer who also holds a black belt in judo.

As you read, consider the following questions:

1. What does Rounds believe accounts for athletes' relative economic success in tennis and golf?
2. Why have women's sports leagues been more successful in other countries than in the United States, according to the author?
3. Why do some men feel compelled to put down female athletes, according to Rounds?

From "Why Men Fear Women's Teams" by Kate Rounds, *Ms.*, January/February 1991. Reprinted by permission of *Ms.* Magazine, © 1991.

Picture this. You're flipping through the channels one night, and you land on a local network, let's say ABC. And there on the screen is a basketball game. The players are sinking three-pointers, slam-dunking, and doing the usual things basketball players do. They're high-fiving each other, patting one another on the butt, and then sauntering to the locker room to talk about long-term contracts.

Now imagine that the players aren't men. They're women, big sweaty ones, wearing uniforms and doing their version of what guys thrive on—bonding. So far, this scene is a fantasy and will remain so until women's professional team sports get corporate sponsors, television exposure, arenas, fan support, and a critical mass of well-trained players.

While not enough fans are willing to watch women play traditional team sports, they love to watch women slugging it out on roller-derby rinks and in mudwrestling arenas. Currently popular is a bizarre television spectacle called *American Gladiators*, in which women stand on pastel pedestals, wearing Lycra tights and brandishing weapons that look like huge Q-Tips. The attraction obviously has something to do with the "uniforms."

The importance of what women athletes wear can't be underestimated. Beach volleyball, which is played in the sand by bikini-clad women, rates network coverage while traditional court volleyball can't marshal any of the forces that would make a women's pro league succeed.

It took a while, but women were able to break through sexist barriers in golf and tennis. Part of their success stemmed from the sports themselves—high-end individual sports that were born in the British Isles and flourished in country clubs across the U.S. The women wore skirts, makeup, and jewelry along with their wristbands and warm-up jackets. The corporate sponsors were hackers themselves, and the fans—even men—could identify with these women: a guy thought that if he hit the ball enough times against the barn door, he too could play like Martina Navratilova. And women's purses were equaling men's. In fact, number-one-ranked Steffi Graf's prize money for 1989 was $1,963,905 and number-one-ranked Stefan Edberg's was $1,661,491.

Team Sports

By contrast, women's professional team sports have failed spectacularly. Since the mid-seventies, every professional league—softball, basketball, and volleyball—has gone belly-up. In 1981, after a four-year struggle, the Women's Basketball League (WBL), backed by sports promoter Bill Byrne, folded. The league was drawing fans in a number of cities, but the sponsors weren't there, TV wasn't there, and nobody seemed to miss the spectacle of a few good women fighting for a basketball.

Or a volleyball, for that matter. Despite the success of bikini volleyball, an organization called MLV (Major League Volleyball) bit the dust in March of 1989 after nearly three years of struggling for sponsorship, fan support, and television exposure. As with pro basketball, there was a man behind women's professional volleyball, real estate investor Robert (Bat) Batinovich. Batinovich admits that, unlike court volleyball, beach volleyball has a lot of "visual T&A mixed into it."

Sport and Patriarchy

A central feature of modern sport is the role it plays in supporting male dominance. Sport has been, and continues to be, an arena that actively and contemptuously excludes females, celebrates "masculinity," and reinforces patriarchy. We need only consider how vigorously and persistently some males have fought female inroads into the world of sport [since the late 1960s]. Also, a part of the ideological content incorporated in the slogan that "sports build character" conceals a subtle message reinforcing, through intention and innuendo, male power and superiority. It is also an endeavor to maintain gender inequality by promoting the building of character traits traditionally associated with "manly" qualities.

George H. Sage, *The World & I*, October 1988.

What court volleyball does have, according to former MLV executive director Lindy Vivas, is strong women athletes. Vivas is assistant volleyball coach at San Jose State University. "The United States in general," she says, "has problems dealing with women athletes and strong, aggressive females. The perception is you have to be more aggressive in team sports than in golf and tennis, which aren't contact sports. Women athletes are looked at as masculine and get the stigma of being gay."

One former women's basketball promoter, who insists on remaining anonymous, goes further. "You know what killed women's sports?" he says. "Lesbians. This cost us in women's basketball. But I know there are not as many lesbians now unless I'm really blinded. We discourage it, you know. We put it under wraps."

People in women's sports spend a lot of time dancing around the "L" word, and the word "image" pops up in a way it never does in men's sports. Men can spit tobacco juice, smoke, and even scratch their testicles on national television and get away with it.

Bill Byrne, former WBL promoter, knows there isn't a whole

lot women can get away with while they're beating each other out for a basketball. "In the old league," he says, "my partner, Mike Connors, from *Mannix*—his wife said, 'Let's do makeup on these kids.' And I knew that the uniforms could be more attractive. We could tailor them so the women don't look like they're dragging a pair of boxer shorts down the floor."

Image-Conscious

The response from the athletes to this boy talk is not always outrage. "Girls in women's basketball now are so pretty," says Nancy Lieberman-Cline. "They're image-conscious." The former Old Dominion University star, who made headlines as Martina's trainer, played with the men's U.S. Basketball League, the Harlem Globe Trotters Tour (where she met husband Tim Cline), and with the Dallas Diamonds of the old WBL. "Everyone used to have short hair," she says. "Winning and playing was everything. I wouldn't think of using a curling iron. Now there are beautiful girls out there playing basketball."

Lieberman-Cline says she doesn't mind making the concession. "It's all part of the process," she says. "You can't be defensive about everything.". . .

There's no doubt that many athletes in the women's sports establishment are leery of fast-talking guys who try to make a buck off women's pro sports, especially when the women themselves don't profit from those ventures. In the old league, finances were so shaky that some players claim they were never paid.

"We weren't getting the gate receipts," says Lieberman-Cline. "They'd expect 2,000, get only 400, and then they'd have to decide to pay the arena or pay the girls, and the girls were the last choice. There was a lot of mismanagement in the WBL, though the intent was good.". . .

Given the track record of women's professional team sports in this country, it's not surprising that the national pastime is faring no better. When Little League was opened to girls by court order in 1974, one might have thought that professional women's baseball could not be far behind. Baseball is a natural for women. It's not a contact sport, it doesn't require excessive size or strength—even little guys like Phil Rizzuto and Jose Lind can play it—and it's actually an individual sport masquerading as a team sport. Still, in recent years, no one's taken a serious stab at organizing a women's professional league.

In 1984, there was an attempt to field a women's minor-league team. Though the Sun Sox had the support of baseball great Hank Aaron, it was denied admission to the Class A Florida State League. The team was the brainchild of a former Atlanta Braves vice president of marketing, Bob Hope. "A lot of the general managers and owners of big-league clubs were mortified,"

Hope says, "and some players said they wouldn't compete against women. It was male ego or something."

The Last Male Bastion

Or something, says softball hall-of-famer Donna Lopiano. "When girls suffer harassment in Little League, that's not exactly opening up opportunities for women," she says. "Girls don't have the access to coaching and weight training that boys have. Sports is a place where physiological advantages give men power, and they're afraid of losing it. Sports is the last great bastion of male chauvinism. In the last eight years [since 1983], we've gone backward, not only on gender equity but on civil rights."

Women of color still face barriers that European American women don't, particularly in the areas of coaching and refereeing. But being a woman athlete is sometimes a bond that transcends race. "We're all at a handicap," says Ruth Lawanson, an African American who played volleyball with MLV. "It doesn't matter whether you're Asian, Mexican, black or white."

Sexual Harassment

Sometimes the enemy isn't policy, but ingrained cultural behavior. Take the case of Julie Croteau, the first woman to play college baseball. First-baseman Croteau won the acceptance of her teammates at St. Mary's College in Maryland. She played hard, traded quips with fellow players and let occasional jibes from the stands roll off her thick skin. For three seasons. Then she hung up her glove, at age 20.

"I'm miserable," she conceded. "I've spent more time fighting and being emotionally destroyed by baseball than enjoying the game." What finished her, she said, was her own team's barrage of sexually degrading comments about women. Knowing the comments weren't aimed at her personally made them no less upsetting. "What they're doing is just the tip of what most teams must be doing," she said. "It's scary."

Susan L. Morse, *CQ Researcher*, March 6, 1992.

Historically, baseball and softball diamonds have not been very hospitable to black men and any women. Despite the fact that even men's softball is not a crowd pleaser, back in 1976, Billie Jean King and golfer Jane Blalock teamed up with ace amateur softball pitcher Joan Joyce to form the International Women's Professional Softball Association (IWPSA). Five years later, without sponsorship, money, or television, the league was history.

Billie Jean King has her own special attachment to the team

concept. As a girl, she wanted to be a baseball player, but her father gave her a tennis racket, knowing that there wasn't much of a future for a girl in baseball. The story is especially touching since Billie Jean's brother, Randy Moffitt, went on to become a pitcher with the San Francisco Giants. But even as a tennis player, Billie Jean clung to the team idea. She was the force behind World Team Tennis, which folded in 1978, and is the chief executive officer of TeamTennis. . . .

On the face of it, TeamTennis is a bizarre notion because it takes what is a bred-in-the-bones individual sport and tries to squeeze it into a team concept. It has the further handicap of not really being necessary when strong women's and men's professional tours are already in place.

In the TeamTennis format, all players play doubles as well as singles. Billie Jean loves doubles, she says, because she enjoys "sharing the victory." What also distinguishes TeamTennis from the women's and men's pro tours is fan interaction. Fans are encouraged to behave as if watching a baseball or basketball game rather than constantly being told to shut up and sit down as they are at pro tour events like the U.S. Open. The sense of team spirit among the players—the fact that they get to root for one another—is also attracting some big names. Both Martina Navratilova and Jimmy Connors have signed on to play Team-Tennis during its tiny five-week season, which begins after Wimbledon and ends just before the U.S. Open.

Past Success

But you have to go back 50 years to find a women's professional sports team that was somewhat successful—though the conditions for that success were rather unusual. During World War II, when half the population was otherwise engaged, women were making their mark in the formerly male strongholds of welding, riveting—and baseball. The All-American Girls Professional Baseball League (AAGPBL) fielded such teams as the Lassies, the Belles, and the Chicks on the assumption that it was better to have "girls" playing than to let the national pastime languish. The league lasted a whopping 12 years after its inception in 1943.

The success of this sandlot venture, plagued as it was by the simple-hearted sexism of the forties (the women went to charm school at night), must raise nagging doubts in the mind of the woman team player of the nineties. Can she triumph only in the absence of men?

It may be true that she can triumph only in the absence of competition from the fiercely popular men's pro leagues, which gobble up sponsorship, U.S. network television, and the hearts and minds of male fanatics. The lack of male competition outside the United States may be partly responsible for the success of women's professional team sports in Europe, Japan, South America, and Australasia. Lieberman-Cline acknowledges that Europe provides a more hospitable climate for women's pro basketball. "Over there, they don't have as many options," she says. "We have Broadway plays, movies, you name it. We're overindulged with options."

Bruce Levy is a 230-pound bespectacled accountant who escaped from the Arthur Andersen accounting firm in 1980 to market women's basketball. "It's pretty simple," he says. "People overseas are more realistic and enlightened. Women's basketball is not viewed as a weak version of men's. If Americans could appreciate a less powerful, more scientific, team-oriented game, we'd be two thirds of the way toward having a league succeed."

Levy, who represents many women playing pro basketball abroad, says 120 U.S. women are playing overseas and making up to $70,000 in a seven-month season. They include star players like Teresa Edwards, Katrina McClain, and Lynette Woodard. "A player like Teresa Weatherspoon, everybody recognizes her in Italy," he says. "No one in the U.S. knows her. If there were a pro league over here, I wouldn't be spending all day on the phone speaking bad Italian and making sure the women's beds are long enough. I'd just be negotiating contracts."

Levy claims that U.S. businesswomen aren't supporting women's team sports. "In Europe," he says, "the best-run and most publicized teams are run by women who own small businesses and put their money where their mouth is." Joy Burns, president of Sportswomen of Colorado, Inc., pleads no contest. "Businesswomen here are too conservative and don't stick their necks out," she says. MLV's Bat Batinovich, who says he's "disappointed" in U.S. businesswomen for not supporting women's team sports, figures an investor in MLV should have been willing to lose $200,000 a year for five years. Would Burns have done it? "If I'm making good financial investments, why should I?"

Dim Prospects

The prospects for women's professional team sports don't look bright. The reasons for the lack of financial support go beyond simple economics and enter the realm of deep-rooted sexual bias and homophobia. San Jose State's Lindy Vivas says men who feel intimidated by physically strong women have to put the women down. "There's always a guy in the crowd who challenges the women when he wouldn't think of going one-on-one with Magic Johnson or challenging Nolan Ryan to a pitching contest."

Softball's Donna Lopiano calls it little-boy stuff: "Men don't want to have a collegial, even-steven relationship with women. It's like dealing with cavemen."

"Homophobia is a problem that affects all women athletes, regardless of whether they are lesbian or straight."

Homophobia Obstructs Women's Sports

Diane Keaton

One of the obstacles many women athletes face is the stereotypical linkage between athleticism and lesbianism. In the following viewpoint, Diane Keaton discusses how this stereotype and the accompanying prejudice against lesbians among both men and women creates problems for all female athletes and their supporters. Keaton is an editor with the *San Francisco Independent*.

As you read, consider the following questions:

1. In what different ways has homophobia affected women's sport, according to Keaton?
2. Why does the author argue that homophobia affects all female athletes regardless of their sexual orientation?
3. How can homophobia be fought, according to Keaton?

"Out of the Closet" by Diane Keaton. This article first appeared in the September 1992 issue of *Women's Sports & Fitness* magazine and is reprinted with the publisher's permission.

The snickers start when Edy Coleman departs the dugout for the playing field. At 5 feet 11 inches, with shaved head and an earring in her eyebrow, the left fielder does stand out.

Coleman came to San Francisco State University, not only to play softball, but also, for the first time, to be true to herself. "I'm the biggest dyke on the team, the one they can see from a mile away," she laughs.

Coleman knows she couldn't be as casual at the "big, big schools with scholarships," schools that generate repeated news coverage that would put her in the spotlight's full glare. "If I were straight I would've gone for the scholarship schools. But [homophobia] intimidated me; it definitely hindered me. I wanted to be where I felt comfortable."

At San Francisco State, Coleman feels no team pressure to be straight or gay. "You do what you want to do," she says. "Our sexual preference doesn't affect the way we are on the softball field."

Homophobia and Athletes

Coleman's choice—to eschew the scholarships and fame that can come from playing for a top university so she could be open about her sexual identity—is but one example of the way homophobia affects women's choices in athletics. And homophobia is a problem that affects all women athletes, regardless of whether they are lesbian or straight.

Observers cite a range of cases: women turning down scholarships at schools unfriendly to lesbians; lesbians getting married and divorced to maintain a heterosexual image; women terrified to reveal they were fired as suspected lesbians; single women who are not hired as coaches; heterosexual women declining athletic careers for fear of being labeled lesbians—perhaps leading to disproportionate numbers of lesbians in sport.

"Oh, God, that's all you hear about with college sports—that the whole team is made up of lesbians," says Mindy Morse, a senior on the softball team at California State University, Chico. Sports opportunities were a big factor in Morse's decision to enroll at Chico State. But as an incoming heterosexual freshman, she was "nervous and scared" about how lesbians would react to her.

As it turned out, Morse says, there were probably lesbian players and coaches on her softball team during her first years of college, but it wasn't always clear who they were. "Then the rumors start, and it doesn't go right. 'She is' and 'she's not,' and then we argue and hate each other. It's better if it's out in the open." Morse says it doesn't bother her to have lesbian teammates, "as long as they aren't flirting with each other."

Now, Morse says, the team makeup is straight—the lesbians have graduated or "been weeded out." When she and her teammates see "obvious lesbian" opponents, they joke about "that

194

guy over there—we just make fun of it." Still, she notes, "everyone is always asking, 'are there any lesbians on your team?'"

Keeping Girls Out of Sports

Homophobia can create bonds, as women find allies and unite to offer support or advice. But it can also erode bonds. Some lesbians resent straight athletes for the media attention they receive. Straight women sometimes avoid lesbians for fear of being contaminated by the "lesbian" label. Even lesbians avoid lesbians. . . .

Perhaps most tragically, homophobia keeps some women and girls out of sports. "I receive more questions about the potential danger to a daughter's sexuality than anything else," says Bruce Ogilvie, a sports psychologist and former consultant to the U.S. Olympic team. "'How can I protect my daughter from succumbing to the seduction of athletes?' parents ask.". . .

Laurie Priest, president of the National Association for Girls and Women in Sport (NAGWS), tells the story of a basketball team on which three of the women were openly lesbian. She told the male coach, "Look, you are heterosexual, and you don't have any influence on these kids' sexuality whatsoever. But if you were a lesbian you'd be held responsible for this. If the parents found out, and wanted to make a stink, it could ruin it for you."

Mariah Burton Nelson, *Are We Winning Yet?*, 1991.

Morse's coach, Chuck Johnson, fields the same questions from parents of would-be college players: They want to know whether his is a "feminine softball team." Johnson, a veteran education faculty member, answers, "I say, 'Yip, they look like all the coeds on our campus,' so I guess that's what the mamas are asking."

Johnson says he thinks all coaches get the same question, because people want to be where they feel comfortable. "There are an awful lot of young, strong, fast women who don't want to be associated with that image, but I don't think it's homophobic behavior."

Discrimination

Others do. In her book, *Are We Winning Yet?: How Women Are Changing Sports and Sports Are Changing Women*, former professional basketball player Mariah Burton Nelson includes a chapter entitled "A Silence So Loud It Screams." In it, an anonymous lesbian Ladies' Professional Golfing Association competitor describes how she is forced to restrict her natural behavior for fear of losing sponsorship and media attention.

Nelson argues that homophobia restricts the behavior of all

women—not just lesbians. "Straight women are afraid to hug each other and cry on each other's shoulders, and they bend over backwards to look feminine," she says, echoing critics who mock makeup classes for athletes and high heels for women coaches at basketball games.

Shortly after Nelson "came out" as a sophomore at Stanford University in the late 1970s, she began addressing high school audiences about sexual preference. "It made me feel good about myself," she says. "College is a time of self-discovery, and in the late '70s there was excitement about the gay movement and lots of support." As the captain of her basketball team, Nelson says she was able to set an example through leadership and that her teammates accepted her.

Nelson, who lives in Arlington, Virginia, says she is a mainstream person who just happens to be gay. But mainstream corporations have told her they would withdraw sponsorship from athletes who come out. "The more that corporations get involved in college sports, the less likely women are to be outspoken about those issues, because corporations are run by straight, white, older men who shy away from controversy," she says.

Arlene Gorton, associate athletic director at Brown University, equates homophobia in sport to racism in the early '60s. "I've heard coaches say, 'I don't care about homophobia, don't tell me. I don't want lesbians on my team. They will destroy my team.' This is where blacks were 30 years ago."

Under the Rug

Lesbianism is "kept under the rug in sporting circles," she says, and there's a "real panic" in trying to talk about it. "If [athletes] talk about it, they'll catch it. They're immediately assumed to be homosexual, or they have to declare that they're not."

Donna Lopiano, executive director of the Women's Sports Foundation, is one of a growing number of heterosexual and lesbian women's sports leaders trying to change this under-the-rug attitude. "The lesbian issue is a very real employment issue," she says. "Whenever a woman departs from a predominantly male idea of what a woman should be, there is discrimination against her. It fits into a whole scenario."

Three years ago [in 1989] the Foundation adopted a nondiscrimination policy that includes sexual orientation. . . . "Our mission is to break down barriers, any 'ism' to limit someone's opportunity in sports," says Lopiano. "It's a crime."

Not everyone feels bringing the issue into the open is the right way to solve the problem. Mary Jo Haverbeck, associate sports information director at Pennsylvania State University, argues that discussion of dating and sexual preferences feeds a tendency to sensationalize women's sports. She says "negative labeling" detracts from opportunities for women and minorities alike.

"It sounds good [to acknowledge lesbians in sport], but I don't think it will work," Haverbeck says. "Sport is a product. It has to be sold. It needs promoting like crazy." Whether the sporting event involves homosexuals, women or minorities, she argues, it is a difficult task to sell it "when a lot of the country is against it. I think [lesbianism] is something much bigger than sport, and this country isn't ready for it." (Penn State has had to respond to a media barrage since 1991, when it was revealed that women's basketball coach Rene Portland made a practice of telling lesbians they were not welcome on the team. The university changed its nondiscrimination policy to include sexual orientation.)

But in fact, homophobia in women's sports is getting more and more attention. Phyllis Howlett, chair of the National Collegiate Athletic Association Committee on Women's Athletics, says that homophobia was on the agenda of the Committee meeting in June 1992. And homophobia was "up there," she notes, in the NCAA's 1988-89 study on perceived barriers of women in intercollegiate athletic careers. "I worry about anything that erodes opportunities and choices for women," she says.

Pat Griffin, associate professor of education at the University of Massachusetts, has been conducting workshops about homophobia on campus since 1987. Griffin, who is credited with helping break the silence on homophobia, came out in 1987, after receiving tenure. "I had been doing homophobia work since 1980, but it took a while to work up to [coming out]," she says. "It's almost impossible to overestimate how thick the fear is among women in sport on this issue."

Griffin faults a precollege education system that "doesn't deal with homophobia and homosexuality." Griffin says heterosexual women are "set up for team divisions" during this "tender time" because they are suspicious or afraid. "They come into the environment warned about coming into contact with these terrible women. It is a terrible burden.

"The way we've tried to address it is to keep it silent and to blame lesbians," says Griffin in a May 25, 1992, article in the *Hartford Courant*. "It doesn't work. It's going to take a lot [of education]. But you have to start someplace. I don't expect it to be radically different in my lifetime."

Education is certainly key. But in the meantime, simply becoming friends with lesbians often helps heterosexual female athletes feel more comfortable around gays. Audrey Nauer, a heterosexual teammate of Edy Coleman, says befriending Coleman helped broaden her views. Now she delights in keeping opponents guessing about her own sexual orientation. "It's up to you to figure out what I am," she says. "I don't care."

> *"No matter how much progress women make toward equal opportunities and accomplishments, someone can always make a buck selling us to men as sex toys."*

Prurient Interest Diminishes Female Athletes

Ruth Conniff

Ruth Conniff is associate editor of *The Progressive*, a monthly liberal magazine, and also teaches girls track at a high school in Madison, Wisconsin. In the following viewpoint, she argues that women can gain a new respect for and sense of themselves by participating in athletics. Such positive gains, however, are threatened in her eyes by society's continuing tendency to view women as sex objects rather than as accomplished athletes and human beings.

As you read, consider the following questions:

1. What images of women does Conniff promote?
2. How are women's images of themselves changing, according to the author?
3. What does Conniff mean by the *"Playboy* image of women"?

From "Awesome Women in Sports" by Ruth Conniff, *The Progressive*, May 1993. Reprinted by permission from *The Progressive*, 409 E. Main St., Madison, WI 53703.

For the last few days I've been tearing pictures out of magazines—*Shape, Runner's World, Sports Illustrated*—collecting photographs of women athletes. I found a great shot of Gail Devers, Olympic gold medalist in the 100 meters, bounding out of the starting blocks, and I ripped out an ad for running shoes that shows two women striding side by side, silhouetted against an enormous blue sky.

I am pinning up these pictures on a bulletin board in the basement locker room of my old high school, Madison East, where I coach girls' track. East is one of those big, fortress-like public high schools you might mistake for a factory—or a prison. Concrete walls and floors, and the bleak, locked-up look of the building contribute to a general feeling of gloom.

I decided to make the bulletin board at the beginning of this year's season, ostensibly to provide information—weekly announcements, work-out schedules, team records, etc.—but also for sneakier reasons. One is to do a little public relations for track (gym classes pass through this locker room every day, and I'm hoping to win a few new recruits). Another reason is to boost the girls' morale. The bulletin board I captured runs the length of one wall of the locker room. Covered with purple and gold paper and glossy photos, it stands out. My hope is that it will reflect a picture to the girls who walk by it of energy and optimism and strength. Hence my hunt through magazines for inspiring images of women in sports.

They're not as easy to find as I thought.

Images of Women Athletes

I have mental images of women sports heroes from when I ran track—Mary Decker Slaney kicking to the finish line with steely determination, Florence Griffith Joyner with her powerful legs and her outrageous long nails and lace tights. When I started my bulletin-board project, I thought of my contemporary, Suzy Favor Hamilton (I raced against her—behind her, I should say—as a student at East and again in college). Favor Hamilton was featured on the cover of *Runner's World* a couple of years ago. I thought it would be easy to find a more recent photo, and hundreds of other good shots of female runners.

But as it turns out, the great pictures I remembered were mostly from stories that only appear every four years, during the buildup to the Olympic Games, and from a few memorable Nike ads. Beyond that, the pictures of women I want to find— strong, beautiful, *serious* athletes—are not so easy to come by.

As I began flipping through a stack of sports magazines I had around the house, I found that the images of women fall into two categories. There are the heroic portraits I've been tearing out. Then there are the more common pictures—sports cuties.

I am fascinated by the gap between these two types of images.

In *Shape* and other high-circulation "fitness" magazines, a plethora of ads for aerobics tapes and exercise equipment focus on female models with no faces, just body parts. A recurring theme is a leotard-clad rear end. No Buts About It . . . one of these ads quips. A similar ad shows a full-page set of buttocks, and below it, a much smaller picture of the owner, dwarfed by her own back-side, and the slogan, A SMALL PRICE TO PAY FOR PERFECTION. . . .

Shape is a typical women's magazine, with articles on diets, relationships, and thin thighs. The fitness hype blends right into the rest of the fashion and beauty market. It is tyrannically trivial: exalting physically "perfect" anatomical features over every other human attribute, quirk, and endeavor. Page after page features anonymous bottoms, bellies, and breasts—nary a whole woman to be seen. Spending a lot of time looking at these faceless fragments is a rather weird and alienating experience.

Sexist Descriptions

Would you believe your ears if the next time you were watching TV sports, you heard:

"Greg Louganis—that charming smile, those tight buns . . . and he can dive, too!"

"Andre Agassi makes the point, his blond locks bouncing."

"Alberto Salazar is a marathoner with a Tom Cruise look."

Ridiculous, outrageous, even sexist, right? But this is how sports commentary often sounds when *women* are competing. Appearance is emphasized, often at the expense of athletic performance. *And what is even worse is, a lot of us don't even hear it.*

Glamour, August 1989.

On the other hand, it is a relief to see, here and there among the health and beauty pages, entire women—faces and all—playing sports. Since I was a kid, more and more women have become involved in sports, and women athletes have become more visible.

Running magazines are clearly the best place to find the pictures I want. Running is a uniquely egalitarian sport. Female runners get coverage that is almost as good as men's, and there are women at every level of competition, including professional athletes. It is also a radically individual sport: People of all shapes, sizes, and ages get their pictures taken crossing finish lines—hometown heroes setting new records at local road races, old women and men winning masters' competitions, adults and kids alike celebrating personal triumphs. But that's in the relatively small, hard-core running publications.

New Ads

As running has gained popularity—pulled along by the yuppie fitness fad—Nike, Reebok, and other companies have been floating ads aimed at women, first for running shoes and now for all kinds of trendy athletic gear in the mainstream magazine world—that sea of body parts and marketing ploys.

In the beginning there were the words: JUST DO IT, and Nike launched its ad campaign, creating its own images of women, running, jumping, looking tough, cavorting in expensive shoes.

Market research must have shown that women like being treated as whole human beings, because the new ads have caught on, spun off, and developed into a whole new genre with a sophisticated "feminist" appeal. Aimed at affluent, athletic women, they combine hip, conversational ad copy with full frontal photographs of smiling, active women. They promise not just well-toned body parts, but health, happiness, attitude, and "lifestyle." Small wonder they're a hit.

Of course, the companies themselves are not nearly so p.c. [politically correct] as the ads. Some—Nike in particular—are major exploiters of their (predominantly female) Third World workers. Their sole purpose in life is not to raise consciousness but to peddle their products, just as other companies peddle nylons, diet pills, and cigarettes.

But the new ads do reflect a significant demographic change in attitude and self-image among American women. It's a change that has everything to do with more women playing sports.

Women's Sports and Fitness—a big, glossy magazine aimed specifically at women athletes—is another good indicator of this change. As the official publication of the Women's Sports Foundation (which, among other things, helps fund girls' sports teams and supports female athletes fighting sex discrimination in their schools), *Women's Sports and Fitness* is a kind of *Sports Illustrated* for women. It is full of stories about women excelling in sports, matter-of-fact profiles of Olympians and other world-class athletes, and advice for weekend jocks. I was practically bowled over the first time I saw it. Here is a slick magazine full of strong, beautiful women who look like people. No condescending beauty tips, no gratuitous cheesecake pictures. Reading it, you'd think women were a bunch of human beings—better yet, serious athletes. I love it. And so do a lot of other women, apparently. It has a paid circulation of 140,000.

Most of all, I see the change in women's images of themselves on a daily basis among the girls I coach.

The other day at practice, some girls on my team were talking about the hard-body heroine of the movie *Terminator 2*. One of the girls said she watched the movie with her boyfriend. "He said he wouldn't mind having a body like that, but he doesn't find her physically attractive," she said.

"Well, excuse me, but I find her physically *awesome*," one of the other girls remarked, to noises of assent from her teammates.

I like eavesdropping on these conversations.

Last year, at the beginning of the season, the girl who considers the Terminator woman awesome didn't want to lift weights, for fear she would get too "built."

That was before she became freshman city champion in the half mile. Now she's hooked. She worked hard to earn her varsity letter in cross-country and showed up for pre-season weight-training for track. She and the other runners on the women's team have developed a touching camaraderie over the past couple of years, as well as a kind of jock swagger that has subsumed some of the cloying cuteness a lot of high-school girls cultivate.

Still the girls who come out for track and other sports at East are far outnumbered by those who do not. (The same is true for boys, but to a lesser degree.) This fact was driven home to me at the beginning of the season, when more than 100 boys showed up for practice, as compared with about 30 girls.

My own experience as an athlete has been so rewarding, and so central to who I am now, that it pains me to think of all the girls in school who might never discover the pride and confidence that come from challenging themselves and excelling in a sport. . . .

Slippery Images

Slowly, over the past several years, *Sports Illustrated* has begun to recognize the appeal of women's sports, and to present women as sports heroes, the way it has long presented men. In [one] issue of the magazine, there's a good story on a women's collegiate basketball game between rivals Vanderbilt and Tennessee. The game sold out weeks in advance, according to the article, and generated more attention than any game in the history of women's basketball. Even Vice President Al Gore felt compelled to comment.

On the other hand, the same issue contains a two-page photo spread of the Dallas Cowboys' cheerleaders, prone on a football field, white booties pointing skyward. On another page there's an ad featuring the Budweiser girls.

It's startling how slippery these images of women are. One minute you're a role model, the next you've been disassembled into body parts.

An old friend from high school came to the indoor city track

202

meet, where I was watching my team. I was lost in the competition, getting nervous before the gun went off, taking times, chewing my nails. Then my friend started talking to me about the girls' bodies as they stood on the starting line. "Don't you think her arms are too big. . . . Her legs look fat. . . . *Those* girls have *great* bodies, though. Maybe I should have run track."

It took the wind out of my sails to listen to her. It's easy to forget, and so annoying to remember, even if you're an athlete giving the performance of your life, some people will still look at you that way.

In March 1993, *Playboy* magazine announced that it is recasting its centerfolds as athletes. Twenty-two Playmate sports teams will be competing in various exhibition events, as part of a campaign to attract new advertisers. "Executives insist that athletic prowess will now be a real factor in selecting future centerfolds," according to an article in the *Toronto Star*.

"All of this comes at a time when the lines between the worlds of sports and racy entertainment are blurring," the article continues. "Some say the Dallas Cowboys' cheerleaders began the trend, and that the Laker Girls took it to a new level.

"'It's simply a marketing project that happens to have the Playmates as the product,' said Michael O'Hara Lynch [*Playboy*'s vice president of marketing]. It's really no different than marketing soap. . . .'"

So there you have it. No matter how much progress women make toward equal opportunities and accomplishments, someone can always make a buck selling us to men as sex toys.

A False Image

That *Playboy* image of women as compliant sex kittens is such a far cry from the experience of being a real, active human being in the world. It's the difference between being a passive, pillow-like object and an engine, hurtling around the track.

You can see it in the way *Playboy* presents pictures of women in hardhats, military uniforms, or athletic gear, as if these occupations were a kind of titillating drag—buxom bunnies masquerading as real people. The sex appeal and the put-down are intertwined in these images. They are supposed to be funny—like cute pictures of children dressed up as adults, playing up the contrast between the hapless female and a serious, adult occupation.

I knew a woman at Yale who posed as one of *Playboy*'s "Women of the Ivy League." She also happened to be the girlfriend of a runner on the cross-country and track teams. I remember seeing her at a cross-country meet. A group of us were standing at the finish line, covered with mud from running, cheering as the men's team came in. She came tripping across the grass, looking radically out of place in a fur coat and high heels, sinking into the soft ground, and waited on the sidelines for her boyfriend. I remember feeling sad when I saw her, outside the circle of happy track people, hugging and laughing, filled with shared, post-race euphoria. She could hardly walk, much less run, and she seemed infinitely far away from taking part in that event.

I felt grateful for my muddy shoes and sweat clothes, grateful that I could be there fully and freely participating, not as a kind of crippled ornament standing on the sidelines.

So that's why I'm busy covering the wall with sports pictures and recruiting girls to run track. If I have anything to do with it, when I'm an old woman I'll be running road races with a crowd of other women, young and old, and every single one of us will be awesome.

"To insist that there is no connection between eros and sports is nonsense."

Eroticism Enhances Female Athletics

Allen Guttmann

Allen Guttmann is a professor of English and American studies at Amherst College in Amherst, Massachusetts. He is the author of several books on sports, including *A Whole New Ball Game: An Interpretation of American Sports* and *Women's Sports: A History*. In the following viewpoint, Guttmann examines the connections between athletics and eroticism, and questions the feminist critique that female athletes are cheapened by being viewed as sex objects. He argues that both male and female athletes can be sexually attractive, and that while this attractiveness may be exploited in harmful ways, its existence need not detract from a true appreciation of women athletes.

As you read, consider the following questions:

1. How has the connection between sports and eros been viewed historically, according to Guttmann?
2. What examples of exploitation of female athletes' appeal does the author disapprove of?
3. How does Guttmann respond to what he calls the "radical feminist" critique of sports as exploitation of women?

From *Women's Sports: A History* by Allen Guttmann, © 1991, Columbia University Press, New York. Reprinted with the permission of the publisher.

When Athenian youths ran races or hurled the discus, when Spartan girls wrestled one another by the banks of the Eurotas, everyone seems to have understood that physically trained bodies, in motion or at rest, can be sexually attractive. The erotic aspects of sports, welcomed by most of the ancients, have always been obvious to the *critics* of sports, then and now. Tertullian's complaints, uttered in the second century A.D., were echoed in 1934 by Cardinal Rodrigue Villeneuve of Quebec. He condemned the "pagan" cult of the body as manifested in sports and deprecated the rampant concern for "hysterical strength, sensual pleasure, and the development of the human animal." For centuries, however, lovers of sports, spectators as well as athletes, have discussed their passion as if the sensual pleasure in sports had no connection whatsoever with human sexuality. They have denied rather than defended the association of eros and sports. Whenever, for instance, outraged religious traditionalists have called attention to the erotic appeal of the female body at play, ingenuous progressive reformers have blandly explained that sunlight, fresh air, and unencumbered movement were their only motives. No wonder that the interminable debates over sportswear for women left both sides frustrated and unhappy.

When Protestant clergymen invented "muscular Christianity" in the mid-nineteenth century, when Pope Pius XII decided in 1945 to affirm the value of modern sports, there was no sudden acceptance of what had been condemned, no reconsideration of the erotic element in sports. Quite the contrary. Christian propagandists for sports seemed to become blind to the sexual dimensions that had been anathema to their clerical predecessors. Ironically, once the mainstream churches took to celebrations of the joy of sports, a number of secular critics, mostly Marxists, began to deplore the "sexualization" of women's (but not of men's) sports. We seem now to be in the midst of what Margaret Hunt has aptly termed "the de-eroticization of women's liberation."

A Conspiracy of Silence

While some of the more ascetic Marxist critics seem to have resurrected Tertullian's indictments of sports, social scientists of a more empirical bent seem to have entered into a conspiracy to avoid mentioning (in public) the erotic element in sports. Numerous studies have documented the fact that exercise programs result in an "improved body-image." The implications of this fact are seldom explored. European and American psychologists and sociologists have discussed an array of motivations for sports participation, including aesthetic dimension. They are reluctant to acknowledge (in public) that "fitness" and "to be in shape" are often euphemisms for the desire to be sexually attractive. . . .

Recognition of simple truths known thousands of years ago is blocked because the topic of eros and sports is obviously, for many people, athletes and spectators both, a taboo, a source of shame and denial. To say this is most emphatically *not* to say that all sports have an erotic aspect or that all athletes are sexually attractive. The heady rediscovery of the erotic component in sports need not impel one to assert, as Christian Messenger does, that the "presentation of female athletes is . . . always eroticized by the fact that . . . any movement of the female body is erotic." The sad truth is that some men and women will, inevitably, deem some male and female athletes, in motion or at rest, unattractive or even repulsive. Nonetheless, to insist that there is *no* connection between eros and sports is nonsense. Happily, the anxious denial of a connection has become less and less plausible.

When Hollywood stripped Johnny Weissmuller of his Olympic swimsuit, wrapped him in a loincloth, and filmed him in the role of Tarzan, the dream-merchants knew what they were doing. Katherine Albert, writing in *Photoplay*, marveled that "a lad who had never been in a picture before, who had been interested in nothing but swimming all his life, and who frankly admits he can't act, is the top-notch heart flutterer of the year."

A generation later, Jean-Claude Killy, the French skier, became an international heart-throb. George Best, the Irish soccer star, joined the Beatles and Mick Jagger as a "teenage 'pin-up.'" Joe Namath marketed his sex appeal almost as successfully as he sold his skills as a quarterback for the New York Jets. Speaking about Canadian football players, anthropologist Robert A. Stebbins remarks mildly that they, too, are "attractive to the opposite sex." Thelma McCormack has anatomized Hollywood prizefight films as a form of "jock appeal." For the benefit of readers who have managed to remain oblivious to their own culture, R. M. Lerner has conducted psychological research in order to prove that women find athletic men attractive.

Eros and Female Athletes

In regard to female athletes too, there is now somewhat less hypocrisy about sports and eros. Australian sportswriter Keith Dunston confesses, "I think I am turned on by Martina [Navratilova]." "Men," remarks American pentathlete Jane Frederick, "go cuckoo for me." She is obviously not offended: "As long as I love my body, everyone else does, too." Noticing that sex and sports are both forms of physical expression, runner Lynda Huey was equally forthright: "Physical strength added to the whole sexual experience. How can anyone want anyone but an athlete? . . . Athletes love physical expression and sex is one of the best forms of it." Ordinary women have admitted that a devotion to sports has done more than improve their cardiovas-

Katarina Witt as "Carmen" (Calgary, 1988).
© Stephane Compoint/SIPA Press

cular fitness. "Sports," comments a thirty-seven-year-old softball player, make "me feel more attractive. . . . I feel sleeker, more fit, more feminine. And that carries over to my marriage." Women who play in the National Women's Football League say that their game has transformed them into better lovers.

In the eighties, mainstream women's magazines became explicit about sports and eros. In April 1983, for instance, *Cosmopolitan* crowed that body builders are "shaplier, firmer, *sexier!*" For advertisers who pay large sums for the right to display "Flo-Jo" [sprinter Florence Griffith-Joyner] in full stride, the message seems equally obvious. Of course, the advertisers have never hesitated to lure consumers with beautiful bodies, male as well as female. Documentation of this fact is hardly necessary for anyone alive and well in the 1990s. That newspapers and magazines now have a special penchant for sexually attractive female athletes is equally evident.

Almost as obvious is the way that sports promoters have capitalized on men's desire to observe women's movements (as opposed to the Women's Movement). When the movements are intrinsic to the sport, as was the case when Colonel McCoombs dressed the "Golden Cyclones" in shorts and jerseys, feminist sensibilities are alerted; when the clothing worn and the poses struck are no longer related to the sport in question, the ethical alarm goes off. During the frantic attempt to keep the failing Women's Basketball League alive, promoters marketed posters of Molly Bolin in shorts and a tank top. The posters sold; the tickets didn't. In 1981, the Ladies Professional Golf Association hired Ray Volpe to improve the appeal of women's golf with photographs of Laura Baugh and other beautiful golfers. Australia's Jan Stephenson suddenly appeared in *Fairway*—in bed with a seductive display of leg. *Fairway* followed this tasteless act with facsimile scenes from sexy films. It was, according to Jaime Diaz, "a shoddy way to sell golf." More abysmal yet, writes Alexander Wolff, was *Vogue's* April 1990 issue, in which Steffi Graf posed in "a black Norma Kamali maillot dress, adjusting her high heel and aiming her décolletage lensward." What the perpetrators of these travesties fail to understand is that the erotic appeal of the female athlete is to a large degree sport-specific. Bolin, Baugh, Stephenson, and Graf are unusually attractive because of the way they move and have moved—*as athletes*. The marvel of their athletic performances eroticizes them as a maillot dress cannot. In fact, an athletic body in an evening gown can cause the same kind of cognitive dissonance as obesity in a track suit.

Feminist Attacks

A number of radical feminists, especially those influenced by Marxism, have waged an energetic and often bitter campaign against the commercial exploitation of the attractiveness which, they allege, transforms women into commodities. European and American Neo-Marxists have sounded variations on themes long familiar to churchgoers (and to mosque-goers too). They have, for instance, condemned the attempt of interested parties to take advantage of the female athlete's "erotic exchange value." Their attack goes beyond the assault on sports promoters, media programmers, and advertisers who use women's bodies to sell tickets, boost ratings, and market products. They also deplore the efforts of women who jog, play tennis, or lift weights in order to brighten their image in the eyes of the opposite sex. Quoting poet Adrienne Rich on heterosexuality as "a beachhead of male dominance," Helen Lenskyj maintains that "a woman's conformity to male-defined standards of heterosexual attractiveness signifies her acquiescence to men's rules."

While admitting that some women have benefited from sports and from the fitness fad, Nancy Theberge still alleges that programs promising enhanced sexual attractiveness represent "not the liberation of women in sport, but their continued oppression through the sexualization of physical activity." After warning in an article that sports are potentially voyeuristic, Margaret Carlisle Duncan has written a sharply focussed attack on the alleged "soft-core pornography" in media coverage of women's sports. Analyzing 186 photographs from the 1984 and 1988 Olympic Games, she notes the intense media interest in sexually attractive athletes like Katarina Witt and Florence Griffith-Joyner. Such athletes are portrayed in ways that emphasize the sexual difference between men and women. Witt, for instance, is shown with "her lipsticked lips drawn up in an exaggerated pout" while four Romanian gymnasts are photographed from behind as they bend over to congratulate their Chinese rivals—a pose which, according to Duncan, accentuates the gymnasts' small stature and makes them seem submissive and sexually accessible. "This is a potentially dangerous combination because it sexualizes a child image and gives viewers visual power over that image." Reviewing the film *Personal Best* for *Jump Cut* magazine, Linda Williams approved of the portrayal of female athletes who were both "tough and compassionate," but she was irked that the women were presented "as so many trained seals flexing their muscles to male awe and approval." (What Williams does *not* acknowledge is the film's recognition that women, too, can find athletic women sexually attractive.)

Feminist Critics

Women who allegedly acquiesce in their own humiliation have not escaped castigation by militant feminists. Margaret MacNeill, for instance, has condemned female athletes who collaborate in the repressions of patriarchal capitalism. Specifically, her ire is aroused less by Florence Griffith-Joyner's iridescent fingernails than by television's treatment of female body builders whose sexuality is accentuated by voyeuristic camera angles.

"Patriarchy," she charges, "is thus reproduced in a newly negotiated form that attracts women by the range of narcissistic commodities." Small wonder that anger sometimes builds to the point where modern sports per se are rejected as wholly evil.

What one makes of all of this is obviously related not only to one's analytic powers and mastery of the evidence but also to one's philosophical stance and personal values. . . . The specific charge that sports are an exploitation of female sexuality requires comment.

I can easily imagine that we might all be better off if advertisements were purely objective statements about the availability of a newly designed automobile, the latest vintage of Beaujolais, or a long-awaited scholarly history of women's sports, but I cannot foresee an austerely rational world in which this kind of advertisement replaces the frantic hype that presently dominates the print and electronic media.

The Root Question

If one understands that advertisements are here to stay and that most advertisements will use physically attractive rather than unattractive models, male as well as female, one can deal with what, for me, is the root question for anyone concerned about the relationship between eros and sports. Why have so many radical feminists condemned the men who have admired physically fit women and their sports performances and why have they sought to discourage women eager for that admiration? Might they not, more logically, have demanded women's right to admire—and even to be erotically stimulated by—physically fit men and *their* sports performances? Although thoughtful scholars are properly leery of efforts to legitimize culture by references to nature, there does seem to be some biological justification for mutual attraction between men and women. Recognition of the legitimacy of this phenomenon need not be tantamount to "compulsory heterosexuality" if we are ready also to recognize, as the film *Personal Best* does, that men and women can also be moved, stirred, excited, and sometimes erotically attracted by athletes of their own sex.

Fears of violence committed against women are certainly involved in the condemnation of an erotic response to sports. Eros, it is argued, is nothing but a fancy name for lust. It motivates men to commit rape and other acts of violence against women. Since the erotic component is ineradicable, this line of argument leads logically to the inescapable conclusion that sports ought to be abolished—along with ballet, modern dance, and most other forms of physical expression. But is there any reason to believe that men who find active women attractive, as dancers or as athletes, are therefore more likely to commit violence against them or against any other woman? I doubt that there is. The undeniable fact that adolescent girls and grown women are sexually attracted to male athletes certainly does not impel *them* to seduce the first hapless male who ambles into their field of vision. The argument that eros drives us to acts of violence reduces us all to the status of Pavlovian dogs.

How can one answer the related argument that men who have erotic fantasies about female athletes are not treating these women as *persons*? The best response is that the charge is often true. The focus on the merely physical *is* partial. But modern societies require partial relationships and differentiated roles as well as the I-Thou relationships celebrated by modern piety. Admiration of Placido Domingo's disembodied voice implies no judgment whatsoever about him as a person. Humanistic philosophers urge us to treat people as ends rather than as means, but do such philosophers really want the clerk at the checkout counter and the attendant at the gas pump to take a serious interest in their personal lives? Civilization is built on civility. Intimacy is for intimates.

Having It All

Some radical feminists have also, as we have seen, charged that sports spectators and sports reporters who concentrate on the appearance of female athletes neglect their performance. There is considerable truth to this accusation (as there is some truth to the related accusation that moviegoers frequently idolize bad actors with good looks). The television camera that skips over the drama of a sports contest in order to linger over "honey shots" trivializes sports. The spectator who admires the performer and ignores the performance might just as well depart from the stadium and scurry to the burlesque theater. We are not, however, trapped in an either-or situation that forces a choice between the athlete and the performance. Motivations are mixed; responses are complex. The athletic body is an inscription of the sports performance. While it may be trite to quote William Butler Yeats on the inextricability of actor from act, no one has said it better than he. How *can* we tell the dancer from the dance?

Why *should* we? One can gasp at Katarina Witt's skill as a figure skater, admire her courage as a competitor, shiver with delight at the beauty of her movements, and simultaneously be stirred by the erotic appeal of her gliding, whirling, spinning, leaping figure. Why not have it all?

Periodical Bibliography

The following articles have been selected to supplement the diverse views presented in this chapter.

Elaine M. Blinde, Diane E. Taub, and Lingling Han	"Sports Participation and Women's Personal Empowerment: Experiences of the College Athlete," *Journal of Sport and Social Issues*, April 1993.
Rick Burns	"Where Have You Gone, Vince Lombardi?" *Harper's Magazine*, September 1992.
Anita Defrantz	"We've Got to Be Strong," *Sports Illustrated*, August 12, 1991.
D. Stanley Eitzen and Maxine Baca Zinn	"The Sexist Naming of Collegiate Athletic Teams and Resistance to Change," *Journal of Sport and Social Issues*, April 1993.
Suzanne Fields	"Feminists Learning the Hard Way," *Conservative Chronicle*, September 15, 1993. Available from Box 11297, Des Moines, IA 50340-1297.
Glamour	"Are Men Taking Over Women's Sports?" September 1991.
Matthew Goodman	"Where the Boys Are," *The Washington Monthly*, April 1989.
Katherine Ingram	"Covering the Bases," *Women's Sports & Fitness*, September 1991.
Constance Johnson	"When Sex Is the Issue," *U.S. News & World Report*, October 7, 1991.
Susanna Levin	"Women's Ways of Winning," *Women's Sports & Fitness*, May/June, 1991.
Susan L. Morse	"Women and Sports," *CQ Researcher*, March 6, 1992. Available from 1414 22d St. NW, Washington, DC 20037.
Joyce Carol Oates	"Rape and the Boxing Ring," *Newsweek*, February 24, 1992.
Ron Scherer	"Women's Sports Are Scoring Despite a Tilted Playing Field," *The Christian Science Monitor*, November 12, 1993.
E.M. Swift	"Bring on the Dancing Bears," *Sports Illustrated*, September 28, 1992.
Alexander Wolff	"The Slow Track," *Sports Illustrated*, September 28, 1992.

Should Steroids Be Banned from Sports?

Chapter Preface

Anabolic-androgenic steroids are drugs synthetically derived from the male hormone testosterone. Since the 1950s they have been used by athletes to increase their muscle mass and improve performance. Officially banned by the International Olympic Committee in 1973, steroids caused a major scandal in the 1988 Olympic Games in Seoul, South Korea. Ben Johnson, a Canadian sprinter, won the 100-meter dash in world record time. However, his gold medal and record time were both taken away when he tested positive for steroid use. Many observers believed that Johnson was unusual only in that he got caught. Michael Janofsky, writing for the *New York Times*, cited medical experts as well as drug traffickers in estimating that around half of the nine thousand Olympic participants in Seoul had used steroids at some point in their training. Steroids are believed to be widely used in other sports as well. Former football player Steve Courson, himself an admitted steroid user, estimated in 1988 that half of the linemen in the National Football League used steroids.

Anecdotal evidence (as well as the performances of users like Ben Johnson) indicates that steroids do work in improving athletic performance. The American College of Sports Medicine notes that when combined with rigorous training, steroids appear to "act to increase the buildup of muscle as well as reduce the breakdown of muscle tissue that occurs during exercise training." Some medical ethicists such as Norman C. Fost argue that athletes at high levels of competition should have the freedom to choose whether to use steroids in their effort to attain performance goals. But the potential harmful side effects of steroids are numerous. They range from acne and balding to liver damage, heart problems, and violent mood swings. Because of these dangers, federal laws were passed in 1988 and 1990 making possession and distribution of steroids without a doctor's prescription a criminal offense.

Both the National Football League and Olympic organizers have increased their efforts to detect and deter steroid use, and steroids are included among the illegal drugs prohibited by other sports leagues as well. The viewpoints in this chapter examine the medical and ethical implications of the use of steroids in sports.

"Anabolic-androgenic steroids can be just as
volatile, just as addictive, and just as . . . deadly
as cocaine, heroin, or any other controlled
substance."

Steroids Should Be
Banned from Sports

Robert Voy with Kirk D. Deeter

Robert Voy served as chief medical officer for the United States
Olympic Committee (USOC) from 1985 to 1989. His resignation
from that post was due in part to frustrations over the problem
of drug abuse in sports. His experiences were recounted in his
book *Drugs, Sports, and Politics*, written with sportswriter Kirk
D. Deeter. In the following viewpoint, excerpted from that
book, Voy describes what anabolic-androgenic steroids are and
how they affect the body. He argues that using steroids gives an
unfair advantage to sports competitors while greatly increasing
their health risks, and calls for tougher testing procedures and
sanctions against the use of steroids.

As you read, consider the following questions:

1. How widespread is the use of steroids in sports, according
   to Voy?
2. What are some of the effects of steroids that the author
   describes?
3. Why do users of steroids become addicted, according to Voy?

From *Drugs, Sport, and Politics* by Robert Voy with Kirk D. Deeter. Champaign, IL: Leisure
Press. Copyright 1991 by Robert O. Voy, M.D. Adapted and reprinted by permission of
Human Kinetics Publishers, Inc.

When Canadian sprinter Ben Johnson tested positive for using the anabolic-androgenic steroid (AAS) stanozolol after he won the gold medal and broke his own world record with a time of 9.79 seconds in the men's 100-meter dash at the 1988 Olympic Games in Seoul, the world of sport was sent reeling from the blow to its image. Sports fans around the globe felt betrayed. For some, this was their introduction to the uglier side of the Olympic Games.

I'm here to say that the use of anabolic-androgenic steroids and other performance-enhancing substances has been commonplace in elite-level amateur and professional sports for years. According to many athletes I've worked with, the only thing that separated Johnson from a great number of others who competed in Seoul in a vast variety of sports is simple: He got caught. . . .

Cheating with Drugs

My position on drug use in sport is simple: I am vehemently opposed to the use of performance-enhancing drugs in any sport at any time.

I base this position on two reasons. First, as a sports enthusiast, I recognize using performance-enhancing drugs as cheating, plain and simple. A world record means nothing to me when I know chemical substances played a significant role in that achievement. I'm sick of watching athletes cheat their way onto the winner's podium at the Olympic Games. Moreover, I'm tired of seeing clean athletes, who sacrifice so much to earn a shot at the gold, fall short because they aren't using drugs to enhance their performances. I'd like to see the playing field made level once again. Restoring a level playing field would mean either that all athletes should be allowed to use these drugs legally or that all drug use should be stopped and controlled by strict precompetition and postcompetition testing programs.

Because I am a physician and realize the dangers inherent in drug use, allowing athletes to use performance-enhancing substances is, in my mind, an irresponsible and completely unacceptable approach to creating a level playing field. This physician's perspective is the second reason I oppose drug use in sport.

The medical profession is now beginning to understand that anabolic-androgenic steroids have serious, in some cases lethal, side effects. We now know that by using anabolic-androgenic steroids, a male athlete exposes himself to many risks, including contracting arterial sclerosis, high blood pressure, heart disease, liver cancer, prostate cancer, sterility, and psychological alterations. With the female athlete, anabolic-androgenic steroid use may mean liver cancer, menstrual irregularity, hypertension, depression, and irreversible masculinizing changes such as a deepened voice and even abnormal genitalia.

Despite our warnings, athletes have stuck to their use of

performance-enhancing drugs—so religiously, in fact, that today anabolic-androgenic steroid sales on the black market are estimated to be a $200 million business. . . .

Anabolic-Androgenic Steroids

Anabolic-androgenic steroids are substances some athletes use to gain a competitive edge by increasing their strength and power.

I should first clarify why I refer to these drugs as "anabolic-androgenic steroids" rather than "anabolic steroids" or just "steroids." The adjective *anabolic* refers to constructive metabolism, here specifically to the muscle-building ability of these synthetic hormones. "Andro-," derived from the Greek word root meaning "man" or "male," combines with "-genic," a suffix meaning "producing" or "forming," to create the word *androgenic*, or "male-producing." *Androgenic* thus refers to masculinizing or male hormonal effects.

All anabolic-androgenic steroids are derivatives of the natural male hormone testosterone. The main female hormone, on the other hand, is estrogen. Both males and females have varying ratios of these two hormones in their systems, ratios that dictate whether we become male or female. People with a testosterone-dominated hormone balance are male. Those with an estrogen-dominated hormone balance are female.

When I talk about androgenic effects of anabolic-androgenic steroids, I am talking about the masculinizing side effects that may cause health problems among the athletes taking them. . . .

I want to make clear that there is absolutely no anabolic-androgenic steroid that affects an athlete anabolically without also affecting him or her androgenically. Dr. John B. Ziegler failed in his attempt to completely rid these substances of androgenic side effects when he introduced Dianabol, as have all others who have attempted to create a purely anabolic drug. There isn't an anabolic-androgenic steroid an athlete can take to increase muscle mass, endurance, or speed without risking dangerous hormonal side effects.

The point is that the athlete who takes anabolic-androgenic steroids gets the whole package. One effect can't be realized (increased muscle mass, etc.) without the other (male hormonal body changes, etc.). In a sense, given the nature of anabolic-androgenic steroids, athletes can't have their cake and eat it, too. It is important for athletes to know this and equally important for everyone to understand that when someone discusses steroids in sport, they are referring to anabolic-androgenic steroids. . . .

The use and abuse of anabolic-androgenic steroids is one of the most controversial topics in sport today. Athletes often refer to these drugs as "the breakfast of champions," which shows just how prevalent and innocent athletes feel AAS use is. Only after Ben Johnson of Canada was stripped of his gold medal and world record after winning the men's 100-meter dash in the Seoul Olympics did this issue erupt into the headlines of sports pages around the world.

YOU CAN RUN BUT YOU CAN'T HIDE

Paul Conrad, © 1988 *Los Angeles Times*. Reprinted with permission.

Nonetheless, these drugs have been used by athletes to gain a competitive edge for the better part of three decades. Dr. Allan Ryan, Dr. Daniel Hanley, and Dr. William Taylor, all former medical advisors to the USOC [United States Olympic Committee], had each spent much time and effort in an attempt to alert the medical profession and the sports community to the abuse of anabolic-androgenic steroids among athletes long before Seoul.

But until very recently, no one had really listened. The USOC and the IOC [International Olympic Committee] didn't officially ban anabolic-androgenic steroids from competition until before the 1976 Olympic Summer Games in Montreal, years after AAS had initially been introduced to athletes.

Anabolic-androgenic steroids are still tremendously popular among a high number of athletes for one simple reason: They work. Any doubters of anabolic-androgenic steroid effects simply needed to watch Ben Johnson blow away the field in the 100-meter dash in Seoul to become believers.

Anabolic-androgenic steroids increase lean muscle mass and strength when used in conjunction with training. It is important to note here that AAS work only in conjunction with an intensive weight training program. AAS can't do anything training and nutrition cannot do, but they can change the body faster than normal. People can't sit on their butts and pop AAS pills and get big! Also, as with any drug, there are positive and negative side effects that may occur. I discuss some of the serious short-term and long-term side effects of anabolic-androgenic steroids later.

A Health Risk

Thus, not only are AAS wrong because they can be used to gain an unfair advantage, but they also present the athlete with a terrible health risk—a situation I believe is a doubly unfair predicament. I have known elite, postcollege athletes who have had to decide between taking AAS to have half a chance to effectively compete internationally, and giving up sport altogether rather than risk their health by taking the drugs. That's one of the most salient arguments I know of against lifting the ban on AAS, assuming that every competitor could be given an equal chance and a fair choice.

Unfortunately, the general public thinks anabolic-androgenic steroids are used mainly by football players, weight lifters, and power event participants in track and field. In actuality, however, AAS use is almost universal in sport today. I have seen anabolic-androgenic steroids used by athletes in all running events, swimming, wrestling, cycling, and most team sports. In fact, the only Olympic sports where I have not witnessed AAS use have been table tennis, women's field hockey, men's and women's figure skating, equestrian events, and women's gymnastics. When I'm asked which sports' athletes take steroids, I usually answer, "You show me a sport where increased power, endurance, or speed can possibly benefit the athlete, and I'll show you a sport where AAS use exists.". . .

Athletes today are skeptical of the medical profession's cautions about bad side effects from anabolic-androgenic steroid use. Yet, despite the little amount of research and information available to physicians, we are well aware from the documented cases that the side effects are real. Additionally, many of us who have followed athletes using AAS have seen the harmful side effects. Athletes need to know this. Physicians and health authorities do know what they're talking about when they discuss the potential dangers of anabolic-androgenic steroids.

Harmful Side Effects

The harmful effects of anabolic-androgenic steroids have been described in various ways by many. In working directly with athletes, I have seen a wide spectrum of side effects resulting from anabolic-androgenic steroids.

I have not witnessed liver cancer, kidney tumors, heart attacks, or death among anabolic-androgenic steroid users. I hope I never do, for AAS have indeed been attributed to well-documented cases of such problems, cases I will describe shortly. In addition, I want it understood that I'm not an alarmist. People aren't continually dropping over dead from the use of AAS. In fact, alcohol claims far more lives in one year alone than AAS will in a decade. But death *is* a possible result of anabolic-androgenic steroid use. . . .

Some of the physical effects go away once the user stops taking anabolic-androgenic steroids. Others—such as male baldness, impotence; female hair growth, deepening of the voice, enlargement of the clitoris; the scarring of cystic acne, certain psychological changes, and stunted growth—are irreversible and permanent. . . .

The detrimental effects anabolic-androgenic steroids have on the liver . . . involve the orally active AAS, such as the derivatives Dianabol, Anavar, Anadrol, and stanozolol. The oral AAS must be metabolized by the liver. Athletes use toxically high doses that cause destruction of liver cells in a way similar to what happens in hepatitis. Such liver toxicity is characterized by symptoms such as nausea, vomiting, and jaundice. Continued anabolic-androgenic steroid use can lead to more significant liver cell destruction and a condition called peliosis hepatitis, or degeneration of liver tissue into blood-filled cysts. These cysts can become quite large and may rupture and bleed. A 27-year-old British bodybuilder recently bled to death, despite surgical efforts to save his life, after a blood cyst in his liver ruptured. . . .

Heart and circulatory diseases are other side effects of anabolic-androgenic steroids that occur after long-term use—sort of a time bomb effect, if you will. Several well-documented studies now show that anabolic-androgenic steroid use may lead to premature arteriosclerosis, or hardening of the arteries. This, in turn, can lead to damage of the heart, the brain, and the kidneys.

Premature arteriosclerosis is believed to be due to the effect anabolic-androgenic steroids have on lowering the body's level of high density lipoproteins (HDLs), the beneficial blood lipid (fat) that protects against cholesterol buildup in the arteries. A lowered level of HDLs provokes premature atherosclerosis or clogging of the arteries with cholesterol, which we commonly see among older individuals but certainly don't expect to see among 17- to 25-year-olds. This aging process leads to high blood pressure and, potentially, heart attacks or strokes. This would seem to be a high price to pay at a young age for a few years of fame and glory on the athletic field.

One athlete who is paying such a price is former Pittsburgh Steeler lineman Steve Courson, who is suffering from cardiomyopathy, which describes a deteriorating heart. He is now on the waiting list for a heart transplant. I have heard that Courson's resting heart rate was, at one time, well over 100 beats per minute. Courson, along with a variety of experts in this field, thinks his religious use of anabolic-androgenic steroids during his professional football career may have contributed greatly to his present condition. . . .

Steven Vallie, a former high school football standout and bodybuilder from New Haven, Connecticut, died of heart failure in the Phoenix Gym in New Haven on March 19, 1989. Vallie's autopsy revealed that his athlete's heart was enlarged and scarred, probably due to his use of anabolic-androgenic steroids. Vallie was 21.

Former bodybuilder Glenn Mauer suffered a stroke in 1983 at the age of 33. One month later he had to undergo a quadruple bypass operation. Mauer's religious use of anabolic-androgenic steroids caused his deteriorated health.

Larry Pacifico, a nine-time American powerlifting champion, was similarly forced to undergo a quadruple coronary bypass operation at the age of 35. His condition was also brought on by anabolic-androgenic steroid use.

Cindy Olavarri, a member of the United States 1984 Olympic Cycling Team, today suffers severe muscle and joint stiffness, a deepened voice, psychological problems, and particular sensitivity to infections. She has publicly attributed this to her use of anabolic-androgenic steroids during her athletic career.

Psychological Effects

Despite the severity of these physical health risks, perhaps the greatest dangers associated with anabolic-androgenic steroid use are the psychological effects these drugs have on the user. The psychological changes brought on by AAS include aggressiveness and feelings of indestructibility and power. Although the advantages these feelings bring on the playing field may be considerable, the athlete cannot turn these feelings off once the competition is over. Consequently, AAS often serve to harm the user or others.

Physiology studies on the limbic area of the brain have identified androgen receptors that cause similar effects to appear when stimulated electrically. Some informal reports indicate that the higher the dose of anabolic-androgenic steroids, the more aggressive the user becomes. There doesn't appear to be a limit to the amount an individual might change. This syndrome closely resembles the classic Dr. Jekyll and Mr. Hyde personality. . . .

I have seen mood swings, increased libido, sexual perversion, violent, uncontrollable behavior, and even psychotic episodes among athletes who used anabolic-androgenic steroids. Minor and temporary behavior changes, though potentially dangerous, may occur while an athlete is on an anabolic-androgenic drug cycle. These episodes of uncontrolled aggressive behavior, described as "roid rage," are fairly common among anabolic-androgenic steroid users. I have heard from girlfriends and wives of AAS users the fears they have when their boyfriends and spouses are "cycling" on these drugs. Relationships are often strained because of insatiable and often aggressive appetites for sex brought on by AAS. . . .

Steroid Addiction

Another danger associated with anabolic-androgenic steroids is their addictive capability. Anabolic-androgenic steroids have been connected with both physiological and psychological addiction. . . .

To understand AAS addiction, one must understand how these very effective muscle-building drugs change the person's basic physical and psychological characteristics. . . . For example, a 130-pound youngster who starts using anabolic-androgenic steroids can, in a matter of weeks, realize an additional 30 or 40 pounds or more of bulging, cut (no-fat) muscle. Not only will he look better in his muscle shirt, but he'll feel more confident. He'll have an increased sex drive, and he won't feel shy around the girls or in the gym where he works out.

Unfortunately, in order to maintain his newfound macho personality and Charles Atlas body, he must continue taking anabolic-androgenic steroids. The instant he stops, the majority of the gains he's made will begin to melt away. He can't face that possibility: He can't be small again and lose the respect and stature he's grown to enjoy. Hence, he feels compelled to continue using anabolic-androgenic steroids.

This type of addiction often begins at an early age, when most youngsters are already experiencing an identity crisis. For many, once they've started on anabolic-androgenic steroids, there's no going back. This psychological dependency is probably the worst form of addiction. It's one thing in sport, where the aggression can be played out on the field, but it's another thing when the addiction sets in among youngsters who don't care as much about performance enhancement as about being big and strong, an identity the average young man could find hard to give up. . . .

The problems with performance-enhancing drugs: (a) they work; (b) athletes can use some drugs in a way that allows them to slip through the current dope testing system; (c) athletes believe if they don't use drugs they will be at a disadvantage competing; and (d) many types of drugs are *not* illegal to use.

Making Steroids Illegal

Though selling anabolic-androgenic steroids without a medical prescription is a punishable crime, possession and personal use of these substances is not. Also, it certainly isn't illegal to get hold of anabolic-androgenic steroids with a doctor's prescription. Unfortunately, many physicians are willing to prescribe these drugs to athletes with little understanding of the dangers they pose. If doctors do not feel ethically compelled to stay out of the anabolic-androgenic steroid business with the athletes, maybe we should legally compel them to do so with tough laws prohibiting such unethical practices and dishing out severe penalties for those who break these laws.

In addition, many athletes feel so long as they're not breaking any law by using these drugs, they aren't really doing anything wrong. I can't tell you how many athletes have said, "Why shouldn't I use steroids? If they're not in my system when I'm competing and if it isn't against the law to use them, what's the big deal?"

The big deal, as I've explained, is that these drugs can give the user an unfair advantage over the competition by helping build muscle mass during training. Using anabolic-androgenic steroids is cheating.

Aside from their impact on sport, these drugs are wrong because they could potentially kill the user or cause serious long-term side effects. We just don't yet know the complete extent of the damage these drugs can cause. The athletes don't either, but they may learn the hard way.

Perhaps the biggest problems these drugs cause can be attributed to the impact AAS can have on the minds of users. Plain and simple, roid rage, the uncontrollable aggressiveness that may result from AAS use, can kill and injure. . . .

Anabolic-androgenic steroids can be just as volatile, just as addictive, and just as potent and deadly as cocaine, heroin, or any other controlled substance. In my mind, solution Number 1 is to treat these drugs accordingly.

"The claim that the ban on steroids is justified by concern for . . . athletes is not only paternalistic without justification, but disingenuous."

Steroids Should Not Be Banned from Sports

Norman C. Fost

The 1988 Olympics were marred by scandal when Canadian sprinter Ben Johnson was stripped of the gold medal he won in the 100-meter dash after he tested positive for steroids. In the following viewpoint, Norman C. Fost, a professor of pediatrics and director of the medical ethics program at the University of Wisconsin-Madison, questions arguments against the use of steroids in sports that were common in the media following that scandal. Fost argues that the arguments commonly heard against steroids do not stand close scrutiny and that athletes should have the right to decide for themselves whether the advantages that may be derived from steroids are worth the possible health risks.

As you read, consider the following questions:

1. What are the four major groups of arguments against steroids, according to Fost?
2. How does the author respond to the argument that steroids are harmful?
3. Why does Fost reject the argument that steroids should be banned because they are unnatural?

"Ethical and Social Issues in Antidoping Strategies in Sport" by Norman C. Fost. In *Sport . . . the Third Millennium/Sport . . . Le Troisième Millénaire*, Fernand Landry, Marc Landry, and Magdeleine Yerlès, eds. Quebec: Presses De L'Université Laval, 1991, 479-485. Reprinted with permission.

My purpose . . . is to question the claim that athletes who use performance enhancing drugs, such as anabolic steroids, violate moral principles other than the obvious duty to obey the rules of competition. I will conclude that the prohibition of such drugs is based on no apparent moral principles, and must therefore serve some other purpose. Finally, I will suggest that the extreme outrage and vilification cast on the Canadian sprinter Ben Johnson is so disproportionate to whatever offense he may have committed, as to raise questions as to the true source of the campaign to discredit him. The task of analyzing the moral basis of prohibiting performance enhancing drugs is complicated by the virtual absence of any strict rationale in the rules governing the subject. Neither has there been much discussion of the moral basis of these rules in the voluminous and raucous literature on the subject over the past decade. I must begin therefore by taking the opponent's view and offering whatever moral arguments might be proposed as a basis for prohibiting drugs in sport.

As best as I can infer from reading commentaries on the subject, there seem to be four moral or quasi-moral concerns:

1. Such drugs provide users with an *unfair advantage* over opponents.

2. The drugs commonly used, particularly anabolic steroids, are *harmful* and there is a duty to protect athletes from harming themselves.

3. The use of such drugs forces competitors to use them, placing them in a situation of *coercion*.

4. Such drugs are *unnatural*, and constitute a perversion of the essence of sports in which they are used.

The problems associated with each of these claims will be examined in turn.

The "Unfair Advantage" Claim

It should be obvious that merely seeking or gaining an advantage over an opponent is not *implicitly* unfair. It is the essence of sport that athletes have or seek to gain an advantage over their opponents. The most obvious advantages are those created by different genetic endowments. We do not say it is unfair that one runner is faster than another, or a wrestler stronger than his opponent, if these differences are due to natural *endowments*. Questions of morality arise only when humans choose certain courses of action. But simply trying or succeeding in gaining an advantage beyond what nature confers is not implicitly immoral. Most athletic training and preparation is indeed guided by the very desire to gain an advantage over one's opponents. Sometimes these efforts are as simple as routine practice and training procedures. But since the first Olympiad, both ancient and modern athletes have explored an infinite variety of natural and unnatural advantages, ranging from better shoes or swimsuits, to better coaches or training equipment, or better diets or nutrition advisors. The mere seeking of an advantage is not implicitly unfair, nor is the gaining of an advantage implicitly unfair. To label it unfair, and prohibit such a practice on the basis of that claim, requires more argumentation than simply showing that an athlete seeks or indeed gains an advantage. Conversely, seeking an advantage by a practice which, in fact, confers no advantage, would not be judged clearly immoral, nor would a ban on such practice seem appropriate. To facilitate discussion of the moral issues I will thus assume for this discussion that anabolic steroids *do* confer an advantage in that they allow some athletes to improve their maximum performance over that which they could have achieved without using steroids. I believe it has been clearly demonstrated that some athletes in some events, particularly weightlifting, can improve upon their previous best performance by adding anabolic steroids to an already intensive training regimen. Whether or not this advantage extends to sprinters, and whether or not Ben Johnson himself in fact was able to run faster *because* of the use of steroids, is less clear. But let us assume for the purpose of this discussion that he was, in fact, able to run faster as a result of using steroids so that we can get to the question of whether he would have violated any moral rule by so doing, and whether officials have a moral basis for prohibiting such a practice.

Steroids and Greasy Swimsuits

One factor which might constitute a moral claim that a given practice confers an *unfair* advantage would be unequal access. In the 1972 Olympic Games, for example, the American pole vaulter Bob Seagren sought to gain an advantage by using a fibreglass pole, a clear improvement on the traditional poles made of other materials. Because his opponents had not had the opportunity to obtain or practice with the new device, it was prohibited. Four years later, when access had been "equalized," the use of that device was permitted. Thus far, I have seen no claim that access to steroids is unequal. On the contrary, it is acknowledged that they are nowadays readily available and widely used. Indeed, it is also widely acknowledged that Johnson is distinguishable from many of his competitors not because he *used* steroids but because he was *caught*. The sophisticated athlete and/or his managers know that the use of such drugs must be scheduled in such a way that hormonal balance is restored at the time of testing; *i.e.*, it is necessary to use the drugs on a schedule that is coordinated with testing, which heretofore has been rather predictable, since it was done primarily at the time of championship events.

In the eyes of many, it is ironic, at least, and hypocritical, at worst, that Johnson was punished and castigated beyond punishment for a practice that had little unfairness (of accessibility), while others publicly boasted of achieving medals by using other types of unnatural assists to victory in ways that appear more clearly unfair. The American swimming coach, for example, gleefully displayed a "greasy" swimsuit which allowed the women swimmers to improve upon their previous best times with the marginal advantage of reducing friction between the swimsuit and the water. He acknowledged that this small differential might well have been the difference between victory and defeat. Similarly, the American volleyball team claimed they had substantially improved their leaping ability with the assistance of expensive computer analyses of their movements and consultation with experts in kinesiology and biomechanics. These advantages, *if* real, could by the same token be judged unfair in that they were *intended* to be kept secret so that opponents would *not* have access to the same technology, even if they could afford it. If there is a rational basis for the ubiquitous steroids to be considered unfair, and the secret greasy swimsuits to be considered objects of praise and admiration, it has not yet been explained.

The "Harmful" Claim

Most published discussions of the steroid controversy emphasize the health hazards and medical harms. A list of dangerous side effects has become a virtual mantra—liver cancer, heart attacks, sterility, hirsutism, psychopathic behavior and others. But good ethics starts with good facts and the first question is whether, in fact, there is unambiguous evidence that steroids, in the doses and duration commonly used by world class athletes, have been shown to cause such harm and, if so, in what incidence.

Much of the data published thus far is anecdotal and of little scientific use. A case report of even a rare event, such as liver cancer in a young adult who had used anabolic steroids, does not prove *causation* or even statistically significant association. Either longterm prospective studies are needed, or at least better retrospective case control studies with careful design and analysis by expert epidemiologists. Many adverse effects which are unquestionably caused by anabolic steroids—such as hirsutism and infertility—are reversible for the vast majority of individuals. But as with the "unfair advantage" argument, we can get to the moral question by stipulating the facts. Let us assume, for the sake of discussion, that steroids do in fact, cause serious, irreversible longterm physical harm, including perhaps death, in some users. What would follow from such a finding? It would not follow that such consequences would justify prohibition

228

among competent adults. Approximately two-thirds of premature mortality in the United States is attributable to personal behavior: smoking, heavy drinking, high fat diets, lack of exercise, inadequate use of seat belts, and so on. For skeptics who would dispute this, there are simpler examples: skiing, sky diving, or automobile racing, to name a few. Indeed, sport itself carries *per se* a substantial risk of death and permanent disability. The majority of professional football players who play for five years or more develop permanent disability. Far more deaths have been attributed to football than to steroids. Quite obviously, it does not follow from these observations that such sports should be banned, or that officials would be morally justified in prohibiting individuals from pursuing these activities. Such paternalism is generally opposed on philosophical and political grounds in western society, particularly in North America. As stated by John Stuart Mill, the dealings of society with the individual should be governed by "one very simple principle":

[. . .] that the sole end for which mankind are warranted, individually or collectively, in interfering with the liberty of action of any of their members, is self-protection. . . . [. . .] His own good, either physical or moral, is not a sufficient warrant. He cannot rightfully be compelled to do or forebear because it will be better for him to do so, because it will make him happier, because in the opinion of others, to do so would be wise, or even right. These are good reasons for remonstrating with him, or reasoning with him, or persuading him, or entreating him, but not for compelling him, or visiting him with any evil in case he do otherwise.

Even proving that an activity is harmful is therefore not a sufficient reason for preventing a *competent* person from pursuing that activity. While there are some exceptions to the general prohibition against paternalism, the burden is on those who would practice it to justify their intrusion into the liberty of those athletes who choose to pursue whatever risks are entailed in exchange for the benefits of athletic success.

Protecting Athletes?

The claim that the ban on steroids is justified by concern for the well-being of the athletes is not only paternalistic without justification, but disingenuous. In sports such as football and hockey, where disability and mayhem are ubiquitous, it is implausible that a drug with few proven harms is singled out as part of a beneficent program to protect athletes from physical harm. If the consequence of roughing the passer were a three point penalty, the practice would disappear and far more disability would be prevented than has been attributed to steroids by even their most severe critics. Similarly, illegal violence in ice-hockey, with its attendant risks, could be dramatically reduced with harsher penalties. The failure of leaders to curtail these clearly dangerous activities suggests that protecting athletes from harm is obviously not the highest priority; presumably, it is balanced with the entertainment objectives, and therefore the economic value, associated with violence. If the health of the athletes were truly the concern and responsibility of the leaders of organized sports, then screening athletes for evidence of heavy smoking and drinking would seem a more justifiable or efficient program.

In summary, the proposition that steroids *are* harmful claims too little and too much. There is little evidence that whatever harms they cause can match numerous other self-destructive activities of world class athletes, including sport itself. And further, the demonstration that any of these behaviors are harmful does not justify, in and by itself, coercive interference with the liberty of competent adults. The concern for liberty would certainly support better research and education on the potential benefits as well as the potential harms of steroids. A competent person remains not truly free to make an informed choice if the data essential for such a choice are not available. A beneficent concern for the well-being of athletes would clearly support expenditure of funds for the development of better scientific and clinical data as well as information.

The "Coercion" Claim

In one of the few attempts to provide a philosophical rationale for the prohibition of anabolic steroids, Thomas H. Murray has argued that their use creates a coercive environment in which use by one or some athletes "forces" others to use them lest they be disadvantaged. Murray's argument, in my view, rests on a wrong use or a misunderstanding of the *meaning* of coercion, which implies restraint "by force, especially by law or authority." I am not aware of any instance or proposal that athletes be forced to use steroids. I believe what Murray means is that an athlete who *chooses* to compete at the highest levels believes, perhaps correctly, that since his/her opponents are using steroids, he is less likely to win unless he too uses steroids, even though he/she might *prefer* not to use them. But this pressure to "pay the price" comes with the territory in many other ways. Competing and winning at the highest levels requires sacrifices and risks imposed by the activities of competitors. Olympic competition requires years of arduous training, involving many risks and discomforts. The ever-increasing intensity, training and performance of other athletes in some sense "forces" one to also seek higher levels, and endure more risk than one otherwise might have wished. In gymnastics, for example, the new "tricks" which one's opponents develop in some sense "forces" current competitors to match or exceed these tricks. Newer maneuvers are always more difficult than older ones. They require more training, and often more risk, either because of the time of exposure on already hazardous equipment, or because of the complexity of the maneuver and the greater possibility of a dangerous slip. It is certainly the case that a modern gymnast is required to make these sacrifices as a condition of competing at the highest levels. But we could not properly say that the success of the competitors coerces or forces the gymnast into making the choice to compete. At least in the western world, athletes remain free to walk away from the arena or the sport. Yet, such athletes appear to be driven by their own internal desires, not by the threats or physical force of others.

Population Estimates of U.S. Anabolic Steroids Users

	Ever Used	Used Past Year
Total	1,042,000	307,000
Age, years		
12-17	120,000	64,000
18-25	384,000	103,000
26-34	220,000	31,000
35 +	318,000	110,000
Sex		
M	897,000	252,000
F	145,000	55,000
Race		
White	874,000	255,000
Black	100,000	28,000
Hispanic	67,000	28,000
Region		
Northeast	151,000	39,000
North central	145,000	40,000
South	539,000	175,000
West	208,000	54,000

Source: National Household Survey on Drug Abuse, 1991.

It may be that the enormous financial rewards awaiting some winners may constitute a strong part of their motivation. A decision to forego competition, including the risks of preparing for competition, whether it be hours of practice on a balance beam or the use of anabolic steroids, may therefore constitute a decision to forego enormous and most tempting rewards and opportunities. But these rewards are discretionary pursuits. They are not requirements for living. If, in fact, an athlete could not provide for the necessities of life other than by competing and succeeding in international competition, and if steroids were essential for success, then the word coercion might indeed be applicable. But that does not seem to be the case. . . .

It may be that athletes who are willing to endure the substantial risks inherent in many sports would prefer not to add to these risks those associated with steroids. That is, if the athletes could make their own rules, a majority might prefer steroid-free competition. Yet it is not clear that such is the case, since professional athletes have the means to negotiate the rules of their employment and they have not heretofore asked for the kind of testing which would be necessary to eliminate the use of such drugs. If they did choose such a system it would not clearly be based on any moral claim, but would appear to be the expression of a preference to endure some kinds of risks—such as those associated with roughing the passer, or more difficult tricks on the balance beam—while foregoing others.

In summary, the claim that the use of steroids is coercive seems to constitute the wrong use of the word. Steroid usage does indeed create pressure on others to conform, but it does not differ in this regard from other pressures implicit in sports. . . .

The "Unnatural" Argument

The most obscure of the claims that use of steroids is immoral is the one based on the distaste for *unnatural* means of assisting performance. Like the other claims, this one lacks internal coherence. Athletes have used unnatural means of improving performance since the first Greeks started training for athletics. Today's training approaches and performances are pervaded by unnatural technologies, from greasy swimsuits to computerized exercise machines to scientifically concocted beverages prepared and packaged in laboratories and factories. To add to the confusion, substances which are completely *natural*, such as testosterone or marijuana, are prohibited as *unnatural*. There do not appear to be coherent principles behind the decisions to allow some performance enhancing chemicals or devices and disallow others. Nor is there an apparent moral issue involved in the claim that some assists should be banned merely because they are unnatural. What moral principle would be involved in allowing a shotputter to lift rocks as part of his training but not manufactured weights or a Nautilus machine? What moral principle is involved in allowing runners to ingest some natural substances, such as vitamins or Gatorade, but not others, such as steroids? Some claim that certain unnatural assists (such as steroids) change the essential nature of the sport. But has sport an essence? Sports are games, invented by men and women, with constantly changing rules. Is pole-vaulting *inherently* something that must be done with a bamboo rather than a fibreglass pole? Has not the forward pass changed the fundamental nature or essence of football more than steroid usage? But such comparisons are, I hope, patently irrelevant, for no sport has an inherent nature or essence. The simplest race requires man-made rules regarding its distance, the width of the lanes, the number of false starts allowed, and I suppose, even the diets or drugs the competitors may or may not use in the hours, days, weeks or years before an event. I certainly do not dispute the right of the athletes and organizers or of the entire sporting community to make whatever rules they wish. I simply dispute the claim that some rules are more "natural" than others, or have an inherent moral basis.

Conclusion

Something is surely amiss in sports. If amateurism means competing for the "love of the thing," it seems to have faded as the sole basis of athletics and of Olympic competition long before the present time. Exploitation, politics, and economic considerations increasingly dominate sports throughout the world, as the third millennium draws near. In the face of these complex and seemingly intractable problems, it is perhaps understandable that scapegoats would be sought as a distraction. The extent and intensity of the vilification cast on Ben Johnson would lead one to believe he has violated some moral principle that is at the bedrock of society. I fail to see what, if any, purely moral principle he violated. He *broke* a rule and most assuredly risked losing (and indeed lost) his medal as a consequence. But the rule is not based on any coherent moral principle the demonstration of which has been offered by those who had promulgated the rules. And whatever moral principles might be involved, such as gaining unfair advantage, or preventing harm, are most everywhere violated in far more obvious and worrisome ways, with little comment or apparent effort at correction.

"Teenagers across America are pursuing dreams of brawn through a pharmacopeia of pills . . . and serums that are . . . often damaging."

Steroid Abuse Among Teen Athletes Is a Serious Problem

Joannie M. Schrof

One area of special concern in the debate over steroid use has been its growing popularity with American teenagers. In the following viewpoint, Joannie M. Schrof examines why steroids are popular with many teens, and describes some of the risks such drugs pose to their physical and psychological well-being. She argues that steroids pose a special health problem for adolescents, whose bodies are still growing, and charges that society's obsession with sports and athletes contributes to the allure of steroids. Schrof is an associate editor for *U.S. News & World Report*, a weekly newsmagazine.

As you read, consider the following questions:

1. Why do many teenagers use steroids, according to Schrof?
2. What are some of the harmful effects of steroids, according to the author?
3. How does Schrof think steroid use among teens could be reduced?

It's a dangerous combination of culture and chemistry. Inspired by cinematic images of the Terminator and Rambo and the pumped-up paychecks of athletic heroes with stunning physiques and awesome strength, teenagers across America are pursuing dreams of brawn through a pharmacopeia of pills, powders, oils and serums that are readily available—but often damaging. Despite the warnings of such fallen stars as Lyle Alzado, the former football player who died of a rare brain cancer he attributed to steroid use, a *U.S. News* investigation has found a vast teenage subculture driven by an obsession with size and bodybuilding drugs. Consider:

• An estimated 1 million Americans, half of them adolescents, use black-market steroids. Countless others are choosing from among more than 100 other substances, legal and illegal, touted as physique boosters and performance enhancers.

• Over half the teens who use steroids start before age 16, sometimes with the encouragement of their parents. In one study, 7 percent said they first took "juice" by age 10.

• Many of the 6 to 12 percent of boys who use steroids want to be sports champions, but over one third aren't even on a high-school team. The typical user is middle-class and white.

• Fifty-seven percent of teen users say they were influenced by the dozen or so muscle magazines that today reach a readership of at least 7 million; 42 percent said they were swayed by famous athletes who they were convinced took steroids.

•The black-market network for performance enhancers is enormous, topping $400 million in the sale of steroids alone, according to the U.S. Drug Enforcement Administration. Government officials estimate that there are some 10,000 outlets for the drugs—mostly contacts made at local gyms—and mail-order forms from Europe, Canada and Mexico can be found anywhere teenagers hang out. . . .

The Risks

The risks are considerable. Steroids are derivatives of the male hormone testosterone, and although they have legitimate medical uses—treatment of some cancers, for example—young bodybuilders who use them to promote tissue growth and endure arduous workouts routinely flood their bodies with 100 times the testosterone they produce naturally. The massive doses, medical experts say, affect not only the muscles but also the sex organs and nervous system, including the brain. "Even a brief period of abuse could have lasting effects on a child whose body and brain chemistry are still developing," warns Neil Carolan, who directs chemical dependency programs at BryLin Hospitals in Buffalo and has counseled over 200 steroid users.

Male users—by far the majority—can suffer severe acne, early balding, yellowing of the skin and eyes, development of female-type breasts and shrinking of the testicles. (In young boys, steroids can have the opposite effect of painfully enlarging the sex organs.) In females, the voice deepens permanently, breasts shrink, periods become irregular, the clitoris swells and hair is lost from the head but grows on the face and body. Teen users also risk stunting their growth, since steroids can cause bone growth plates to seal. One 13-year-old who had taken steroids for two years stopped growing at 5 feet. "I get side effects," says another teen who has used steroids for three years. "But I don't mind; it lets me know the stuff is working."

The Death of Benji Ramirez

On a cool October night in 1988, Benji Ramirez, a defensive tackle for the Ashtabula (Ohio) High School Panthers, played the game of his life. Making tackles and fumble recoveries all over the field, Benji led his team to a 21-6 victory. The 17-year-old glowed with pride when named the defensive lineman of the game.

Three nights later, during practice, Benji collapsed and died.

His mother was shocked: Benji, 6'3" and 201 pounds, had always been healthy and strong. In fact, in some ways during the year before his death, the teenager had seemed stronger than ever, gaining weight and building up his body like never before.

But according to the coroner's report, that sudden growth spurt may have caused the fatal weakening of Benji's heart. As Benji's mother soon learned, her son had been injecting illegal drugs called anabolic steroids.

Katie Monagle, *Scholastic Update*, May 1, 1992.

In addition to its physical dangers, steroid use can lead to a vicious cycle of dependency. Users commonly take the drugs in "cycles" that last from 4 to 18 weeks, followed by a lengthy break. But during "off" time, users typically shrink up, a phenomenon so abhorrent to those obsessed with size that many panic, turning back to the drugs in even larger doses. Most users "stack" the drugs, taking a combination of 3 to 5 pills and injectables at once; some report taking as many as 14 drugs simultaneously. Among the most commonly used are Dianabol ("D-Ball"), Anavar and Winstrol-V, the same type of steroid Ben Johnson [Canadian Olympic sprinter] tested positive for in 1988. "You wouldn't believe how much some guys go nuts on the stuff," says one teen bodybuilder from the Northeast. "They turn into walking, talking pharmacies."

Despite massive weight gains and sharply chiseled muscles, many steroid users are never quite happy with their physiques—a condition some researchers have labeled "reverse anorexia." "I've seen a kid gain 100 pounds in 14 months and still not be satisfied with himself," reports Carolan. If users try to stop, they can fall into deep depressions, and they commonly turn to recreational drugs to lift their spirits. Even during a steroid cycle, many users report frequent use of alcohol and marijuana to mellow out. "I tend to get really depressed when I go off a cycle," says one Maryland teen, just out of high school. "On a bad day, I think, 'Gee, if I were on the stuff this wouldn't be happening.'"

"Juicers" often enjoy a feeling of invincibility and euphoria. But along with the "pump" can come irritability and a sudden urge to fight. So common are these uncontrolled bursts of anger that they have a name in the steroid culture: "roid rages." The aggression can grow to pathological proportions; in a study by Harvard researchers, one eighth of steroid users suffered from "bodybuilder's psychosis," displaying such signs of mental illness as delusions and paranoia. So many steroid abusers are ending up behind bars for violent vandalism, assault and even murder that defense attorneys in several states now call on steroid experts to testify about the drugs' effects.

What steroids do in the long run is still unknown, largely because [as of 1992] not one federal dollar has been spent on long-term studies. Although Lyle Alzado was convinced that steroids caused his brain cancer, for example, there is no medical evidence to prove or disprove the link. But physicians are concerned about occasional reports of users falling ill with liver and kidney problems or dropping dead at a young age from heart attacks or strokes. Douglas McKeag, a sports physician at Michigan State University, is compiling a registry of steroid-related illnesses and deaths to fill the gaping hole in medical knowledge. McKeag sees preliminary evidence that steroid use might cause problems with blood-cell function that could lead to embolisms in the heart or lungs. "If that turns out to be true," he says, "then bingo—we'll have something deadly to warn kids about."

Steroid Subculture

Unfortunately, even that sort of documented health threat is unlikely to sway committed members of the steroid subculture. One widely shared value among users is a profound distrust of the medical community. Their suspicion is not totally unjustified. When steroid use was first becoming popular in the late 1950s, the medical community's response was to claim that they didn't enhance athletic ability—a claim that bulked-up users knew to be false. When that failed to deter users, physicians turned to scare tactics, branding steroids "killer drugs," again without hard evidence to back up the claim. As a result, self-styled "anabolic outlaws" and "Dianabol desperadoes" have sought guidance not from doctors but from the "Underground Steroid Handbook," a widely distributed paperback with detailed instructions for the use of more than 80 performance enhancers. "I know that proper steroid therapy can enhance your health: it has enhanced mine," writes author Daniel Duchaine. "Do you believe someone just because he has an M.D. or Ph.D. stuck onto the end of his name?" Or kids simply make up their own guidelines. "If you take more kinds at once, you get a bigger effect, and it's less dangerous because you're taking less of each kind," reasons one 18-year-old football player who has been taking steroids for two years.

Schwarzenegger's Views on Steroids

There is no one who has ever gone the long haul relying on drugs. So many kids have this misconception that all you need to do is take a few pills and work out a little bit, and that will take you over the top. But that's not the way it works. That extra 20 pounds that you may lift from using those steroids is not going to be worth it. No one will know about it. But you will know when you get sick and when the side effects come out. It doesn't pay off. I think it is very important that someone like myself who has been there—someone they idolize—gets that message out.

Arnold Schwarzenegger, *U.S. News & World Report*, June 1, 1992.

Although even the steroid handbook mentions health risks particular to children and adolescents, in the end most young users seem unfazed by the hazards. In one poll, 82 percent said they didn't believe that steroids were harming them much, and, even more striking, 40 percent said they wouldn't stop in any case. Their motto: "Die young, die strong, Dianabol."

The main drawback to steroids, users complain, is that many brands must be administered with huge syringes. The deeper the needle penetrates the muscle, the less juice squandered just under the skin. Inserting the 1½-inch needles into their buttocks or thighs leaves many teens squeamish, and they often rely on trusted friends to do the job. "The first time I tried to inject myself, I almost fainted, and one of my friends did faint," remembers a 19-year-old from Arizona. . . .

Local "hard core" gyms, patronized by serious weight lifters, are the social centers of the steroid culture. Teenagers caught up in the bodybuilding craze—typically white, middle-class suburbanites—commonly spend at least three hours a day almost every day of the week there, sometimes working out in the morning before school and again after school is out. Here they often meet 20- to 30-year-old men using steroids to bulk up for power lifting and bodybuilding shows or members of what steroid experts call the "fighting elite"—firefighters, bouncers, even policemen—synthetically boosting the physical strength they need to do their jobs. "Our role model is this older guy, the biggest guy at the gym," says one 17-year-old. "He's not a nice guy, but he weighs 290 pounds without an ounce of fat . . . that's our goal."

The older steroid veterans not only inspire kids to try the drugs but often act as the youngsters' main source for the chemicals. Sometimes, it's the gym owner who leads kids to a stash of steroids hidden in a back room; sometimes, it's a lifter who keeps the drugs in a dresser drawer at home and slips kids his phone number. Once in a while, it's a doctor or veterinarian who writes out endless prescriptions for the boys or for an unscrupulous coach. And too often, it's overzealous parents who push the drugs on their children. "My stepdad says he's going to start me up on steroids as soon as I'm done growing," says one freshman who wants to play pro football, "But I think he's just joking." Greg Gaa, director of a Peoria, Ill., sports-medicine clinic, says he has gotten calls from up to a dozen parents a year who want him to supply illegal performance enhancers to their children.

A vast black market across America guarantees kids ready access to steroids in big cities and small towns alike. Typically, the drugs are shipped via private couriers from sources in other countries. . . .

The Desire to Belong

Ultimately, to reach children, educators will have to crack the secretive steroid subculture. So inviting is the underground world that, according to one study, 1 in 10 users takes steroids primarily out of desire to belong to the tightknit group. Those who opt out are quickly ostracized. Bill, a 17-year-old junior from New England, says he was a wallflower with only a couple of friends before he got into steroids. Two and a half years and 16 cycles of steroid use made him part of the fellowship. But Bill vividly remembers one day last winter: It's the day his parents found a needle he forgot to discard. Since then, he hasn't seen much of his friends. "I had to switch gyms because they were all teasing me about shrinking up and pressuring me to use the stuff," he says. "I never see them now—we don't have anything to talk about anymore—but they're all betting I'll go back on it. Right now, the only way I know I'll stay off steroids is if I can find a guarantee that I'll reach 220 pounds without them. No, make that 230."

"Steroid use has been linked to kidney, liver and heart damage. . . . When women take steroids, they upset their hormonal balance as well."

Steroid Abuse Among Women Athletes Is a Serious Problem

Marcia J. Pear

The abuse of steroids is widespread among athletes, female as well as male. Because the drugs are based on the male hormone testosterone, there have been special concerns about their effects on women. In the following viewpoint, Marcia J. Pear contends that steroid use poses serious health problems for women athletes. Pear is a health writer based in San Francisco, California.

As you read, consider the following questions:

1. Why is it difficult to determine how many women athletes use steroids, according to Pear?
2. What is the difference between "stacking" and "cycling" steroids, according to the author?
3. According to Pear, how do some coaches encourage steroid use?

When the International Olympic Committee announced that the 1984 Games would feature the first-ever women's cycling event, Cindy Olavarri's life changed forever. A competitive racer since 1979, Olavarri was in a perfect position to make the Olympic team. "I decided I would do whatever it took," she remembers. In her quest for quick results, Olavarri began using steroids.

During her three and a half years of stealthy steroid abuse, Olavarri suffered liver inflammation, ligament and joint damage, facial hair growth, acne, the loss of her periods and a cancerous back tumor, which a depressed immune system allowed to flourish. But with her eyes on the prize, Olavarri ignored what was happening to her body.

She made the team in the Olympic trials, though her ecstasy was short-lived. While preparing for the Games in Colorado, she received a call informing her she'd tested positive for steroids, thereby forfeiting her chance to compete.

"I knew it was cheating," the 37-year-old health club fitness director says today. But she acknowledges that in the single-minded pursuit of her goal, "I forgot my values. I'd been tested before and never gotten caught." If she hadn't been caught in 1984, Olavarri says, "I probably would've taken steroids until I was too sick to continue."

Mimicking Men

Anabolic steroids are synthetic derivatives of the male hormone testosterone that not only build muscle but also halt protein breakdown, permitting longer, greater-intensity workouts.

The downside is that steroid use has been linked to kidney, liver and heart damage and degenerative joint diseases. When women take steroids, they upset their hormonal balance as well. Because a woman has about 0.1 mg. of testosterone in her body compared with a man's 5 to 10 mg., many women who use steroids develop masculine traits along with muscles. Track star Diane Williams, who took steroids in the early '80s, grew a mustache and developed a deeper voice and an enlarged clitoris. Menstrual disorders, breast shrinkage and uterus atrophy can also occur.

Charles Yesalis, professor of health and human development at Pennsylvania State University, has found steroid abuse by women to be most prevalent in track-and-field, swimming and body building. It's difficult to tell how many women take steroids—an estimated one to three million U.S. athletes are users—because most are extremely tight-lipped, and many are in denial. Michael Scott, Jr., physician crew chief with the U.S. Olympic Committee, recalls a swimmer who tested positive for steroids, yet steadfastly maintained her innocence, claiming the positive reading was the result of the testosterone in her birth control pills.

One reason some women athletes ignore the risks is that little research has explored the long-term effects on females—for instance, no one has investigated how steroids affect a woman's fertility. Yet while research remains in its infancy, Yesalis cautions that "absence of evidence isn't evidence of absence."

© Hofoss/Rothco. Reprinted with permission.

In fact, a study conducted by William Malarkey, professor of internal medicine and director of the Clinical Research Center at Ohio State University Medical Center, suggests that women weight lifters who use steroids may be inviting premature heart disease. Nine women steroid users, ages 23 to 41, showed a marked drop in good HDL cholesterol and a corresponding rise in harmful LDL cholesterol. "These are the kinds of metabolic profiles of people who develop heart disease," Malarkey says.

Stacking the Deck

An important factor that affects possible side effects—and their potential reversibility once an athlete goes off the drugs—is the way someone uses steroids. For example, Olavarri was "stacking"—taking several different anabolic steroids simultaneously, a practice that could have accelerated her risk. Also, by initially taking them orally, she may have caused her liver damage. When a drug goes through the intestinal tract, it goes through the liver.

Another common practice is "cycling"—taking an anabolic steroid for a specific interval, say 8 to 12 weeks, then stopping to clear the drug from the system. While athletes may believe this approach safeguards them from serious problems, Scott warns that "in women, side effects may occur even after only one cycle of steroid use." A 34-year-old cyclist developed increased facial hair, hair on her chest and back and loss of scalp hair after two cycles. "I've followed her for four years now [since she stopped taking the drug] and she's only improved about 10 percent, so these changes appear permanent," Scott says. Reproductive changes—menstrual problems, shrinking breasts and uterus—are more likely to return to normal.

Emotional Roller Coaster

What about the much-ballyhooed 'roid rages? Mood swings are "a primary and early indication that an athlete is taking steroids," Scott asserts. "Someone can feel euphoric and invincible or become belligerent while she's on the drug, then get depressed and delusional when off it."

Yesalis believes that our win-at-any-cost mentality is "absolutely driving the train" on steroid abuse. Athletes feel "enormous pressure to keep up with other members of the team," adds Scott—a mindset that coaches often encourage.

"It's important for coaches to realize how they influence athletes," counsels Olavarri. "When coaches suggest that athletes reach an unrealistic goal—they're basically telling them to take steroids."

However, Olavarri places the ultimate responsibility for her steroid use squarely on her own shoulders. She admits that steroids substituted for her self-confidence. "My whole athletic career is tarnished, because I'll never know what was the drug and what was me. That's the hardest part—wondering if I could have made the Olympic team without steroids."

Periodical Bibliography

The following articles have been selected to supplement the diverse views presented in this chapter.

Anne Marie Brooks	"No Place for Steroids," *Current Health*, September 1992.
Virginia S. Cowart	"Blunting 'Steroid Epidemic' Requires Alternatives, Innovative Education," *Journal of the American Medical Association*, October 3, 1990. Available from 515 N. State St., Chicago, IL 60610.
Peter Gambaccini	"The Unfair Advantage," *Sport*, October 1992.
David Gordon	"The Rumored Dope on Beijing's Women," *Newsweek*, September 27, 1993.
Herbert A. Haupt	"Deadly Search for Beautiful Bodies," *USA Today*, February 1993.
Katie Monagle	"The Devil's Juice," *Scholastic Update*, May 1, 1992.
Kenny Moore	"Great Wall of Doubt," *Sports Illustrated*, September 27, 1993.
Merrell Noden	"Shot Down," *Sports Illustrated*, March 15, 1993.
Scott Ostler	"Ban Drug Testing for Life," *Sport*, June 1993.
Butch Reynolds, interviewed by David Kuehls	"Back on Track," *Runner's World*, June 1993.
Lynn Rosellini	"The Molecules of Sport," *U.S. News & World Report*, February 17, 1992.
Michael H. Stone	"Anabolic-Androgenic Steroid Use by Athletes," *NSCA Journal*, March/April 1993. Available from PO Box 81410, Lincoln, NE 68501.
Tung-Ping Su et al.	"Neuropsychiatric Effects of Anabolic Steroids in Male Normal Volunteers," *Journal of the American Medical Association*, June 2, 1993.
Kenneth Tanner	"Are We Pushing Our Kids to Use Steroids?" *The Family*, July/August 1991. Available from 50 St. Paul's Ave., Boston, MA 02130.
Rick Telander	"Mail-Order Muscles," *Sports Illustrated*, November 22, 1993.
Charles Yesalis et al.	"Anabolic-Androgenic Steroid Use in the United States," *Journal of the American Medical Association*, September 8, 1993.

For Further Discussion

Chapter 1

1. If you have ever participated in organized sports, do your experiences reflect more the positive views of Lyle J. Micheli and John Leo or the criticisms of Rick Wolff and Alfie Kohn? Explain.

2. Do the reforms proposed by both Lyle J. Micheli and Rick Wolff suggest a common ground between the two on the value of sports? Why or why not?

3. Do professional or college athletes have any responsibility to their fans beyond playing their best, as Karl Malone suggests? What responsibilities do you think they should have?

4. Have any of your past or present role models been athletes? What qualities about them did you admire? What qualities found in many athletes does Matthew Goodman describe? Do Goodman's generalizations about athletes describe your role models? Why or why not?

Chapter 2

1. What social factors described by this chapter's authors, including Shannon Brownlee, Nancy S. Linnon, Raymie E. McKerrow, Norinne Hilchey Daly, Charles B. Reed, and Louis Barbash, might account for the familiar "dumb jock" stereotype? Do these authors exploit this or other stereotypes to support their arguments? Explain.

2. The National Collegiate Athletic Association forbids student-athletes on athletic scholarships being paid cash stipends or holding jobs during the school year. An August 30, 1993, article by the Associated Press tells the story of Bennie Blades, who admitted to receiving between $30,000 and $40,000 from sports agent Mel Levine while playing college football for the University of Miami, Florida, in 1987, thus breaking NCAA regulations. Levine later became Blades's agent when Blades started his professional career in the National Football League. Blades was quoted as saying, "A lot of kids are rich at Miami. They are students, but they are driving BMWs and even Jaguars. You see that, and you realize you are busting your butt practicing to play a game that makes millions. . . . I think if someone offers you something you should take it."

Do you agree with Blades? Why or why not? Which of the authors listed in the previous question do you believe would support Blades? Which would disagree? Explain.

3. What reforms are described by the Knight Commission? Do you believe they are enough to satisfy critics like Tom McMillen, who believe federal legislation is necessary? What laws, if any, do you believe are necessary? Explain why.

Chapter 3

1. Jeremy M. Jacobs believes the lot of the average sports fan has improved in recent decades. Bob McCabe argues that the average fan has been treated unfairly. Who do you believe presents the stronger argument? Explain.

2. Are Dick Schaap and Frank Dell'Apa simply attacking two different groups of people (athletes and owners), or do their arguments reveal fundamentally different concerns about sports? Explain your answer.

3. Do you believe professional athletes are overpaid? That team owners make too much money? Why or why not? Defend your answer.

4. Which of the viewpoints in this chapter reflect the belief that sports is more than a business and professional athletes and team owners have a responsibility to their community beyond making money? What does this belief have to do with such things as antitrust laws? Do you agree with the idea that sports is more than a business? Why or why not?

Chapter 4

1. What stereotypes about black and white athletes are explored in the viewpoints by Jim Myers and George Gilder? Why might people object to "positive" stereotypes such as "blacks are naturally athletically gifted"?

2. What different explanations do Myers and Gilder offer for the fact that most NFL football quarterbacks are white? Which do you agree with? Why?

3. Wayne M. Barrett charges many of the people who decry racism in sports with being racist themselves. Is this an adequate answer to their accusations? Why or why not?

Chapter 5

1. Do the differing views of Kathleen Sharp and Thomas K. Hearn Jr. on discrimination in college athletics reflect the differences between an "outsider" (female journalist) and an "insider" (male college president)? Explain your answer.

2. Make a list of the "negative" and "positive" values described by David Whitson and Gail Whitaker, respectively. Are they

mutually exclusive? Which are closer to any values and lessons you may have learned from your own experiences with sports?

3. Why do you believe professional women's basketball has failed to establish itself in the United States? Do you agree with Kate Rounds that male chauvinism is the primary reason? Why or why not?

4. What are your own mental images of female athletes? Which words would you use to describe them? Are they much different from your mental images of male athletes? Which of the viewpoints by Allen Guttmann, Ruth Conniff, and Diane Keaton come closest to reflecting your own impressions of female athletes?

Chapter 6

1. What criticisms of the arguments of Robert Voy does Norman C. Fost make concerning steroids? What responses might Voy make to Fost's arguments?

2. Are Fost's arguments supporting steroids applicable to the teenagers described by Joannie M. Schrof? Should steroids be allowed for some people and not for others? Explain your answer.

3. What impels people to use steroids, according to the viewpoints in this chapter? What do these motives say about the role sport plays in our society?

Organizations to Contact

The editors have compiled the following list of organizations concerned with the issues debated in this book. The descriptions are derived from materials provided by the organizations. All have publications or information available for interested readers. The list was compiled on the date of publication of the present volume; names, addresses, and phone numbers may change. Be aware that many organizations take several weeks or longer to respond to inquiries, so allow as much time as possible.

Black Coaches Association (BCA)
PO Box J
Des Moines, IA 50311
(515) 271-3010

The BCA is a membership organization of minority college athletic coaches, assistants, and administrators established to address issues pertaining to minorities in sports. Through conventions, meetings, youth clinics, educational workshops, and other activities, the BCA seeks to explore alternative solutions on combating racial discrimination and other problems faced by minorities in sports. It publishes an annual *Newsletter*.

Center for the Study of Sport in Society
Northeastern University
360 Huntington Ave., 161 CP
Boston, MA 02115
(617) 373-4025
fax: (617) 373-4566

The center promotes research into sport and its relation to society and endeavors to develop programs that identify problems and promote solutions in sports-related areas. It produces an annual *Racial Report Card* on the racial discrimination records of professional sports leagues. The center also publishes the *Journal of Sport and Social Issues* and the *Center for the Study of Sport in Society Digest*.

Knight Foundation Commission on Intercollegiate Athletics
John S. and James L. Knight Foundation
One Biscayne Tower, Suite 3800
2 S. Biscayne Blvd.
Miami, FL 33131-1803
(305) 539-0009

The Knight Commission was established in 1989 to examine problems facing intercollegiate athletics and to propose a reform agenda. The commission produced three reports which are available to the public: *Keeping Faith with the Student-Athlete*, *A Solid Start*, and *A New Beginning for a New Century*.

National Association for Girls & Women in Sport (NAGWS)
1900 Association Dr.
Reston, VA 22091
(703) 476-3450
fax: (703) 476-9527

NAGWS is an educational organization that serves the needs of administrators, teachers, and participants involved with sports programs for girls and women. It has produced several position papers on coaching certification, national high school championships, separate and mixed teams, and other women's-sports-related issues.

National Association for Sport & Physical Education (NASPE)
1900 Association Dr.
Reston, VA 22091
(703) 476-3410
fax: (703) 476-9527

NASPE is a national membership association of teachers, coaches, and others involved with school sports and physical education. It makes and distributes guidelines and brochures for elementary and secondary school sports programs and publishes numerous position papers, including *"No Fail" Rule* and *Exploitation of the Interscholastic Athlete*.

National Association of Intercollegiate Athletics (NAIA)
6120 S. Yale Ave., Suite 1450
Tulsa, OK 74136-4223
(918) 494-8828

The NAIA works to develop intercollegiate athletic programs as an integrated part of the total educational program of the college. It organizes and administers national championships and other competitive activities between colleges with a similar philosophy of athletics. Among its publications are the monthly *NAIA News* and annual *Media Guides* for football and basketball.

National Collegiate Athletic Association (NCAA)
6201 College Blvd.
Overland Park, KS 66211-2422
(913) 339-1906

The NCAA is the national administrative body overseeing intercollegiate athletic programs. It publishes reports on student-athlete graduation rates in colleges, transcripts from its annual conventions discussing academic and athletic rules, special reports on sports programs, finances, and television. Among its publications are *NCAA: The Voice of College Sports* and *Guide for the College-Bound Student-Athlete*.

National Federation of State High School Associations (NFSHSA)
11724 NW Plaza Circle
Kansas City, MO 64195-0626
(816) 464-5400

NFSHSA is the national administrative organization of high school sports and activities. Among its subsidiary organizations are national associations for high school athletic directors and sports coaches. The federation publishes rule books, sports handbooks, athletic contest rules, the *National High School Sports Record Book* and the *Interscholastic Athletic Administration* magazine.

National Football League Players Association (NFLPA)
2021 L St. NW
Washington, DC 20036
(202) 463-2200

The association consists of active and retired NFL players. It conducts research on player issues and compiles salary information and statistics. Among its reports on NFL players are *Aftermath of an NFL Career: Injuries* and *Life After Football: A Survey of Former NFL Players*.

National High School Athletic Coaches Association (NHSACA)
PO Box 5020
Winter Park, FL 32793
(407) 679-1414

The organization of high school coaches and athletic directors seeks to promote cooperation among coaches, school administrators, the press, and the public. It holds seminars in sports medicine and promotes educational programs on drug abuse awareness. It publishes *National Coach: The Voice of High School Coaches in America*, a quarterly magazine.

National Strength and Conditioning Association (NSCA)
PO Box 81410
Lincoln, NE 68501
(402) 472-3000
fax: (402) 476-6976

The NSCA is an organization of professional coaches, athletic trainers, physical therapists, and others involved with strength and fitness conditioning. It publishes the *NCSA Journal*, a bimonthly publication featuring articles and research on strength training practices. The association also produces position papers, including a statement denouncing the use of anabolic-androgenic steroids as a performance enhancement, and distributes coaches' manuals, instructional videos, and other materials.

National Youth Sports Coaches Association (NYSCA)
2611 Old Okeechobee Rd.
West Palm Beach, FL 33409
(800) 729-2057

NYSCA conducts research and educational programs that seek to make sports a positive experience for all children. It publishes the periodical *Youth Sport Coach*.

North American Society for Sport Management (NASSM)

106 Main St., Suite 344
Houlton, ME 04730-9001

NASSM is a professional organization consisting of sports managers as well as professors and students in the field of sports. It publishes the quarterly *Journal of Sports Management*.

North American Youth Sport Institute (NAYSI)

PO Box 957
Kernersville, NC 27285
(910) 784-4926

NAYSI provides technical assistance for fitness centers, hospitals, sport centers, sport medicine clinics, corporations, and schools that have programs, products, and services for children and teenagers involving fitness, recreation, education, sport, and health. Its services are described in the *NAYSI Resource List*. It publishes a quarterly newsletter, *Sport Scene*.

Sporting Goods Manufacturers Association (SGMA)

200 Castlewood Dr.
North Palm Beach, FL 33408
(407) 842-4100
fax: (407) 863-8984

SGMA is a national trade association for businesses that produce and sell athletic footwear, apparel, and sporting goods equipment. It is also involved in promoting and supporting school sports programs. It publishes brochures and reports on sports participation by Americans and on sales of sporting goods equipment.

Sports Fans United (SFU)

352 Seventh Ave.
New York, NY 10001
(212) 736-3267

SFU is a consumer organization that seeks to represent the interests of sports fans by making spectator sports more accessible and affordable to them. It opposes the move to pay-per-view televised sporting events and what it views as unreasonably high prices for attending sports events. The organization publishes brochures and the newsletter *Fan Advocate*.

United States Athletes Association (USAA)

3735 Lakeland Ave. N, Suite 200
Minneapolis, MN 55422
(612) 522-5844

USAA is an organization for junior high, senior high, and college students involved in athletics. Through its chapters in schools and colleges the organization seeks to promote academic achievement, community service, and drug abuse prevention. It distributes the book *Beating the Odds* and publishes a newsletter and directory.

Women's Sports Foundation (WSF)
Eisenhower Park
East Meadow, NY 11554
(800) 227-3988
fax: (212) 949-8024

The foundation supports the participation of women in sports activities and seeks to educate the public about athletic opportunities for women. It publishes a quarterly newsletter *The Woman's Sports Experience*, books, including *Aspire Higher—Careers in Sports for Women* and *A Woman's Guide to Coaching*, as well as an annual *College Scholarship Guide*.

Bibliography of Books

Judith Andre and David N. James, eds. — *Rethinking College Athletics*. Philadelphia: Temple University Press, 1991.

Wilford S. Bailey and Taylor D. Littleton — *Athletics and Academe*. New York: Macmillan, 1991.

Eliot Berry — *Tough Draw: The Path to Tennis Glory*. New York: Henry Holt, 1992.

H.G. Bissinger — *Friday Night Lights: A Town, a Team, and a Dream*. Reading, MA: Addison-Wesley, 1990.

Paul B. Brown — *My Season on the Brink*. New York: St. Martin's Press, 1992.

Darrell Burnett — *Youth, Sports and Self-Esteem*. Indianapolis: Masters Press, 1993.

Jay J. Coakley — *Sport in Society: Issues and Controversies*. 4th ed. St. Louis: Mosby-Year Book, 1990.

Sebastian Coe, David Teasdale, and David Wickham — *More Than a Game: Sport in Our Time*. London: BBC Books, 1992.

Howard Cosell with Shelby Whitfield — *What's Wrong with Sports*. New York: Simon & Schuster, 1991.

Steve Courson and Lee R. Schreiber — *False Glory*. Stamford, CT: Longmeadow Press, 1991.

Eric Dunning and Chris Rojek, eds. — *Sports and Leisure in the Civilizing Process*. Toronto: University of Toronto Press, 1992.

D. Stanley Eitzen and George H. Sage — *Sociology of North American Sport*. 5th ed. Madison, WI: Brown & Benchmark, 1993.

D. Stanley Eitzen, ed. — *Sport in Contemporary Society: An Anthology*. 4th ed. New York: St. Martin's Press, 1993.

Charles C. Euchner — *Playing the Field: Why Sports Teams Move and Cities Fight to Keep Them*. Baltimore: Johns Hopkins University Press, 1993.

John Feinstein — *Play Ball: The Life and Troubled Times of Major League Baseball*. New York: Villard Books, 1993.

Roy Firestone with Scott Ostler — *Up Close*. New York: Hyperion, 1993.

Arthur A. Fleisher III, Brian L. Goff, and Robert D. Tollison — *The National Collegiate Athletic Association: A Study in Cartel Behavior*. Chicago: University of Chicago Press, 1992.

Bill Geist — *Little League Confidential*. New York: Macmillan, 1992.

Jeffrey H. Goldstein, ed. — *Sports, Games, and Play*. 2d ed. Hillsdale, NJ: Lawrence Erlbaum Associates, 1989.

Allen Guttmann	*A Whole New Ball Game: An Interpretation of American Sports*. Chapel Hill: University of North Carolina Press, 1988.
John M. Hoberman	*Mortal Engines: The Science of Performance and the Dehumanization of Sport*. New York: Free Press, 1992.
Dale Hoffman and Martin J. Greenberg	*Sport$biz*. Champaign, IL: Leisure Press, 1989.
Alan G. Ingham and John W. Loy, eds.	*Sport in Social Development: Traditions, Transitions, and Transformations*. Champaign, IL: Human Kinetics Books, 1993.
Grant Jarvie, ed.	*Sport, Racism and Ethnicity*. New York: Falmer Press, 1991.
Peter King	*Inside the Helmet: A Player's-Eye View of the N.F.L.* New York: Simon & Schuster, 1993.
Richard E. Lapchick and John Brooks Slaughter, eds.	*The Rules of the Game: Ethics in College Sport*. New York: Macmillan, 1989.
Helen Lenskyj	*Out of Bounds: Women, Sport and Sexuality*. Toronto: The Women's Press, 1986.
Tom McMillen with Paul Coggins	*Out of Bounds*. New York: Simon & Schuster, 1992.
Art Manters	*SuperBookie: Inside Las Vegas Sports Gambling*. Chicago: Contemporary Books, 1991.
Eric Margenau	*Sports Without Pressure*. New York: Gardner Press, 1990.
Michael A. Messner	*Power at Play: Sports and the Problem of Masculinity*. Boston: Beacon Press, 1992.
Michael A. Messner and Donald F. Sabo, eds.	*Sport, Men, and the Gender Order*. Champaign, IL: Human Kinetics Books, 1990.
Michael Mewshaw	*Ladies of the Court: Grace and Disgrace on the Women's Tennis Tour*. New York: Crown, 1993.
Lyle J. Micheli with Mark D. Jenkins	*Sportswise: An Essential Guide for Young Athletes, Parents, and Coaches*. Boston: Houghton Mifflin, 1990.
Marvin Miller	*A Whole Different Ball Game: The Inside Story of Baseball's New Deal*. New York: Simon & Schuster, 1991.
Dan E. Moldea	*Interference: How Organized Crime Influences Professional Football*. New York: William Morrow, 1989.
Mariah Burton Nelson	*Are We Winning Yet? How Women Are Changing Sports and Sports Are Changing Women*. New York: Random House, 1991.

James Quirk and Rodney D. Fort — *Pay Dirt: The Business of Professional Team Sports*. Princeton, NJ: Princeton University Press, 1992.

Randy Roberts and James Olson — *Winning Is the Only Thing: Sports in America Since 1945*. Baltimore: Johns Hopkins University Press, 1989.

George H. Sage — *Power and Ideology in American Sport: A Critical Perspective*. Champaign, IL: Human Kinetics Books, 1990.

Jack Sands and Peter Gammons — *Coming Apart at the Seams: How Baseball Owners, Players, and Television Executives Have Led Our National Pastime to the Brink of Disaster*. New York: Macmillan, 1993.

Robert L. Simon — *Fair Play: Sports, Values, and Society*. Boulder, CO: Westview Press, 1991.

C. Fraser Smith — *Lenny, Lefty, and the Chancellor: The Len Bias Tragedy and the Search for Reform in Big-Time Basketball*. Baltimore: Bancroft Press, 1992.

Paul M. Sommers, ed. — *Diamonds Are Forever: The Business of Baseball*. Washington, DC: Brookings Institution, 1993.

Paul D. Staudohar and James A. Mangan, eds. — *The Business of Professional Sports*. Chicago: University of Illinois Press, 1991.

Neil J. Sullivan — *The Diamond Revolution*. New York: St. Martin's Press, 1992.

William N. Taylor — *Macho Medicine: A History of the Anabolic Steroid Epidemic*. Jefferson, NC: McFarland, 1991.

Rick Telander — *The Hundred Yard Lie: The Corruption in College Football and What We Can Do to Stop It*. New York: Simon & Schuster, 1989.

Robert Voy with Kirk D. Deeter — *Drugs, Sport, and Politics*. Champaign, IL: Leisure Press, 1991.

Christine L. Wells — *Women, Sport and Performance: A Physiological Perspective*. 2d ed. Champaign, IL: Human Kinetics Books, 1991.

Don Yaeger and Douglas S. Looney — *Under the Tarnished Dome: How Notre Dame Betrayed Its Ideals for Football Glory*. New York: Simon & Schuster, 1993.

Charles E. Yesalis, ed. — *Anabolic Steroids in Sport and Exercise*. Champaign, IL: Human Kinetics Books, 1993.

Andrew Yiannkis and Susan L. Greendorfer, eds. — *Applied Sociology of Sport*. Champaign, IL: Human Kinetics Books, 1992.

Index

258